Palgrave Executive Es

Today's complex and changing business environment brings with it a number of pressing challenges. To be successful, business professionals are increasingly required to leverage and spot future trends, be masters of strategy, all while leading responsibly, inspiring others, mastering financial techniques and driving innovation.

Palgrave Executive Essentials empowers you to take your skills to the next level. Offering a suite of resources to support you on your executive journey and written by renowned experts from top business schools, the series is designed to support professionals as they embark on executive education courses, but it is equally applicable to practicing leaders and managers. Each book brings you in-depth case studies, accompanying video resources, reflective questions, practical tools and core concepts that can be easily applied to your organization, all written in an engaging, easy to read style.

Tim Baines · Ali Ziaee Bigdeli · Kawal Kapoor

Servitization Strategy

Delivering Customer-Centric Outcomes
Through Business Model Innovation

Tim Baines
Aston Business School
Aston University
Birmingham, UK

Ali Ziaee Bigdeli
Aston Business School
Aston University
Birmingham, UK

Kawal Kapoor
Advanced Services Group Ltd.
Birmingham, UK

ISSN 2731-5614   ISSN 2731-5622   (electronic)
Palgrave Executive Essentials
ISBN 978-3-031-45428-8   ISBN 978-3-031-45426-4   (eBook)
https://doi.org/10.1007/978-3-031-45426-4

This Palgrave Macmillan imprint is published by the registered company Springer Nature Switzerland AG
The registered company address is: Gewerbestrasse 11, 6330 Cham, Switzerland

Paper in this product is recyclable.

*We make money
when our customer
buys products*

*We make money
when our customer
repairs products*

*We make money
when we repair
products for
our customer*

*We make money
when our customer
uses products*

*We make money
when our customer
gets the outcomes
they need to
succeed*

For JB, JMB & SEC.

—TB

To the irreplaceable presence that continues to guide me from within—my mother.

—AZB

To those puzzled by the intricacies of servitization, including my beautiful family.

—KK

Preface

In the Spring of 1999, I gave a research presentation in California presenting a set of ideas about how industrial firms could compete in the upcoming millennium; how businesses in developed economies could react to the then prevailing trends to 'lean-out' and 'offshore' production and do so by building competitive strategies that embrace services rather than products alone. The paper was titled 'Total Service Manufacture'. My passion and background in engineering and manufacturing meant I could deliver a paper that empathised with practitioners yet was rooted in internationally acclaimed research about strategy and supply chains. My argument was that there is a healthier, wealthier and more sustainable future for those businesses that see beyond 'just' production. Yet, the paper also reflected a disappointment— all too often executives and policymakers lack a vision for industry beyond investing in new machines and factories. It's a frustration I still feel today.

Little did I know at the time, but this presentation heralded a fascinating journey: an attempt to persuade the decision-makers, regulators and influencers to recognise and embrace the opportunities of competing through competitive strategies based on services rather than just products and production. I was not, and still am not, advocating just 'shifting' to services, abandoning or offshoring all aspects of production. Rather, I believe in a future based on a synergy of integrated and innovative products and services, and achieving this by transforming businesses with a production legacy to focus on delivering customer outcomes. Going beyond just 'making it' and 'moving it'! Today, this is the phenomena widely known as servitization.

A key steppingstone in this journey was my earlier book, *Made to Serve*. It described servitization as an innovation, laid the foundations of advanced services and identified some of the main practices and technologies that are key to their delivery. *Made to Serve* was published in 2013, a culmination of a decade's work and, although much of the content remains relevant today, our knowledge has evolved and the time is now right for our next major step in this journey. I recently turned down a dinner invitation from a senior executive, explaining that we were finalising this book. He asked how long we had been working on it and thought I was being flippant when I said ten years; yet, it really is a decade's worth of ideas, experience and learning since *Made to Serve* that have shaped the content we present here.

This journey has been immensely challenging for all involved. Servitization contests ideas about industry that have been prominent for at least 250 years! As you will see in this book, though, the rewards are worth it. Personally, I have only been able to face these challenges by having the good fortune to come together with an incredibly capable and like-minded set of individuals now known as the Advanced Services Group—or ASG to our friends—and, in particular, to research this topic with Professor Ali Bigdeli and Dr. Kawal Kapoor. As a group, we all share a mission to directly increase the adoption of servitization within industry, and as a team, we have worked to bring together the international research community and leading businesses around this challenge. During this time, we have ourselves been fortunate to work with some extraordinarily talented researchers and practitioners, and in the later sections of this book, we acknowledge those who have helped to shape our thinking.

We have written this new book to equip business leaders with up-to-date and comprehensive insights into the concepts and evidence that will help them to understand, embrace and apply servitization. It builds on the foundations laid by our earlier book but extends these significantly to help enable companies to move from a focus on just selling products, to providing advanced services which help customers to achieve the results that they need to be successful. Indeed, one of our underlying ambitions is to help elevate the conversations within businesses to widely embrace the concept of management by outcomes. Using the creation and delivery of advanced services to spearhead a wider change towards an outcome-based organisation; thinking both about outcomes for our customers, the way we manage our business and those that supply to us.

Our motivation is simple: through servitization we want to help deliver industrial practices that make the world a better place to live—healthy, wealthier and more sustainable. The legacy of the Industrial Revolution is that industries around the globe are wedded to business models built on the principles of 'make-sell-dump'. These models played a vital role in the development of the economic and political systems that we benefit from today, but their time is over and slowly businesses are realising that, to grow and be more sustainable, they have to change their ways of doing business. Our goal in writing this book is to accelerate this change and, as a university-based research centre, we have the privilege of a neutral platform, unrivalled access to research and industry and no ulterior motives.

To conclude, those readers familiar with our work will see that this book refines, integrates and extends a range of ideas published in our research papers and practitioner guides. It combines these with dozens and dozens of examples from industry as to what does work and what does not. Indeed, so rich is the collage of knowledge from research and practice that my co-authors and I could not have drawn this together without our friends and colleagues in the broader academic and industrial community that have helped to shape and influence our work. In the acknowledgements, we thank and recognise some of the very special contributions that have made this book possible.

Professor Tim Baines
Professor Ali Ziaee Bigdeli
Dr. Kawal Kapoor
The Advanced Services Group
Birmingham, UK

Acknowledgements

This book is based on our research on servitization and advanced services over the last two decades, drawing on our extensive collaborations and engagements with some of the world's leading businesses and senior executives. It was well after publishing Made to Serve in 2013 that we realised it is now the right time for the next major step in better understanding the what, why and how of servitization and advanced services.

There were many people who helped in bringing this book to fruition, and we are grateful to all of them. Writing this book was harder than we thought and more rewarding that we could have ever imagined. None of it would have been possible without a team of brilliant and dedicated people who not only put up with us while writing this book, but also invested hours in listening to our ideas, reading drafts, sharing thoughts and feedbacks and feeding us with more information on what and where needed to be improved—our dearest colleagues at the Advanced Services Group (ASG). ASG is a group of specialists in servitization research and practice, and through an ongoing portfolio of programmes and initiatives, it has established a clear 'line-of-sight' from the discovery and development through to the exploitation of servitization and advanced services.

So, we would like to express our sincere gratitude to Kristina Anders (Marketing Manager), Daniel Andrews (Research Fellow), Mustabsar Awais (Research Fellow), Ahmad Beltagui (Senior Lecturer in Operations Management), Sandra Benbow (Senior Industrial Fellow), Paula Cresswell (Partnership Development and Operations Manager), Katja Dmitrijeva (Visiting

Industrial Fellow), Jill Forrest (Servitization Engagement Coordinator), Gill Holmes (Senior Research Manager), Ian Machan (Managing Director and Industrial Fellow), Iain McKechnie (Director of Strategic Partnerships), Antonio Masi (Visiting Doctoral Researcher), Eleanor Musson (Senior Partnerships Manager), Raveen Menon (Research Fellow), Parikshit Naik (Business Development Manager), Chris Owen (Senior Teaching Fellow In Operations Management), Dipti Rathi (Doctoral Researcher) and Andreas Schroeder (Associate Professor of Information Systems).

We are also grateful for the support and contributions of our visiting professors and industrial fellows, including Alec Anderson (Managing Director at Koolmill Systems) a flag bearer for changing a global industry, in this case rice milling through a technological and business model revolution, Luke Benton (Managing Director at MNB Precision) an early example of achieving significant revenue growth, and cost savings, through adopting a servitization mindset, Peter Bruch (former Managing Director of AE Aerospace) as a developer of a 'glass factory' to support supply-chain evolution, Lee Cassidy (CEO at Tactile Technology), Jim Euchner (former Vice President of Global Innovation at The Goodyear Tire & Rubber Company) who was instrumental in creating our Advanced Services Research partnership in 2015, Des Evans (retired CEO of MAN Truck and Bus UK), Richard Glover (former International Director of Technical Service at Xerox Corporation), Andrew Harrison (retired Engineering Fellow at Rolls-Royce) for his insight into design for service, Charlotte Horobin (Region Director at Make UK) for feeding us a regular stream of suitable businesses that are able to grow their services, Ian Hughes (former Director of Services at Tetra Pak), Mike Hulme (Managing Director at Alstom) who demonstrated how large value contracted advanced services can be negotiated, Paul Jackson (Managing Director of UV Light Technology) for his work as co-chair of our SME Partnership, Paul Jennings (retired Managing Director of JCB Finance), Dimitris Karamitsos (Senior Energy Efficiency Business Developer Specialist at BASE), David Mackerness (Director at Kaer Pte Ltd) one of the most impressive examples of providing services and becoming carbon-neutral in doing so, Tom Palmer (Former Group Director of Services Strategy at Rolls-Royce) and Greg Parker (former Senior Director, Product Management and Business Development at Johnson Controls).

In addition to our ASG colleagues, two other groups of people greatly helped us to make this book more relevant and interesting—our academic colleagues and friends, and industrial partners and executives.

In 2010, we formed an academic conference called the Spring Servitization Conference (SSC). SSC was created to build and formalise a research community around servitization, and to genuinely support and accelerate academic endeavour in this area. The conference is entirely focused on servitization and advanced service business models, attracting scholars from across disciplines including marketing, operations management, strategy, information systems, innovation, and leadership. SSC has come a long way since its humble beginning as a workshop at Aston Business School, and has now become the largest international gathering of researchers interested in servitization. We have been very fortunate that this platform has enabled collaborations and friendships with like-minded and leading researchers, who have greatly helped us with our ideas for this book, through meeting, peer-reviews, discussions and joint publications.

Of our academic colleagues, we are especially grateful to Rui Sousa (Catholic University of Portugal), Marko Kohtamäki (University of Vaasa, Finland), Mario Rapaccini (University of Florence, Italy), Rogelio Oliva (Texas A&M University, USA), Chris Raddats (University of Liverpool, UK), Christian Kowalkowski (Linköping University, Sweden), Vinit Parida (Luleå University of Technology, Sweden), Judy Zolkiewski and Jamie Burton (University of Manchester, UK), Nicola Saccani (University of Brescia, Italy), Keiko Toya (Meiji University, Japan), Vicky Story (Loughborough University, UK), Shaun West (Lucerne University of Applied Sciences, Switzerland), Ferran Vendrell-Herrero (University of Edinburgh, UK), Oscar Bustinza (University of Granada, Spain), Paolo Gaiardelli (University of Bergamo, Italy), Henk Akkermans (University of Tilburg, the Netherlands), Lino Cinquini and Andrea Tenucci (Scuola Superiore Sant'Anna Pisa, Italy).

We have also been very fortunate to engage and work closely with many multinational companies and gain first-hand insight and knowledge about servitization in practice. Most of the engagements, interviews, discussions and workshops were facilitated through our Advanced Services Partnership, which is a consortium of multinational companies seeking to excel at servitization through the adoption and implementation of advanced services. To each of the following people, we express our hopes that this book has captured the best of what they have accomplished with servitization: James Galloway (former Baxi), Kris Swiderski (former Baxi), David Willetts (former Baxi) for his continued input on open innovation, Jill Lawrence (Crown Equipment Corporation), Andrew Barrett (Domino Printing), Will Edwards (Domino Printing), Jeremy Jones (Domino Printing), Lee Metters (Domino Printing), Kate Rattigan (Domino Printing), Dawie Kriel (Energy Partners Refrigeration), Ross Townshend (Ishida), Lee Vine (Ishida), Oliver Moffat (Jaguar

Land Rover), Christian Rudebeck Holm (Kamstrup), Chris Dodd (Legrand), Tony Greg (Legrand), Frank Van Keulen (Nederman), Glynn Lloyd (Moog), Aage Snorgaard (former Nederman), Mark Butters (Omron), who recognised the need to develop his company's involvement in advanced services at a European not national level, Almudena Marcos Bardera (Omron), Andy Bates (Omron), Maurizio Poli (Omron), Sam Tilley (Omron), Jessica Hard (Öresundskraft AB), Ben Wilson (Schneider Electric), Matthew Skipworth (Terex), Alejandro Chan (Tetra Pak), Dean Griffin (Tetra Pak), Dave Madsen (Tetra Pak), Marcus Olausson (Tetra Pak), Johan Paulsson (Tetra Pak) for their strategic services vision and development of insights from engagements with their customers, Gary Whitehead (Tetra Pak), Kayvan Zadeh (Tetra Pak), Chris Borrill (Thales) who has demonstrated how to influence a large organisation with a service mindset, Philippe Chassin (Thales), Cindy Mamer (Waters Corporation) who continued to pursue a services strategy wherever she worked and Rinze van Kammen (Yanmar).

Summary

This is a book for people who would like to help businesses to compete through services which shamelessly focus on delivering outcomes for customers; offering Products-as-a-Service, and regularly earning revenue when the customers get the results they value. It introduces these as advanced services business models, explains why they are of growing importance and then describes how a product-centric firm can innovate these services through a process known as servitization.

Servitization, and especially competing through advanced services, offers businesses a pathway to improve both economic productivity and sustainability. It can create greater value for customers, while also improving resource efficiency and the dematerialisation of the supply chain. It has the potential to reshape the industrial landscape for businesses, markets and consumers around the world.

This book should be especially helpful to industrial and manufacturing firms, as for them servitization is both an acute opportunity and an intense strategic threat. Yet, it is also relevant for managers and scholars working in and with organisations which are already services focused, but don't necessarily deliver business outcomes for their customers. Irrespective of whether you are in a firm interested in offering 'services-around-products' or 'products-around-services', much of what we share will be relevant.

We have two ambitions with this book. The first is to accelerate the widespread adoption of servitization and advanced services across industries globally. To do this, we draw on internationally acclaimed research from over the last decade with some of the world's leading industrial firms. We share insights and experiences from this to explain the *what*, *why* and *how* of servitization. The second ambition is to more broadly accelerate the growth of outcome-based management in industrial firms and their supply chains. We deal with this implicitly by taking the innovation of the business model as an essential foundation—it all should start with the customer.

Members of the advanced services group
Team Strategy Day, June 2023

First row: Raveen Menon, Mustabsar Awais, Zoe Whitmarsh, Gill Holmes, Andreas Schroeder, Jo Parkes, Tim Baines, Kawal Kapoor, Ali Ziaee Bigdeli, Jill Forrest, Dipti Rathi, Iain McKechnie, Shriram Dusane, Daniel Andrews

Second row: Antonio Masi, Paula Cresswell, Parikshit Naik, Ian Machan, Ahmad Beltagui

Not Pictured: Kristina Anders, Sandra Benbow, Katja Dmitrijeva, Eleanor Musson, Chris Owen

Praise for *Servitization Strategy*

"Through an honest, practical and 'real-world' approach to understanding and implementing servitization strategy, Tim Baines and the Advanced Services Group. From my own first-hand experience of utilising the tools, processes and frameworks outlined in this book, I wholeheartedly support these practical methods as a demonstrate that while challenges certainly exist, they can be overcome, and in doing so provide significant opportunity for increased revenue capture and business resilience."

—Ross Townshend, *Former Business Unit Manager at Ishida*

"Working with Tim and his team provided the tools to develop a viable Machinery (Hardware) as a Service (MaaS) Business Model and the confidence to launch this into an antiquated global industry, where such a Business Model is an alien concept. MaaS is the catalyst that will transform a global food system delivering demonstratable benefits for all stakeholders."

—Alec Anderson, *Managing Director at Koolmill Systems*

"Tim Baines and Ali Bigdeli have been studying servitization in the real world for decades. In this book, they translate their observations into insights and models that are very useful for practitioners trying to move from product-led to services-led businesses. I can speak from experience to say that we would not have been as successful in building our services businesses at Goodyear without their insight."

—Jim Euchner *Former Vice President for Global Innovation at The Goodyear Tire & Rubber Company*

"SERVITIZATION STRATEGY is a "must have" book, a phenomenal tool to Thanks to the great help of Prof. Tim Baines and members of the ASG team, we have managed to effectively involve our European organization in the development of an integrated value proposition strategy of "services and products", where advanced services are perceived not only as a great door opener in strategic accounts, but also as the key element in establishing long-term relationships and generating revenue streams. Guide industrial companies in the development path of services business model and advanced services and in its successful implementation."

—Maurizio Poli, *General Manager Strategy Implementation at Omron*

"Finally, a publication containing all the good practices for a company to embark on the journey of Servitization. The passionate work Tim and the ASG team have been performing deserved to be compiled in a book that can help transforming the way we do business."

—Alejandro Chan, *Vice President of Global Services at Tetra Pak*

"The Advanced Services Group have been instrumental in inspiring new ways of thinking about customer-centric propositions and supporting business model innovation to fit. This book is a must-read bible for any entrepreneurial senior leader who wants to get ahead in their sector and remain relevant for current and future customers. Read the book, be bold and experiment to win."

—James Galloway, *Formed Head of Product Management, UK and Ireland at Baxi*

"The authors challenge business leaders to look beyond internal process efficiencies for productivity improvements. In addition, they advocate business model innovation, to enable delivery of outcomes for customers with economic, societal and environmental impact. The results can be spectacular, but it's not easy and their practical application frameworks help to create a pathway. On our servitization journey so far, we've changed the conversation from lowest price to highest value, whilst building customer trust and loyalty."

—Paul Jackson, *Managing Director at UV Light Technology*

"I enjoyed reading Tim Baines' previous book, Made to Serve, and his new follow up has gained valuable insights into the current and increasing trend towards adoption of Servitization. The wealth of explanations and real-life practical examples provided by so many first-class businesses are coupled with plenty of guidance to aid readers new to the field. The pursuit of Net Zero and growing competition from low-cost producers give added urgency to exploring and adopting advanced services and this book provides an excellent blueprint for the necessary actions to be taken."

—Paul Jennings, *Former Managing Director at JCB Finance*

"I would like to thank Tim and the ASG for their invaluable support and advice in helping us navigate a journey towards outcome-based services, one that still has a long way to run. It is the blend of insightful theory and real-life practise that has been most compelling and that is why this book is essential reading for any business leader embarking on a similar journey."

—Will Edwards, *Director of Channels at Domino Printing*

Contents

About the Authors

Professor Tim Baines is a leading international authority on servitization and advanced services and is the co-founder of the Advanced Services Group (ASG). ASG is an international leader in research underpinning the adoption of servitization within the manufacturing industry. This research provides executives with the knowledge, skills and networks that allow them to understand, evaluate and accelerate the adoption of high-value service-based business models within their organisations. Professor Baines has been at the forefront of the development of new thinking in manufacturing operations strategy and servitization for over twenty-five years. He has published in a range of world leading and internationally excellent journals, and is widely cited for his research. His impact and contribution to practice is reflected in the extensive global collaborations he has established with companies such as Airbus, Boeing, Caterpillar, Ford, Goodyear, Rolls-Royce and Thales. He has also been influential in Regional, National and European policy, is regularly invited to participate in academic and industrial events around the world and has been central to fostering an international community of researchers on servitization. His career began with a technician apprenticeship, and after graduating with an M.Sc. and Ph.D. from Cranfield University, he studied as a post-doctorate at the Massachusetts Institute of Technology and Auburn University in the USA. He has published over 300 articles including 70 refereed journal papers, and a further 30 books and chapters. He is a chartered engineer, a fellow of both the Institution of Mechanical Engineers and the Institution of Engineers and Technologists and has held a number of senior positions and directorships within universities and business.

Professor Ali Ziaee Bigdeli is internationally recognised for his research on innovative business models for industrial services. He is a Professor of Industrial Service Innovation and the co-director of the Advanced Services Group within Aston Business School, Aston University. Professor Bigdeli has been among the first researchers to directly investigate industrial service from business model design and innovation aspects, rather than traditional viewpoints around manufacturing systems. His research has had direct impacts on over 300 multinational and small/medium-sized firms, guiding them in the development and implementation of innovative business models focused on industrial services, which has bolstered their growth and resilience. Through his active involvement in industry engagement, he has played a pivotal role in establishing a strategic partnership among multinational manufacturing organisations and spearheaded the creation and delivery of over 50 interactive seminars, specifically designed for senior executives, aimed at fostering an in-depth exploration and expeditious adoption of servitization practices. Professor Bigdeli has a strong publication track record in leading international journals with over 100 peer-reviewed journal publications, book chapters and conference papers, most of which have been co-developed through close collaborations with leading scholars from various institutions and countries.

Dr. Kawal Kapoor is an international researcher and expert in servitization concepts, innovation adoption and business management. She specialises in leading-edge product, service, digital and social innovations, committed to translating complex concepts into practical solutions that drive tangible results for businesses. She is the research manager for the Advanced Services Group (ASG), and leads the research activities within ASG by collaborating closely with both global corporations and SMEs in the manufacturing sector, seeking to embrace servitization. She is a trusted research authority and her expertise in service and outcome-based business models puts her work at the forefront of industry-driven innovation. She develops resources with practical insights and actionable strategies that resonate with industry professionals, empowering them to enable service transformations. She has a multidisciplinary background. After graduating with a degree in Industrial Engineering and Management, she worked as a software engineer at Accenture Services that provided her the exposure to operational dynamics and industry-specific processes of the retail and Life Sciences domains. She then pursued her research career and earned an M.B.A. degree and a Ph.D. in product innovations. She has held pivotal post-doctoral positions in contributing to three prominent EU commissioned projects. Through these projects, she has collaborated with international partners and played an instrumental role in addressing industry challenges and spearheading initiatives for driving sustainable innovations. She has published over 50 articles in high-impact peer-reviewed journals, book chapters and influential conference proceedings. Her contributions have also been published in industry reports, media outlets and magazines reaching a broader audience.

List of Figures

List of Tables

1

Introduction

You might focus on making it and moving it, but the customer only gets value from using it!

In our lives, we might strive to achieve outcomes, but most businesses only see this as an opportunity to sell us products. We want to keep food fresh, but we have to buy a refrigerator; we want to keep our homes hygienic, but we have to buy a vacuum cleaner; we want to keep clothes and dishes clean, but we have to buy washers; we want to travel, but we have to buy a car. Businesses might profit by selling us products, but we only get value when we use these to get our desired outcomes, and we often must reluctantly take on the risk that products underperform in helping us to achieve these.

As customers, we often want to just get the job done. As Peter Drucker put it: 'What a customer buys and considers value is never a product, it is always utility, that is, what a product or service does for them' [1]. This gap represents a significant opportunity for wealth creation, and yet many executives simply don't realise what they are missing. Even when they do, they rarely have the language, skills, and tools to grasp the opportunity. This is especially the case in industrial firms that have a legacy of products and production.

Let us offer you an example by introducing Mike, a pseudonym for a real Chief Executive of a Japanese-owned industrial company producing food processing equipment. In his home life, Mike is an avid consumer of services rather than products; rather than purchasing CDs or DVDs he streams music

© The Author(s), under exclusive license to Springer Nature Switzerland AG 2024
T. Baines et al., *Servitization Strategy*, Palgrave Executive Essentials, https://doi.org/10.1007/978-3-031-45426-4_1

through Spotify[1] and movies through Netflix[2]; he listens to his favourite books via Amazon's Audible[3]; uses Uber[4] for his travelling needs; hires fitness equipment from Homegym,[5] and rents clothes through The Devout.[6] His aspiration is for easy living and peace of mind, and this helps ensure he has the time and energy to focus his attention on business. His business life, however, is a totally different story.

He was chosen for the role of Chief Executive because of his expertise in business finance and accounting. In his mind production is king, making things and moving things! Mike is motivated by the volume of equipment sales and the profit returned against these. When he thinks of innovation, it is all about the shopfloor: new robots and machines to replace people and so improve efficiency. He is not anti-services; indeed, he is an advocate of the customer having to invest in expensive maintenance programmes which generate further income from replacement spare parts and technician time—every site visit is a revenue opportunity. He wouldn't like to think that the equipment is unreliable; certainly, customer satisfaction is very important to him, but so too is recurring revenue through spare-part sales. He's confident that the equipment will perform well but wouldn't like to offer that as a longer-term guarantee. The market for food processing equipment is growing, his business is profitable, and yet the market share won by his business is shrinking and productivity is stale. There is an ever-growing threat of competitors from lower-cost economies, and he doesn't really know what to do next when it comes to NetZero.

We encounter many Chief Executives and Vice Presidents like Mike; what they value as a consumer (in B2C) themselves, is disconnected from the values they project towards customers in their own (B2B) organisations. Most don't even realise this is the case. As everyday consumers, we buy electricity as we use it, we buy water as we use it, so why not heat, refrigeration, or mobility? We continually meet people in senior roles, especially in large industrial firms, that don't see the opportunity. They have a static view of customer appetite. They don't appreciate how this is shifting away from products and more towards services, and that services can enhance the value of existing products, and so they leave value on the table. And when it comes to innovation and improving productivity, they are internally focused and really can't see beyond

---

[1] https://www.spotify.com/.

[2] https://www.netflix.com/.

[3] https://www.audible.co.uk/.

[4] https://www.uber.com/.

[5] https://www.homegymuk.com/.

[6] https://www.thedevout.com/.

the factory gate. Overcoming this disconnect is a pathway to business growth, and achieving this requires the executives of organisations to strive towards and focus more on the delivery of outcomes for their customers. This is the process of servitization.

Servitization offers compelling opportunities. The Goodyear Tire & Rubber Company is a multinational corporation (20.80 billion USD revenue in 2022 [2]) with over 72,000 employees worldwide, and its global research centre is based in Akron Ohio, USA. In 2013, we were introduced to the then Vice President for Global Innovation, Jim Euchner. Jim was exploring new services-led models for Goodyear, which was becoming increasingly exposed to competition from tyre producers in countries that had a significantly lower cost base. We looked together at a range of internationally leading and relevant businesses, such as Alstom Rail and MAN Truck & Bus in the UK, along with Caterpillar Dealers in the USA. In each case looking to understand their more advanced services and how they innovated these services.

Within Goodyear, Jim was especially concerned with Truck and Off-road tyres. He was convinced that the opportunity for growth was not simply trying to sell more tyres, but by also selling an integrated package of products and services focused on 'keeping the truck on the road'. This meant for example, mitigating the business disruptions that a customer experiences when a tyre wears excessively because the operator has failed to manage tyre under inflation. Jim then led the innovation of a service offering now known as Proactive Solutions. A full suite of data-based services featuring advanced telematics and patented predictive analytics technology providing road haulage companies with the precise and real-time monitoring of tyres, resulting in reduced tyre wear and re-treading and improvements in safety and fuel savings.

Proactive Solutions was incubated in Germany, starting in 2014 and was launched as a Pan-European business in 2015/16. Success then followed in Austria, Belgium, France, Germany, Italy, Luxembourg, the Netherlands, Poland, Portugal, Spain, Switzerland, and the United Kingdom, and it was further rolled out in North America and Brazil [3]. Following these successes in 2020, Goodyear developed its Total Mobility offering [4], an integrated fleet management system that brought together truck tyres and a range of other after-sales services. As the company states: Goodyear Total Mobility is '… a bespoke portfolio of solutions that allows you to take a strategic approach to driving better results and delivering the measurable, year-on-year improvements you want' [5].

The experiences of Goodyear illustrate that services offer an opportunity for business growth worldwide. This is indicative of a fundamental shift in

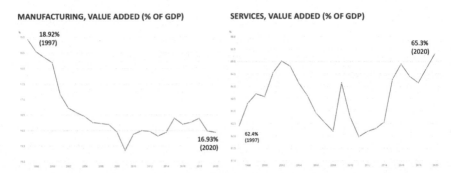

Fig. 1.1 Growth of a services society (*Note* Value added is the net output of a sector after adding up all outputs and subtracting intermediate inputs. It is calculated without making deductions for depreciation of fabricated assets or depletion and degradation of natural resources. *Source* The World Bank [7])

economic activity globally. Looking back into history, for centuries the agriculture sector led economic development, and then following the industrial revolution the manufacturing sector led the world economies. However, over the last three decades there has been a continual increase in the contribution from services to the Gross Domestic Product (GDP) in value added globally. Figures from 2019 show that services accounted for an average of 55% of the GDP in developing economies and, as of 2020, this figure is at 65.3% across world economies (Fig. 1.1). Generating about two-thirds of the world's GDP, services are a significant part of the world economy. While GDP measures the production of goods and services within a country's borders, the world trade figure is a measure of the exchange of those goods and services between different countries. Reports also show that services accounted for an average share of 22.1% of the world's trade in 2020. And it is estimated by the World Trade Report that services will make up for nearly one-third of the world's trade by 2040, which is a 50% rise in services share in just another 17 years [6].

This is not to say that manufacturing is no longer important to economies, or that all services are a result of servitization. Rather, it is simply indicating that it has been the services sector which has experienced the most growth, and so those firms which intend to trade only in the production of goods may put themselves at a disadvantage. As Robbie Kellman Baxter in her work on the membership economy [8] puts it, so much of our economy has operated historically on the principles of ownership. Companies manufacture and sell things; consumers and organisations buy them and then own them, taking on the rights and responsibilities of private ownership. As individuals grow

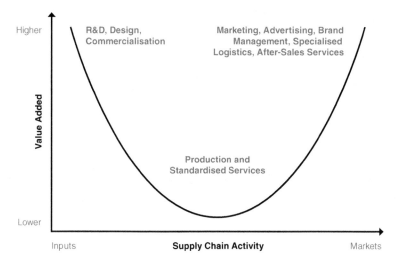

Fig. 1.2 Value creation and capture in the supply chain (*Source* Adapted from various publications, including Mudambi [11], Aggarwal [12] and Rungi and Prete [13])

frustrated with the responsibilities of owning too much stuff, they want to cut back and find new ways to access the products and services they want.

Other evidence of opportunities for growth is illustrated by Stan Shih's Smile Curve (Fig. 1.2). The smile curve divides a typical firm's supply chain into three parts: upstream (i.e., research and development, design and branding), midstream (i.e., production and assembly); and downstream (i.e., distribution, sales and services), and international studies have suggested, argued, and evidenced that value creation and capture are higher in the stages of pre- and post-production than within production itself [9, 10]. Largely this is because the entry barriers to competitors are higher in these regions, whereas in the middle it is relatively easy to replicate capabilities and so subject to more intense competition. So, for a firm in a developed country to stay ahead of competitors from lower-cost economies, it is necessary to climb from the midstream assembly stage to the pre- and post-production stages.

All this helps to illustrate that competing just through products is rarely enough. 'Making it' and 'Moving it' are the essential activities on which many industrial firms are founded, and yet in developed economies that strive for sustainable wealth creation, this focus is insufficient. The customer only gets value from 'using it', and business leaders and economic advisors who fail to grasp this will put their firms at a competitive disadvantage. Those executives that do will better position their firms to grow and become more sustainable.

Our Purpose with This Book

The international industrial data sends a powerful message to businesses: overlook the potential value of servitization at your peril. Yet many business executives, particularly those in firms with a heritage of products and production, focus on making and moving 'things'. They leave a gap which their customers are expected to fill themselves if they want to get the outcomes they desire. This gap represents an opportunity for business growth and sustainability through the process of servitization. It is a gap that is frequently overlooked by policymakers, executives, researchers, and consultants alike.

The principal objective of our book is to help this potential of servitization to be appreciated, understood, and addressed. To help both practitioners and researchers in contextualising servitization amongst the very many closely associated topics and innovations that now exist—from Subscriptions to Digital, from Product-Service Systems to Smart Connected Products—and to understand these, their relevance, and differences. We do this by bringing together leading research and practice in servitization, embracing both, to deliver insights and guidance that is rigorous and relevant. This will help to give business executives their best chance of success if they set out to apply servitization in their firms.

Our Target Audience

We have written this book for those people who are influencing and shaping practice and policy for the industry today and tomorrow; whether an experienced senior executive leader within a large multinational, an entrepreneurial director of a smaller enterprise, or a Master's student preparing themselves for a career in business. Although job titles and roles may differ, what our readers will have in common is a desire to protect and grow businesses through innovative services-led business models.

We expect that our readers will vary in terms of their knowledge of servitization. For those starting out, with little previous exposure to this topic, we want to help them understand the core concepts, language, and what to expect when they introduce servitization into their firm. For those people already on this journey, we want to help refine their thinking and set out what may still lie ahead. And for those who are well advanced and experienced, such as the very many people we have interviewed in the process of creating this book, we want to provide them with a means of communicating their experiences for the benefit of others.

This book should be especially beneficial for people dealing with firms that have a legacy of product design and production, firms that we generally refer to as manufacturers and industrial. Much of this book is also relevant to firms without this specific heritage. Every day we see more and more technology vendors converging on the services space that many industrial firms see as uniquely theirs. Indeed, as you will read in our concluding pages, we believe that these vendors are more likely to be the disrupters and exploit servitization faster than traditional manufacturers.

Our Focus and Positioning

This is a big-picture book about servitization. Sometimes servitization is thought of relatively narrowly: a manufacturing firm growing a portfolio of more conventional services such as selling more spare parts and repair; and there are many articles, conferences and special interest groups that deal with just this. Yet we have a wider focus. Our attention is on a broader and bolder innovation; that of enabling industrial firms which are historically product-centric, and output orientated, to compete strategically through more advanced services. These are higher value business models which target 'business outcomes'; offerings that treat Product-as-a-Service and earn revenue when the desired customer outcomes are achieved. And, while servitization is usually seen from the perspective of 'services around products', it can also feature as 'products around a services core' [1]. We embrace both.

Servitization is our principal theme as it places an unprecedented emphasis on the customer. Servitization also serves well as an integrating theme, drawing upon a wide range of popular topics (i.e., Product-Service Systems, Subscription, Smart Connected Products, IoT, etc.), some of which have strong theoretical underpinning (i.e., research on business model innovation) and others with strong roots in the practice community (i.e., Field Service, XaaS, EaaS, etc.). Our Fig. 1.3 helps to illustrate the principal topics that have become associated with, drawn into, and have influenced the development of servitization thinking.

From a research perspective, there are a wide range of authors from a variety of disciplines that are directly or indirectly contributing to the development of knowledge about servitization. Many of the scholars are regular and longstanding contributors to the Spring Servitization Conference (SSC)[7]

---

[7] https://www.advancedservicesgroup.co.uk/research/spring-servitization-conference/.

Fig. 1.3 Servitization within an ecosystem of research and practice (*Note* Publications by the authors named in this figure can be found in the bibliography. © The Advanced Services Group Ltd)

which is the principal forum for the world's foremost researchers coming together to share and progress this topic. We have positioned this book to embrace and draw together such contributions. For example, a popular topic is 'digital servitization', a term used to emphasise the almost essential role of digital tools (e.g., AI, IoT, remote condition monitoring, dashboards, etc.) in servitization with contributions from key authors such as Heiko Gebauer [14], Marko Kohtomaki [15] and Theoni Paschou [16]. In this book, we include these exciting evolutions, galvanising them together under the big picture of servitization.

Another key topic is Product-Service Systems (or PSS). There is excellent Scandinavian/Northern European-led PSS research mainly established by researchers seeking to improve social, economic, environmental and industrial sustainability [17, 18]. PSS researchers will talk about 'outcomes' under the notion of results-orientated services, where the product's functional results are sold and the ownership of the product remains with the provider [19]. Attention to delivering 'outcomes' is also growing in research communities around Industry 4.0 and the Internet of Things (IoT). The 'Fourth Industrial Revolution' (or Industry 4.0) originated from a project focused on developing high-tech strategy for the German government in 2011 [20]. The discussions started by focusing on the use of digital technologies (interconnectivity, smart automation, machine learning and real-time data) to enhance manufacturing processes, but more recently have coalesced around how such transformations can deliver more value for the customers. Several authors describe the IoT technology as a prerequisite for outcome-based business models [21].

From the perspective of the business community, servitization draws on the debate around leading thinking in Field Service, where publications such as *Field Service News* led by Kris Oldland have engaged and made an excellent contribution. Similarly, there is a wide range of practitioner- and vendor-sponsored conferences that regularly accommodate presentations, discussions and posts around topics, such as 'Everything-as-a-Service (XaaS)', 'Equipment-as-a-service (EaaS)', and 'Product-as-a-Service (PaaS)'. These often draw on examples of 'Software-as-a-Service' (SaaS), which is dealt with specifically by organisations such as the Technology Services Industrial Association [22]. Associated with this is work on 'Subscription' for which there is a wide range of practitioner-focused publications now available, such as the work by Stephan Liozu [23], Paul Dunn and Ronald Baker [24]. The work on Subscription is promoted and somewhat extended by concepts such as the 'Membership Economy' [8], heralded by authors such as Robbie Keller Baxter, which help to embrace the more social and community aspects of Subscription. Intriguingly, here there are links with the broader research on PSS and illustrated the linkages that exist (often implicitly) across all these topics.

Our Foundational Research

This book shares the findings from a structured research programme launched in 2014. A year earlier, we had published *Made to Serve* [25] which captured the state-of-the-art in servitization at that time. It introduced the concept of advanced services, and benchmarked the practices of leading international businesses engaged in servitization, such as Caterpillar, Rolls-Royce, Alstom, Xerox Corporation and MAN. While *Made to Serve* established the concept, it offered little information on how to innovate advanced services in organisations.

Since publishing Made to Serve, our research programme has studied the interplay of theory and practice and set out to understand and help industrial firms that have a strong product heritage to transform, so that they can compete through advanced services. All this has helped us to develop better knowledge and refine our understanding of these services as business models,[8] and their relevance and application in industry. For example, we have thoroughly examined the mechanisms for both creating and capturing value. We have also significantly extended our knowledge of the practices and technologies for servitization, beyond that captured in *Made to Serve*, and examined more closely the motives and benefits realised through success. Along the way, we have published over 80 articles in peer-reviewed journals and conferences, and our work has been cited nearly 30,000 times by others in the research community. Indeed, during this time, research interest in servitization has grown exponentially. Up to 2010 there were only about 49 peer-reviewed articles on servitization, but between 2010 and 2023, some 850 journal articles have been published in this field.

During this decade, we have also designed and executed research with a wide range of multinational businesses across sectors including defence, health, food and aerospace. Table 1.1 provides an overview of those that have been most influential in our work. Sometimes we have simply observed businesses as they have taken this journey, while other times we have directly informed their decisions to bring about servitization. Some businesses have helped us dive deeper into specific aspects of services, providing a small but essential nugget of knowledge. With others, such as Goodyear, Domino, Omron, Tetra Pak, Thales and Baxi, their executives have helped us gain a complete picture of the transformation process. We have learned about these companies' challenges, helped to inform their decisions, and shared their successes and frustrations. Our core insights and frameworks have been influenced, evaluated, and are now practised within a wide range of such multinationals.

In addition, we have engaged with over 200 smaller businesses as they too have explored and adopted servitization [27]. Collectively, we have witnessed their development and widespread adoption of new business models, strategic investments, cultural change, and improved business performance. We have observed impacts across the global markets of Europe, USA, China and Brazil; from large American multinationals to small businesses in the West Midlands of the United Kingdom. We also recorded the consequences of these changes in terms of employment, sales and growth. In this book, we share accounts of these successes, along with more grim reports of where companies have failed, why, and in what way.

Much of the research in this book has been carried out by our team, the Advanced Services Group, based in Birmingham, UK. In addition, many

---

[8] The business model concept is underpinned by an integration of various theoretical perspectives, including both variance and process theories [26].

Table 1.1 Overview of the firms studied through our research programme

	PARENT/HOLDING COMPANY	INDUSTRY/BUSINESS FOCUS	TEAMS/DEPARTMENTS ENGAGED WITH	SIZE (TURNOVER/NO OF STAFF) [1]
1	The Goodyear Tire & Rubber Company	Passenger, commercial and aircraft tyre	Global Innovation and Proactive Solutions Europe	~ $12bn / ~ 72,000
2	Rolls-Royce	Aerospace and defence	Civil Aerospace, Defence, and Electrical Aviation	~ $13bn / ~ 50,000
3	Alstom	Rail transportation	Train Life Services UK	~ $15bn / ~ 75,000
4	Thompson Tractor USA & Finning UK (Caterpillar Dealership)	Heavy equipment supply and service	Service and Equipment Management	~ $440m / ~ 1,500 (Thompson Tractor) ~ $102m / ~ 1,400 (Finning UK)
5	Xerox Corporation	Manufacturer and provider of document solutions and services	Technical Service, Xerox International	~ $7bn / ~ 20,000
6	MAN Truck & Bus	Truck and trailer manufacturer	MAN Truck & Bus UK	~ $11bn / ~ 34,000
7	Ishida	Packaging equipment	Proactive Services EMEA	~ $1bn / ~ 3,500
8	Nederman	Manufacturer of air filtration equipment	Services and IoT Platforms	~ $4bn / ~ 1,900
9	Yanmar	Heavy equipment	After Sales Services Europe	~ $6bn / ~ 18,000
10	Moog Inc.	Manufacturer of precision motion control systems	Industrial Services	~ $3bn / ~ 10,700
11	Crown Equipment Corporation	Industrial forklift trucks	Service Design and Customer Support	~ $4bn / ~ 16,000
12	Genie	Lifting and material handling	Services Operations	~ $1.6bn / ~ 3,800
13	Domino Printing Sciences	Developer of industrial and commercial inkjet printing	Connected Services	~ $900m / ~ 2,800
14	BAXI	Manufacturer and distributor of domestic and commercial water and space heating systems	Product Management UK and Ireland	~ $2.2bn / ~ 6,400
15	Thales	Manufacturer of electrical systems and equipment for the aerospace, defence, transportation and security sectors	Land and Air Systems	~ $16bn / ~ 80,000
16	Legrand	Producer of switches and sockets	Assisted Living and Healthcare	~ $7bn / ~ 38,000
17	Yamazaki Mazak Corporation	Manufacturer of machine tools and equipment	European Services Sales Engineering	~ $328m / ~ 7,800
18	Donaldson Company	Manufacturer of air filtration equipment	Business Development and After Market Services	~ $328m / ~ 11,000
19	Omron	Manufacturing and sales of automation components, equipment and systems	Service Business Development EMEA	~ $8bn / ~ 39,500
20	Tetra Pak	Multinational food packaging and processing manufacturer	Global Services Business	~ $11.5bn / ~ 25,500

[1] All company information and statistics captured in this table are as of 2022/23.

academic and industrial colleagues have provided critiques of our work and made suggestions on how to improve it. We are immensely grateful for their input. In the acknowledgments section, we have recognised their participation and contribution to this study.

Our Structure

We have constructed this book around three principal questions: *What is servitization and what are advanced services? Why are these important?* and *How can businesses with a heritage of products and production go about innovating and exploiting these services?* Using this structure, we provide a series of chapters which take you through a logical, digestible, and hopefully interesting journey. Throughout, we have attempted to use straightforward language, helpful illustrations, and examples taken from businesses we know and have researched. In particular, we use the example of 'heat-as-a-service' to help ground and enrich our description of an advanced services business model. Finally, we have also developed a series of complementary resources to help you apply servitization in practice, and these can be accessed via our online store: https://www.advancedservicesgroup.co.uk/store/.

References

1 Linz, C., G. Müller-Stewens, and A. Zimmermann, *Radical business model transformation: Gaining the competitive edge in a disruptive world*. 2017: Kogan Page Publishers.

2 Goodyear. *Form 10-K for The goodyear tire & rubber company*. 2022 [cited 2023 20/03/2023]; Available from: https://corporate.goodyear.com/us/en/invest ors/financial-reports.html.

3 Goodyear. *Goodyear launches new business—Connected fleet management solutions*. 2016 [cited 2023 4/01/2023]; Available from: https://news.goodyear.eu/goodyear-launches-new-business---connected-fleet-management-solutions/.

4 Goodyear. *Goodyear launches end-to-end fleet offer, goodyear total mobility*. 2019 [cited 2023 04/01/2023]; Available from: https://news.goodyear.eu/goodyear-launches-new-end-to-end-fleet-offer-goodyear-total-mobility/.

5 Goodyear. *What's goodyear total mobility?* 2023 [cited 2023 4/01/2023]; Available from: https://www.goodyear.eu/en_gb/truck/Goodyear-Total-Mobility.html.

6 TheWorldBank. *Manufacturing and service value added indicators*. 2021.

7 WorldTradeReport, *The future of service trade*. 2019.

8 Baxter, R.K., *The membership economy find your superusers, master the forever transaction, and build recurring revenue*. 1st edition ed. 2015: McGraw-Hill. 272.

9 Shih, S., *Reconstitution of acer: Start-up, growth and challenge*. 1992: Taipei Commonwealth Publishing: Taipei, Taiwan.

10 Shen, J.H., K. Deng, and S. Tang, *Re-evaluating the 'smile curve'in relation to outsourcing industrialization*. Emerging Markets Finance and Trade, 2021. **57**(5): p. 1247–1270.

11 Mudambi, R., *Location, control and innovation in knowledge-intensive industries*. Journal of economic Geography, 2008. **8**(5): p. 699–725.

12 Aggarwal, S., *Smile curve and its linkages with global value chains*. Journal of Economics Bibliography, 2017. **4**(3): p. 278–286.

13 Rungi, A. and D. Del Prete, *'Smile curve': Where value is added along supply chains*. 2017.

14 Gebauer, H., et al., *Organizational capabilities for pay-per-use services in product-oriented companies*. International Journal of Production Economics, 2017. **192**: p. 157–168.

15 Kohtamäki, M., et al., *Digital servitization business models in ecosystems: A theory of the firm*. Journal of Business Research, 2019. **104**: p. 380–392.

16 Paschou, T., et al., *Digital servitization in manufacturing as a new stream of research: a review and a further research*. A Research Agenda for Service Innovation, 2018: p. 148–165.

17 Mont, O., *Product-service systems: panacea or myth?* 2004: Lund University.

18 Goedkoop, M.J., et al., *Product service systems, ecological and economic basics*. 1999.

19 Tukker, A., *Eight types of product–service system: Eight ways to sustainability? Experiences from SusProNet*. Business Strategy and the Environment, 2004. **13**(4): p. 246–260.

20 Xu, X., et al., *Industry 4.0 and Industry 5.0—Inception, conception and perception*. Journal of Manufacturing Systems, 2021. **61**: p. 530–535.

21 Spring, M. and L. Araujo, *Product biographies in servitization and the circular economy*. Industrial Marketing Management, 2017. **60**: p. 126–137.

22 Lah, T. and J. Wood, *Technology-as-a-service playbook: How to grow a profitable subscription business*. 2016: Point B, Inc.

23 Liozu, S.M., *The industrial subscription economy: A practical guide to designing, pricing and scaling your industrial subscription*. 2021: Value Innoruption Advisors Publishing.

24 Dunn, P. and R.J. Baker, *Time's up!: The subscription business model for professional firms*. 2022: John Wiley & Sons.

25 Baines, T. and H. Lightfoot, *Made to serve*. What it takes for a Manufacturer to Compete, 2013.

26 Hedman, J. and T. Kalling, *The business model concept: theoretical underpinnings and empirical illustrations*. European Journal of Information Systems, 2003. **12**: p. 49–59.

27 Baines, T., et al., *Servitization applied, an insight into small and medium-sized businesses innovating their service strategies.* The Advanced Services Group. 2019: Birmingham: Aston Business School.

Part I

What Is Servitization and What Are Advanced Services

#servitization: outcomes rather than just outputs

2

Servitization, Advanced Services and Outcomes

We sell servitization! Just a short while ago I delivered a keynote on servitization at a conference for senior and influential asset financiers in London. Interest in servitization and charging customers through Subscription has been rapidly growing within this community, and I had been invited as the principal authority to share lessons from other industries. My session was in the afternoon, and so in the morning I sat in the audience and listened to the other speakers. The event was launched by the Chief Executive of a powerful multinational financier and his opening remark was simply 'we sell servitization; we have been selling servitization for years'. This comment was picked up and repeated by many of the other speakers that then followed, each tempted to outdo the previous—the overriding message they were all trying to give was that their businesses were mature in their understanding and application of the concept. So, I made no friends when I took the stage and started by pointing out, 'You can't sell servitization!'.

Terminology is important: words and phrases are to be used with sensitivity, and the names and definitions given to a phenomenon are to be respected. This clarity is essential for science to progress, for knowledge to be established and taught, and for actions to be precise, appropriate and understood. This is just as important for research within business as it is for the laboratory. And so, in this section, we clarify what we mean by servitization, advanced services and outcomes. At the end, you will appreciate why it really doesn't make much sense to talk about selling servitization. But, perhaps more importantly, this section will help you to understand what we mean by an advanced service—what the customer is actually receiving, and how they will typically pay.

T. Baines et al., *Servitization Strategy*, Palgrave Executive Essentials, https://doi.org/10.1007/978-3-031-45426-4_2

Servitization: A Working Definition

To begin, we need to prepare you for the following chapter by providing a working definition of servitization. When our work began to gain traction in the early 2000s, we brought together contributions from a range of authors and practitioners, and characterised servitization as 'the innovation of a company's capabilities and processes to better create mutual value through a shift from selling products to selling integrated product-service systems' [1]. Over the succeeding years, our definition has become very popular amongst the research community, and this largely reflects how we and many others still think about and write about servitization today. This definition makes a good starting point for our book, but there are a couple of small, yet significant, caveats to keep in mind as you read the following chapters.

First, you will find that we no longer refer to servitization as a 'shift' or a 'transition' 'from' products 'to' services. This is partially because these words have unintended side effects. They suggest that servitization is restricted to manufacturing firms [2], and that adoption in such firms will directly and potentially dramatically lead to disinvestment. The term 'shift' is all too easily interpreted as a 'shift away' and suggests a reduction: less production, less people, some redundancy, and eventually factory closure. This can lead employees to feel threatened by servitization and so create barriers to adoption. Christian Kowalkowski, in his excellent book on service strategy, challenges business leaders to question whether indeed a change should be so radical [3]. In addition, the terms 'shift' and 'transition' do not necessarily reflect what we see in practice; Rolls-Royce still maintains a healthy product-centric business activity which complements their services business. As a consequence, we favour the more inclusive term of 'transformation' over 'shift'.

Second, we have found that defining servitization only in terms of products and services doesn't do justice to the ambitions of leading firms in this space. This is because people struggle to define these. All too often a product is taken to be something that is material (it will hurt if you drop it on your toes), whereas a service is 'everything else which is not a product'. This is generally consistent with a Goods-Dominant Logic. Some scholars provide a tighter definition by treating a service as a process—a collection of inputs (people, technologies, information) that are applied and, in doing so, can create value [2, 4]. This is taken from Service-Dominant Logic (SDL) [5], which goes on to treat services as the fundamental basis of economic activity and a unit of exchange.

We now think of servitization as a move towards delivering 'outcomes'. Take a look at the services marketing literature and you will find the term 'outcomes' is gaining popularity (more on this later). The notion of an outcome helps to avoid a distracting debate about the distinction between a product and service. And so, if traditional factories are all about 'outputs', then *servitization can be thought of as transforming a firm to also compete through offering 'outcomes' to customers*. We refer to business models that are based on delivering such outcomes as advanced services business models. You will find that we present servitization in this way as the common thread throughout the book. It is a working definition, and you will also see that in the later sections of Chapter 7, when we tell you much more about servitization and advanced services, we return to reflect more deeply on the definition of servitization.

Business Model Thinking: A Powerful Lens to Unpack Servitization

When Sandra Vandermerwe and Juan Rada [6] first introduced the term 'servitization' in the late 1980s, they saw it as a process where companies add more and more value to their core offering through bundling and combining customer-oriented goods and services. They also asserted that not only service industries but also manufacturing industries should focus on innovative value-added service development. They carefully pointed out that servitization referred to the evolutionary pathway of organisational change, from a pure product perspective towards an integrated product–service orientation, so that the firm providing the offering is better able to lock out competitors, lock in customers and increase market differentiation.

So how is servitization thought about today? The foundations put forward by Vandermerwe and Rada have stood the test of time, though often servitization is seen to concern businesses with a strong production heritage bundling services with products to strengthen their value proposition for customers. So much so, that while earlier research papers on servitization made an explicit link to 'manufacturing' in their titles, today this association is often taken for granted. It is generally assumed that any article dealing with servitization is concerned with industrial or manufacturing firms.

Yet, there is a growing appreciation (or re-acknowledgment) that businesses which are often thought of as pure service can also apply servitization by bundling products into their service offering to strengthen their value proposition for customers. Serco [7] is a good example of this. Traditionally, it provided relatively ordinary services such as catering and site maintenance to the UK Armed Forces. Over time, it has become more involved with asset support, such as aircraft maintenance, engine maintenance, and modification and upgrades. Serco doesn't necessarily go as far as production, but its orientation towards products has grown. This has been a necessary step in order to provide the outcomes that its customers now seek.

Quite often servitization is conceptualised as a firm's movement along a continuum, ranging from pure products or goods (outputs of the manufacturer) to pure services provision [8]. This representation, put forward by Oliva and Kallenberg in 2003, helped to foster the idea that servitization was a 'shift' from products to services [9]. An idea complemented by researchers such as Mathieu (2001) who saw servitization as a movement from 'services supporting the product' to 'services supporting the customer' [10].

While the integration of products and services remains core to servitization, this is now better understood through the lens of business models. In the past, there were often debates about the composition of a business model; in practice, the term was often used loosely, simply being thought of as being synonymous with how much is charged for a service or how the customer might pay. Over the last decade, research on business models has advanced significantly, and now it provides a means of systematically expressing what is being offered to customers, how this is delivered, and how value is then captured by the provider of the offering. A business model is now seen as the architecture through which a firm creates, delivers, and captures value, and how it achieves competitive advantage from these processes. It is the logic for value creation and appropriation [4].

Commonly, there are seen to be three principal components of a business model [4]: (i) the customer-centric front end (value proposition and customer/consumer interaction), (ii) the organisational back-end (the operating model, the coordinated activity/resource system needed to realise and deliver the value proposition), and (iii) the monetisation mechanics (the approach to value capture, what is paid and how value is appreciated over time). Some scholars see a fourth element that captures the basis of competitive advantage Some scholars see a fourth element that captures the broader economic, market and social context within which the business model operates. The external environment plays a crucial role in shaping the opportunities and challenges faced by a firm and determining its potential for sustained competitive advantage (how to be better than the competition). The framework illustrated in Fig. 2.1 captures these four components.

A competitive product or service offering gives customers some benefit for which they are willing to pay. The combination of the offering (what

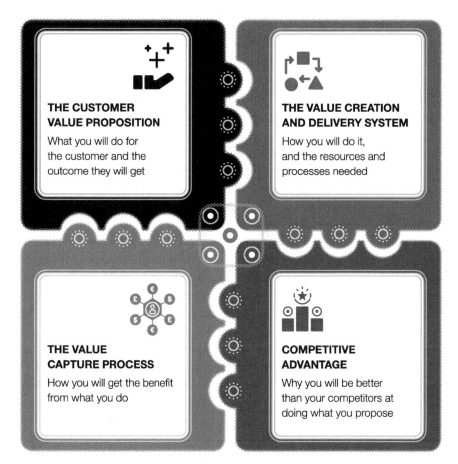

Fig. 2.1 Framework illustrating the principal components of a business model (© The Advanced Services Group Ltd)

is provided) and the benefit (the results for the customer) is termed the customer value proposition. The business model framework is helpful because it forces a distinction between the actual service that is being offered to the customer, from how a service is delivered and rewarded. For example, it is quite common to hear an executive say, 'We're offering Condition Monitoring', or 'We're offering Digital Services', or 'We're offering Pay-as-you-go Services'. Yet, none of these are actually offerings. Rather they tend to describe services in terms of 'what it is' rather than 'what it offers' customers. The customer receives a confusing message, the potential value isn't clear, and this slows the sale. What they are really saying is that '*If you buy this machine, we will put in place a digital system, which will allow us to monitor the machine as it works, and if its condition or performance declines then we will alert you*'. Here, the actual offering is a form of 'advice'—the provider is offering to advise the customer of any changes in condition or performance of the machine.

Here, the business model framework is especially useful during discussions about 'digital services'. The mantra from many tech companies exaggerates the problem: *How can you not embrace digital in today's day and age?* So powerful is the messaging that many executives are simply too cautious to ask, '*What are these new digital services?*' Here, the business model framework leads executives to question whether a 'new digital service' is either a new customer value proposition or an existing proposition which uses digital to improve the efficiency of its delivery. The first occurs, for instance, if a producer of machine tools were to develop a digitally-enabled condition monitoring capability and then begin to offer 'advice' to customers—just as mentioned above. This is a new customer value proposition which didn't previously exist. If, however, the machine tool producer already sold such advice to customers, perhaps in the form of consulting support provided by field service technicians, then this would be an example of exploiting digital innovation in the service delivery process. In this instance the producer is replacing a physical form of consulting with a form of online performance dashboard.

The business model framework also helps with discussions about financial innovations and services. For example, subscription-based payments are becoming increasingly popular, whether for streaming music through Spotify or leasing a car from a dealership. Executives might describe these innovations by saying, 'We're offering pay-as-you-go or subscription-based services.' Once again, by using the business model framework, it becomes clear that such a change in the payment process is actually a revenue model innovation rather than new service. Leasing and rental are similar examples, and all part of financing which enables new services in turn enable customers to gain access to equipment, but not themselves defining an innovative service offering based on such equipment. Leasing and rental are similar examples, and all part of financing which enables new services that which enable customers to gain access to equipment. Leasing and rental, though, so not themselves define an innovative service offering based on such equipment.

We saw how a business model framework could aid servitization during our work with Jim Euchner at The Goodyear Tire & Rubber Company. Jim was leading on the exploration of new business models for truck tyres based around 'truck mobility'. Some of his colleagues assumed that these were the same as existing 'pay-per-use' models. However, Goodyear had 'sold' truck tyres for many years on the basis of 'pence per kilometre' (PPK). This typically meant that the fee the customer 'paid' for the tyre was broken down into instalments based around distance travelled. The truck operator typically still took ownership of the tyre and many of the responsibilities for tyre mainte-nance. The innovations of Jim's team differed significantly, but because the names seemed similar, he faced internal barriers to adoption. By applying the business model logic, he was able to delineate the service innovation (poten-tially Goodyear offering a whole package of services to keep the truck on the road) from conversations about the ways in which the customer might pay for such a service. Slowly this helped Jim's ideas to gain traction.

All this helps to illustrate how the business model framework (Fig. 2.1) is invaluable in unpacking servitization. It provides a clear distinction between what is being offered to customers, how this is delivered, and how value is then captured by the providers of the offering. It allows us to covey that servi-tization is principally concerned with the innovation of the customer value proposition, and while such innovations are often accompanied by changes to the revenue model and delivery system, these changes taken alone don't necessarily mean that servitization is taking place within a firm. The next step, therefore, in understanding servitization is to explore the various forms a customer value proposition might take, and to do this we use another framework known as the 'services staircase'.

Services Staircase: Understanding Value Propositions for Servitization

Servitization is concerned with the bundling and integration of product and services, and differing combinations support different types of customers. Our earlier book, *Made to Serve*, drew upon the practices observed in Cater-pillar Dealerships who grouped their customers into three distinct types based on their buying behaviours. Each type necessitating a specific combination of integrated products–services to be offered by the Dealership:

- Customers who want to '*do it themselves*': we refer to the integration of products and services that fit this customer type as base services.
- Customers who want the provider to '*do it with them*': we refer to the inte-gration of products and services that fit this customer type as intermediate services.
- Customers who want the provider to '*do it for them*': we refer to the inte-gration of products and services that fit this customer type as advanced services.

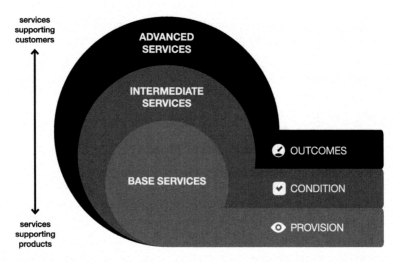

services
supporting
customers

ADVANCED
SERVICES

INTERMEDIATE
SERVICES

OUTCOMES

BASE SERVICES

CONDITION

services
supporting
products

PROVISION

Fig. 2.2 The three principal types of services of an industrial firm (© The Advanced Services Group Ltd)

This is a quick and helpful grouping of service offerings. Base services are where customers simply want to buy the product, and perhaps spare parts, along with the usual assurances of safety and compliance (i.e., guarantees and warranties). Intermediate services are for customers who might buy the product, but on occasion also ask for help with some periodic maintenance, repair and overhaul. Advanced services are for customers who tend to be results-orientated and just want to achieve business outcomes. These three sets of service offerings build on each other as illustrated in Fig. 2.2, and services can be thought of as differing, based on whether they focus on supporting the product or supporting customers. This grouping can be further subdivided by reflecting on the differing levels of bundling and responsibilities that providers take on behalf of customers. This is the basis of the 'services staircase' as seen in Fig. 2.3.

We first came across the concept of a services staircase in the defence industries. Shortly after its formation, the UK's Defence Logistics Organisation (DLO) began transforming the support arrangements for its various defence platforms, systems and equipment so that more of responsibilities were transferred to industry partners. A staircase illustration was developed to represent the successive steps that were needed to move away from traditional support arrangements (from the DLO paying for items to be repaired) to a point where it paid to receive specified levels of military capability. We took this concept and by working with a cross-section of businesses, developed a generic staircase that can be used to represent service-based customer value propositions more widely across industry.

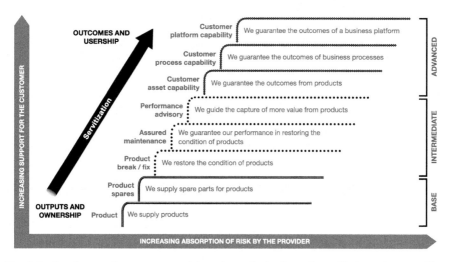

Fig. 2.3 Services staircase summarising the principal service offerings (*Note* Offerings higher up the staircase mean that the provider is giving increasing support to customers, and taking on responsibilities that would have otherwise sat with the customer [or another provider]. *Source* Adapted from Baines et al., 2019. © The Advanced Services Group Ltd)

Our staircase (Fig. 2.3) shows eight steps, each representing a different services offer made by the provider to the customer. The vertical (y axis) reflects the distinction we mentioned earlier—whether a service is supporting a product (spare parts, repair) or directly supporting the customer [11]. On the horizontal axis is the responsibility taken on by the provider which would have otherwise sat with the customer (or another partner) [12]. In moving up the staircase to solve a customer's problem, the provider increasingly combines and integrates products and services [13]. In doing so, the provider takes on greater responsibilities for risks and (if all goes well) can capture greater value in return. For example, if a provider offers to 'restore the condition of a product' they are integrating services (i.e.: identifying worn components, supplying spare parts and organising repair), and inevitably they will offer a set of assurances about the work they carry out (i.e.: faults will be resolved, performance will be restored).

The staircase is helpful for illustrating servitization. Firms that are product-centric, just supplying products and spare parts, are positioned on the lower levels of the staircase. Firms that go a step further to offer intermediate services, such as repair and maintenance programmes, are positioned on the mid-levels of the staircase. Those firms that offer even more to customers, such as outcome-based advanced services, are on the higher levels of the staircase. The extent and plans for servitization can be illustrated by determining the current position of a firm against the staircase, and then reflecting on the footprint of the firm in the past and its intentions for the future.

Most executives are fully conversant with services on the lower levels of the staircase. Spare parts are extra components for parts that may fail or wear out in a system or product, to be used for repair or replacement. Break-fix programmes are support services that customers can pay for on an as-needed basis, typically when there is an issue with the product that needs to be fixed. Assured maintenance programmes (mid-levels of the staircase) are maintenance service agreements that provide customers with scheduled maintenance and repair services for their products or equipment, typically for a fixed period of time or a certain number of service visits. These programmes offer a higher level of assurance and predictability than the break-fix programmes, giving customers greater confidence that their equipment or products will be properly maintained and serviced according to a pre-defined schedule.

Most of the attention given to servitization concerns services that are higher on the staircase. In particular, there are a growing number of successful industrial applications of Performance Advisory services. Table 2.1 illustrates a variety of these. Most Service Executives will have come across these services as digital innovations offering remote monitoring, usage analytics and dashboards. The basis of a performance advisory service is that it offers the customer guidance on how to get greater value out of a product.

An example of such a service is the Ecostyle driver and vehicle performance reporting from MAN Truck & Bus UK. The history behind this is that MAN recognised that fuel consumption was heavily dependent on the way a truck was driven. A driver who drove erratically, braked heavily, and accelerated hard, would burn more diesel than an equivalent truck driven smoothly. So, MAN developed a digital system to monitor how their trucks are driven to be able to provide a detailed breakdown of drivers' performance, across metrics such as harsh braking, idling and green-band driving. All of which translates into a financial impact on the customers' operations [14]. This service innovation has helped MAN to achieve differentiation in the marketplace and to win market share from its rivals. Additionally, this has helped to bring about a significant reduction in fuel consumption and CO_2 emissions from the trucks. And, as we will discuss later, digital technologies are at the core of many servitization strategies [15].

The very top levels of the staircase focus on advanced services. We will explain these in depth shortly, but for the moment just think of these as the

Table 2.1 Examples of performance advisory services

Company	Example offering	Description
GE Energy	Remote monitoring and diagnostic (RM&D) service	GE Energy offer active monitoring for aeroderivative gas turbine plants. It provides early warning of changing operating conditions and prompts on-site action for issue resolution. This enables faster response to unplanned events, diagnosis and correction of faults, and analysis to seek out emerging trends to enable proactive intervention against potential outages and extended downtime
Siemens	Condition-based monitoring of baggage carts at airports	Siemens offers a condition-based monitoring service, for airports, which gathers acoustic and vibration data from rail mounted luggage carts that transport checked-in baggage around the airport. Analysis of the data indicates likely future breakdowns and Siemens advises the customer that maintenance is needed. This is intended to prevent breakdowns that cost time and money, to prevent penalties for the airport operator due to luggage not being loaded onto flights and to improve the passenger experience through the punctual delivery of baggage

(continued)

Table 2.1 (continued)

Company	Example offering	Description
Nicklin Transit Packaging	Monitoring packages in transit	Nicklin makes packaging (crates, pallets, etc.) used by businesses to transport a wide range of manufactured goods. It uses tracking units and sensors placed on packaging containing delicate items to monitor the location of the packaging, whether it has experienced shocks (e.g. from being dropped), and exposure to moisture or extreme temperatures. The data that is collected can be used by Nicklin and its customers to identify whether (and if so, where and when) items have been damaged in transit
Emerson Retail Solutions	Refrigeration efficiency monitoring	Emerson Retail Solutions sells temperature controls and monitoring systems to customers in food retail and transportation, and restaurants. Sensors on Emerson's equipment collect intelligence regarding the performance of refrigeration units. This is used to sell an advisory service to customers to advise on the efficiency of the design of their refrigeration units

Company	Example offering	Description
Domino Printing Sciences	Safeguard service	Domino Printing Sciences develops and manufactures coding, marking and printing technologies and aftermarket products. Its products are used to apply variable and authentication data, barcodes and unique traceability data onto products and packaging, such as 'use by' dates for food products, batch or lot information for industrial manufacturing, and serialised codes for regulated industry compliance. Domino's SafeGuard service provides status and performance data from its equipment to a dedicated Cloud service, accessible to Domino and the customer via a web dashboard. Today, simple automated alerts help customers prevent avoidable production outages, while remote diagnostics allows issues to be resolved more quickly and accurately
UV Light Technology Ltd	Sterile environment	UV Light Technology Ltd sells UV equipment for a wide variety of applications, including food (reduction of bacteria), medical (show contamination and improve hygiene) and industrial (detection of cracks and leaks, curing paint). Data is collected from its machines and sold to customers on a subscription basis as a service that enables them to monitor and control the running of the equipment

'outcome-based' services. Pioneering examples of such include Rolls-Royce with 'power-by-the-hour' to airlines, and Xerox Corporation with 'pay-per-copy' on document printing machines.

Providers progress up the staircase with their offerings by doing more to support their customers' business processes. More responsibilities and so more risk. Indeed, much of the appeal of advanced services for customers is that they don't need to expend time and resources to get a job done and done right (because they are buying an outcome). For customers, using an advanced service should result in lower risks, lower upfront expenses and lower maintenance [16], and this is because providers are now being contracted to take on responsibilities that previously sat with the customer themselves. Each new responsibility comes with new risks for the provider.

Executives with a background in asset management will often view servitization as a means to risk management. In the construction industry, for example, building a road might necessitate a range of excavators and heavy machinery. For each of these assets, there will be a variety of risks or hazards that could result in financial loss; for instance, the equipment might not be up to the job, or possibly be expensive to maintain, or it might take longer to repair, and be difficult to operate properly or not be reusable on other projects. A customer may choose to take on the responsibility for such risks; or, alternatively, it could buy services so that some or all of this responsibility is transferred to a provider. Servitization takes place where a customer, who has traditionally taken on such responsibilities (i.e., selected, maintained, repaired, monitored, and disposed the equipment), instead contracts for these from a willing and able equipment provider. There is a change with regards to who takes on the responsibilities involved—and this can be regarded as managing risk.

The risks themselves don't change—whoever takes the responsibility for them. However, if a provider offers a customer new advanced services (it moves higher up the services staircase), then there may be a greater awareness of the risks involved, and their consequences. To deal with this new awareness, it is possible to categorise risks, and there are various ways of doing this. One approach is to identify internal and external risks: internal risks relate to the broader aspects of the business model design, whether the organisation has the right competencies, resources and processes; and external risks relate to aspects such as shifting markets and disruptions (i.e. technological, social, environmental or regulatory) [17, 18].

Figure 2.4 introduces a risk and responsibility axis of the services staircase to illustrate how these are typically associated with different service offerings. While these responsibilities may vary from one business application to another, it helps to show how responsibilities change. For example, in a situation where the offering to the customer is for the sale of a product (envelop 1), then the provider is only undertaking to supply a safe and functional product. However, should the provider offer an assured maintenance programme (envelop 2), then it is also taking on additional responsibilities around spare parts, repair, and maintenance. This changing footprint of responsibilities occurs with servitization, some of these can, of course, be offset by partnerships, etc., and we will discuss these later in Chapter 4.

The profile of risks illustrated in Fig. 2.4 also helps to explain the competencies necessary to successfully deliver an advanced services business model. We explain in Chapter 5 that there are a variety of incentives for an industrial firm to embrace servitization and supply services bundled with their products. Done well, it is a largely linear relationship between the firm moving up the services staircase and the value generated from a customer. Put simply, the more you do for a customer the more money you can expect to earn. The situation with profitability is though more complex. Although the total value of profits increases in line with the services staircase, the margins themselves are impacted by a variety of factors, especially the firm's capabilities to manage their new responsibilities for risk. Industrial firms often have some inherent capabilities from which they can take advantage. For instance, manufacturers like to think that since they design and produce a product, they are also in the

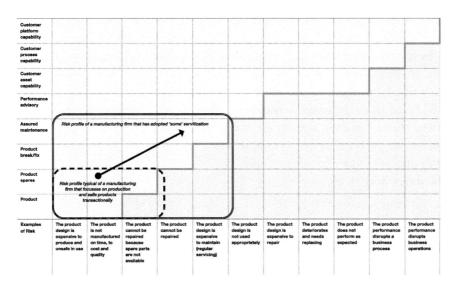

Fig. 2.4 Risks and responsibilities and how these can change with servitization (© The Advanced Services Group Ltd)

best position to monitor, repair and maintain that product. In reality additional capabilities will be needed, and if these are not in place to support a contract, then the firm will be exposed, and their financial performance can be severely affected.

Advanced Services: A Working Definition

In the early days of our servitization research we recognised that there were a group of services-based business models, beyond those that focused on spare parts and maintenance contracts, which were more exciting and valuable to businesses. These came in many guises, such as Outcome-Based Contracts' (OBC), Capability Contracts (CC) [19] or Performance-Based Contracts (PBC). Yet they all aspired to delivering outcomes associated with customers' business processes, for example, flight hours or passenger movement [20]. This notion of 'outcomes' when the service is 'used' is often explicit in the popular names given to these, such as 'power-by-the-hour', 'pay-per-click', 'pay-per-pack', and 'pay-per-print'.

We found none of the existing terminologies entirely adequate to describe all the differing forms these services could take, and so we created the term 'advanced services' to represent this group. Although this is a broad collective of services, they characteristically focus on delivering outcomes for customers rather than improving the accessibility or condition of products. Customers benefit from these outcomes as a result of using the service (value-in-use). These are integrated product-service systems with the customer paying mainly (and in some cases, entirely) for the contracted outcomes, and typically benefiting from reduced and more predictable operating costs [21].

This led us to define an 'advanced service' as an '*integrated products-service system, that when used, delivers outcomes that directly align with value creation and capture processes within a customer's own organisation*'. To help you understand these services in more depth, we will now say a little more about 'outcomes' and 'usage'.

Advanced Services: Outcomes Rather Than Outputs

An outcome refers to the way a thing turns out, a consequence or change resulting from an action or activity. In a business context, the notion of an 'outcome' is often introduced alongside the associated nomenclature of 'input', 'activity', 'output', and 'impact'. Each means something different:

- Input: resources needed to carry out the activity
- Activity: conversion process
- Output: primary deliverables from the activity
- Outcome: results from the deliverables
- Impact: consequences from the results

The way in which these terms interrelate to each other presupposes a cascading cause and effect. A wide range of systems and scenarios can be described using these terms and Table 2.2 gives a set of examples which help to illustrate this application to practice.

Outcome-Based Thinking (or OBT) is a recognised management practice and is the process of setting goals and measuring progress according to the desired effect (rather than the actions taken to get that effect). An illustration of this is provided by Elon Musk, who is demonstrating outcome-based thinking when he talks about SpaceX, describing the project in terms of getting humans to Mars and making humans a space-faring species; whereas

Table 2.2 Examples of scenarios and associated outcomes

Scenario	Process descriptors				
	Input	Activity	Output	Outcome	Impact
Personal fitness	Self, time, tread-mill	Running	Calories burnt	Weight loss	Wellbeing
Field technician supporting domestic boilers	Self, time, van, parts	Boiler repair	Operational boiler	Warm room	Comfortable building
Using drilling equipment	Pistol drill, drill bit, elec-tricity	Operate drill	Rotational speed and torque	Hole in a wall	Able to fix shelf
Organisation's IT department	People, time, hard-ware, soft-ware	Computer support	Software installa-tion	Effective word processing	Document production
Provision of internet connection at home	Provider, cable, router, computer	Connection to internet	Download and upload speed	Able to use MS Teams	Good communication

other people might have seen the project as it being all about the feasibility to re-land a rocket (Technology Thinking) or solving the problem of costly satellite delivery (Problem Thinking) [22]. Thinking in terms of outcomes can be challenging for people; we have a very long history of thinking in terms of activities (for example, running, repairing or operating equipment) and the associated outputs (for example, distance, an operational machine, parts or products).

Outcome-based thinking has been advocated and practised in a range of sectors such as education and health for some time. There are also some examples in the industrial sector, with perhaps the most well-known being in marketing. Theodore Levitt, an American economist, once famously stated that 'customers may purchase quarter inch drill bits, but what they really want is a quarter inch hole'. Although this remark is accredited to Levitt (see Clayton M. Christensen [23]), this understanding has been used in the marketing literature for some time. Levitt himself attributed the remark to McGivena in 1969 and earlier works from 1947 [24], and today almost every marketer we know agrees with Levitt's insight.

The services staircase embodies this thinking. The upper steps encompass three levels of outcomes: outcomes around a product, a business process, or a business platform. Indeed, as we mentioned above, when contracts are formed at these levels they are often referred to as outcome-based and associated with revenue models based on 'pay-per-outcome'. The opportunity offered by focusing on outcomes is summed up well by the authors Lah and Wood, who state that a focus on business outcomes opens the door to all kinds of new value-adding opportunities. Tasks that used to be performed by customers—or didn't get done at all—can now be performed by providers. This is a chance to replace classic product-attached services with new, much higher value-adding services [21].

A fitting example of outcome thinking can be observed in the case of the ICI-Nobel Explosives Company in Great Britain. Back in the 1990s, they produced explosives for coal mining, but the decline of that industry led its product to be used mainly in quarries. The price competition was fierce and there was little to no brand loyalty. Quarries demanded last-minute deliveries and ICI-Nobel had to fulfil these orders or risk losing business. Varying order amounts and unpredictable delivery patterns meant the capacity of the firm's delivery trucks was underutilised, also impacting profits [25]. So, given its expertise on blasting, ICI-Nobel began working on a new software program that could be used to optimise the location of drilled holes for the explosives and also the timing patterns for the blast. The new software gave the firm the competitive and productivity advantage that had been missing. It started offering a complete service to the quarries, right from planning the blast to drilling holes and firing the blast. The quarries no longer paid for the explosive (the product) but for the 'rock on ground' (the outcome). Equally, the quarries didn't need to employ blast planners, drillers, and shot firers, nor did they need to do inventories for their explosives. For its part, ICI-Nobel now had a way to extract some loyalty from its customers and build a barrier against the competition [25].

The idea of management by customer outcomes is appealing but there a couple of important cautions to note. The term should be applied with care and precision. Marketing slogans can easily be misleading, giving customers the impression that they are being sold an outcome when, in practice, they are not. To work out whether what is being offered is an outcome, ask: *What is actually being promised? What is it that the provider is 'contracting' to offer?* In the earlier days of studying MAN, we had the impression from some conversations with colleagues that they were selling 'mobility-as-a-service', but when we looked closely and asked these questions, we could see that these were actually offerings around monitoring driver behaviour that we described earlier.

Similarly, business models where the provider is rewarded entirely only when an outcome is achieved are still quite rare within industry. Why is this? While most executives will embrace the notion of outcomes (once properly understood), putting contracts into place which are only outcome-based can be too risky for many firms. For instance, offering customers a coffee-making service entirely on the basis of 'pay-per-cup' is one thing, but offering an expensive machine tool just on the basis of 'pay-per-part' is a wholly different matter. Investment is high and there are a wide range of risks that could impact performance. For example, Alstom couldn't provide 'pay-per-passenger' or 'pay-per-mile' as there were too many factors outside of their control, and so they contract for the availability, reliability, and performance of their trains [26]. We refer to these indirect measures of an outcome as 'proxy indicators'. Although customers are not strictly paying for outcomes, they are getting the next best thing.

Advanced Services: Usership Rather Than Ownership

Where an advanced service is based around the use of a product then this invariably leads to conversations about ownership. Sometimes an emotional conversation. It is quite usual to hear people will say that they own their own homes and their own cars, so surely, they should own their own heating boiler, vacuum cleaner and lawn mower. Similar thinking can underpin their decisions in business.

The truth is, of course, more complex. Houses are often mortgaged, and the title deeds are held by banks (over 30% percent of German households and 60% of Dutch households had a mortgage in 2020) [27]. Most cars are leased; around 90% of new car sales in the UK and 82% in the United States are purchased on finance [28]. As Ben Wilson from Schneider Electric in Australia sees it: '*The world is moving away from hardware ownership and thinking about how you can make it easier to access the services you need.*' So, what we casually believe about ownership differs to what we practise, and, in practice, we are less sensitive to ownership than it might appear.

An illustration of how market forces are changing is indicated by the car parked in front of your house [29]. Ownership of a car was once a symbol of freedom, mobility and success. In the latter half of last century it became, for many, essential for moving between the suburbia and the cities. Today, if you live in a congested metropolis, driving a car can be decidedly lacklustre, no longer fast and convenient, expensive to park and subject to congestion charges. So why own a car? Maybe simply buying a service (if one is available) is a better way to gain mobility [16, 30]. Traditionally, people tend to own their lawn mowers; but why should they have their garages and sheds cluttered with them? Perhaps these are just applications waiting for As-a-Service business models.

Ownership does have more practical implications in, for example, the case of a heating boiler system that is installed within a home. It is easier to find financing for products and assets that can be retrieved, should the customer default on payments. Houses, cars, and even vacuum cleaners and lawn mowers can all potentially be repossessed. Boilers and lighting systems are built into the fabric of a property and are not so easily retrieved, and what happens should the house be sold? This doesn't prohibit advanced services; it just means that the financing arrangements are a little more involved.

Ownership also has practical implications for the manufacturer of the product. The economic process associated with transactional product sales is readily understood. Put simply, the customer buys the product from the manufacturer by transferring a single sum of money, and this then allows the manufacturer to fund production of further products which are then offered for sale. No sale, no funds transferred, no production; the cycle stops. Indeed, there are actually financial accounting regulations (IFRS 15 and 16[1]) that

---

[1] IFRS 15 and 16 are International Financial Reporting Standards.

IFRS 15 establishes the principles that an entity applies when reporting information about the nature, amount, timing and uncertainty of revenue and cash flows from a contract with a

expect a sale to take place. So how can a manufacturer contemplate retaining ownership of a product?

The confusion is deep seated. In the early 2000s, research papers describing Rolls-Royce's 'power-by-the-hour' began to emerge. These suggested that 'the customer would no longer own an engine; they would buy thrust'. If the customer didn't consume the thrust, they would have nothing to pay. *How could Rolls-Royce afford to do this?* Rolls-Royce is internationally renowned for its operations excellence—it is best in class in the cost, quality and delivery of its product. *How could they now take on the financial burden of engine ownership? When one component alone might cost $1,000,000?* We spent considerable time with Rolls-Royce to disentangle what was actually going on, but it was actually an executive from Alstom that beautifully summed up the situation.

This executive was Mike Hulme. Mike, at the time, was the Operations Director for the network of Alstom's high-speed Pendolino trains operating on the West Coast mainline in the UK. We held discussions with Mike around three simple questions. First, we asked '*With an outcome-based business model does the customer own the product?*' His answer was simply, '*No, there are sometimes exceptions, but usually ownership is not transferred to the customer.*' So, our second question was, '*Does the provider, who is quite often the manufacturer, own the product?*' Mike replied, '*No, there are sometimes exceptions, but usually ownership is not retained by the manufacturer either.*' And so, our third question was, '*Who owns the asset?*' Mike's answer was succinct: '*Usually it's the financier who takes legal ownership.*' In other words, although the manufacturer always sells the product, it isn't necessarily the customer who buys it.

This helped clarify matters. The confusion over ownership is partly caused by some firms, such as Rolls-Royce, GE, Caterpillar and JCB having their own financial organisations. These organisations are referred to as Captives and will take on the ownership of a product. Often these Captives are joint ventures with financial institutions, for instance JCB Finance [31] is a joint venture with the banking group Nat West Group PLC and was created to

---

customer. The entity recognises revenue to depict the transfer of promised goods/services to the customer in an amount that reflects the consideration to which the entity expects to be entitled in exchange for those goods or services. https://www.ifrs.org/issued-standards/list-of-standards/ifrs-15-revenue-from-contracts-with-customers/.

IFRS 16 is to report information that faithfully represents lease transactions and provides a basis for users of financial statements to assess the amount, timing and uncertainty of cash flows arising from leases. As a single lessee accounting model, it requires a lessee to recognise assets and liabilities for all leases with a term of more than 12 months unless the underlying asset is of low value. A lessee is required to recognise a right-of-use asset representing its right to use the underlying leased asset and a lease liability representing its obligation to make lease payments. https://www.ifrs.org/issued-standards/list-of-standards/ifrs-16-leases/.

provide a source of funding to JCB customers. This helps to explain why it has been said that 'Rolls-Royce no longer sold aircraft engines, but rather power-by-the-hour'. Ownership is often transferred, but from one operating business to another within the broader organisation.

Taken overall, this arrangement can be thought of as the provision of 'user-ship' rather than ownership. The offering is an integrated product-service system that delivers outcomes, and from the providers' perspective, a product sale takes place; product ownership is transferred, funds are released and transferred back to the provider. Yet, this ownership is rarely transferred to the customer, and instead is taken on by a third party (usually a financier). The product is delivered to the customer, and the customer can then make use of the product as part of the integrated product-service offering; and, in doing so, value co-creation takes place. Funds are transferred back (possibly as one combined payment) to both the financiar (to enable usership of the asset) and the provider (for services that enable the desired outcomes). A high-level representation of this tripartite structure is illustrated in Fig. 2.5, and we will return to this discussion again in Chapter 3.

Finally, the notion of usership rather than ownership helps to define advanced services. However, while this can be thought of as a form of leasing or rental, it's important to emphasise that this arrangement alone does not define advanced services. These models alone provide the customer with 'access' to a product or asset for a specified period of time in exchange for regular payments and securities. To be an advanced service, a raft of services is offered and integrated with the product to provide outcomes for the customer.

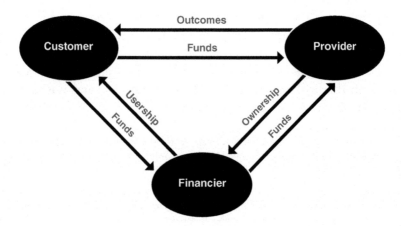

Fig. 2.5 The service provider sells ownership and the customer gets usership (© The Advanced Services Group Ltd)

Different Forms of Advanced Services

When we speak to practitioners and academics, we find that there are three types of advanced services which differ based around scope of the responsibilities for outcomes; outcomes around a product (or asset), outcomes around business processes within which there are a number of products (or assets), or outcomes around multiple business processes within which there are a variety of products (or assets). In this section, we will explain these three types of services by using an illustrative example based around 'heat-as-a-service' within an average home. Our example is informed by our work with a business named Baxi which is part of the BDR Therma group. Baxi is a global heating and hot-water solutions supplier with an established client market and well over one million domestic and commercial customers in the UK.

This example effectively showcases the different forms of advanced services, and as most households have heating and hot-water systems, it should resonate with most people who can relate to this common scenario in their own homes. Typically, heating and hot-water systems are built-in when a house or apartment is constructed. The homeowner takes on ownership when the building is purchased, and they are responsible for the maintenance and repair should it be needed.

Many of the domestic heating systems are based around natural gas, a fossil fuel that is directly contributing to climate change, and so, to fulfil its net zero ambitions, the UK government is introducing regulations that will outlaw these systems. Alternative technologies such as heat pumps are, however, more expensive and disruptive to install, and, though more efficient, they benefit from monitoring and adjustment to tune them to the fabric of the building. Market adoption in the UK is therefore slow and lagging other countries.

Advanced services have the potential to unlock the opportunity by reducing initial costs and ensuring performance. There are various forms of advanced services that could be applied to domestic heating as illustrated in Table 2.3. In this section, we will explain these forms to help you appreciate the different 'scope' of each service. For simplicity in these examples, we avoid the energy conversation, as here we only seek to demonstrate how advanced services can differ based around the scope of responsibilities in a familiar and practical application.

Table 2.3 Illustrating different forms of advanced services

	Examples of advanced services and how they might be measured		
	Product	Process	Platform
Might be known as	Boiler-as-a-service	Heat-as-a-service	Comfort-as-a-service
Outcome offered to customers	Hot water supply within a home	Warm rooms within a house	Warm, safe and secure house
Typical products/ systems associated with the offering	Heating boiler	Heating boiler and heat distribution system (pumps, valves, pipes, radiators, thermostats)	Heating boiler, heat distribution system, water supply system (pipes, values, pumps), electrical supply system (consumer unit, wiring, sockets, lighting), and alarm systems (fire, security)
Direct measure of outcome	Reliable supply of hot water leaving boiler	Ambient air temperature of all rooms in the house	Ambient air temperature of all rooms, water flow at taps, electricity at sockets, and alarms detecting heat and movement
Proxy-indicators of outcome	Boiler is working (operating) when required	Radiators are working (operating) and emitting heat within house when required	Radiators are working (operating) and emitting heat within house, water pressure, no electrical faults at consumer unit, alarms operational
Basis on which customer might pay	Boiler availability and reliability	Heating system availability and reliability	Heating, water, electrical, and security system—availability and reliability

Advanced Services Around Products

The most common form of an advanced services business model focuses on the product or asset that is supplied by the provider and used by customers. In our example, the product is a 'boiler' which is often the primary heating source in a home. Keep in mind that what we will now explain differs from a more conventional 'boiler maintenance contract' that just deals with periodic maintenance and (eventual) repair, should a fault be reported by the homeowner.

An advanced service around this might be termed 'Boiler-as-a-Service' (Table 2.3); the asset is a heating boiler which supplies hot water to a domestic heating system (Fig. 2.6). The offering made to the customer is based on the outcome from the boiler—in this case, the supply of hot water. This might be delivered by the heating boiler, integrated with a range of services, to ensure that it is fully functional and delivering hot water when needed. The customer would pay a fee to the service provider only when hot water is delivered.

A measure of such an outcome being achieved would be the temperature and the flow rate of the water leaving the boiler. Monitoring this would need sensors at the out-flow of the boiler and the data from these recorded and reported. Such an additional system might be expensive. A less costly approach is to monitor whether or not the boiler is operational (is it turned on and working), and to assume that when it is then sufficient hot water is

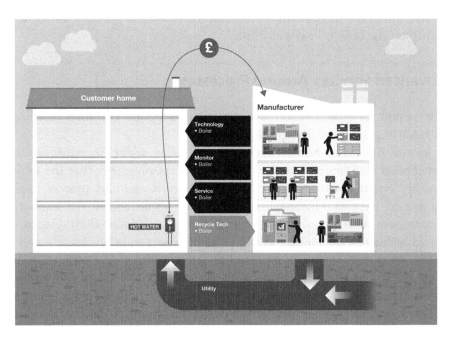

Fig. 2.6 Typical example of outcomes at the level of the product or asset (© The Advanced Services Group Ltd)

being produced. Here, the boiler functioning (i.e., the boiler operates when needed) is taken as a proxy-indicator that hot water is being produced.

A B2B example of an advanced service based around a product is of Domino Printing. Domino produces and sells world-leading industrial equipment for printing barcodes on food products. It can also offer customers an advanced service to print barcodes on packaging for items such as lettuce, eggs and bread. Here, Domino provides the printing machine and supporting services, and its customers receive the outcome of correctly printed codes. These codes are essential for the sale of their correctly packaged and labelled foods to their own customers (supermarkets). Conversationally, people at Domino refer to its service as 'pay-per-pack' or 'pay-per-code', and this is regarded as being an offering where the only time/way customers pay is in return for each code correctly printed.

Another example is Eden Springs, a supplier of 'coffee service solutions' offering a fully managed vending service [32]. The service bundles together the machine, its maintenance and cleaning, as well as monitoring the use of coffee beans and replenishing these for its customers when needed. It guarantees regular fills of the machine by monitoring the range of drinks in demand; cleaning the machine to the manufacturer's standards; counting and banking all the cash in the machine then crediting the customers' account. Revenue is earned on the basis of 'pay-per-drink'.

Advanced Services Around Processes

The second form of advanced services is based around customer processes, within which the provider's product operates.

In our Boiler-as-a-Service example, the boiler might be providing the outcome of 'hot water' but this does not necessarily mean that the entire heating 'system' is working. An advanced service around process might be termed Heat or Heating-as-a-Service and would extend the measured outcomes to cover the complete heat generation and distribution systems. It would include all the pumps, valves, pipes, radiators and thermostats– everything that comes together as a process to deliver warm rooms within a house (Fig. 2.7). Some of these components (for example, the valves and pumps) won't necessarily have been supplied by the provider but would need to be adopted and managed to deliver the desired outcome. A direct measure of the outcome being achieved would be the ambient air temperature in these rooms.

A direct outcome such as ambient air temperature would need control of a range of factors beyond just the heating and distribution system. The

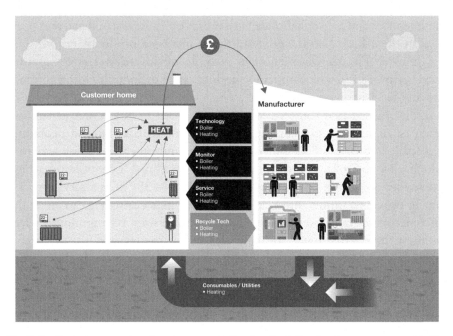

Fig. 2.7 Typical example of outcomes at the level of the business process (© The Advanced Services Group Ltd)

insulating properties of the building, the efficiency of the heat distribution system where radiators are located, and whether doors and windows are left open, all affect whether room temperature can be attained and sustained. The service provider could measure and mitigate for some factors; for example, digital technologies could be used to identify if and when windows and doors were open, though this is not necessarily straightforward technologically and contractually. An alternative approach would again be to use proxy-indicators of the outcome being achieved, such as radiators achieving and sustaining a set temperature for a number of hours each day. Some digital technologies might still need to be installed, such as temperature sensors on valves and pipes, though these are readily available components.

A B2B example from Xerox here shows how advanced services around the product differ to those around the process. Xerox is widely associated with— its 'pay-per-copy' model for printers [33]. Based around a product, customers receive an integrated product-service printing system, and they pay for this based on the number of documents printed. However, Xerox also offers a process-based system which consolidates the print devices, and also supports the digitisation of some customer documents. With this service, Xerox guarantee process functionality and uptime, which means customers can access documents, seamlessly collaborate with others on those documents, and print them in the office or on the go, resulting in increased productivity [34].

Schneider Electric gives another example of advanced services around customer processes. The company's product range includes building automation and electric power distribution. The Vice President for Field Services in Australia realised that some customers didn't want to buy power generation products, or have them maintained, updated or replaced at end of its life. As a result of a series of customer engagement and experimentation activities (which took about 18 months), the business developed 'EcoStruxure', which it describes as 'Secure Power-as-a-Service' (SPaaS) [35]. It is a service which aims to provide a unique lifecycle experience, where customers can enjoy the outcomes of secure power without product ownership, paying monthly fees based on their actual usage. Initially, this was at the level of just the generator, but then the service was developed into 'EcoStruxure Building'. So, now the company has a process-based offering which securely connects hardware, software and services over an Ethernet IP backbone to help customers maximise their building efficiency, optimise comfort and productivity and increase building value.

Advanced Services Around Platforms

The third form of advanced services are around customer platform. Platforms are a broad integration of products and services, of which online marketplaces and meta platforms are all examples [4]. Outcomes are offered at the level of the platform, and in Table 2.3 we give the example of a 'warm, safe, and secure' house. Here, the provider has expanded beyond 'heat-as-a-service' to also provide safety and security in the home—'Comfort-as-a-Service'. This would mean the adoption and management of products and services well beyond the heating system, such as the cold-water supply system (pipes, values, pumps), the electrical supply system (consumer unit, wiring, sockets, lighting), and any alarm systems (fire, security) (see Fig. 2.8).

There might be a variety of direct measures of outcomes. So, in addition to a warm room mentioned above; the cold-water supply might be measured by the water flow from the taps, the electricity supply at the sockets, and the alarms demonstrating that they are capturing smoke, heat and movement within the home. Measuring such outcomes directly would again be expensive. So, proxy indicators can be used; for example, the water pressure can be measured to ensure that there are no leaks (the assumption being that this indicates a healthy water supply), similarly the condition of the electrical

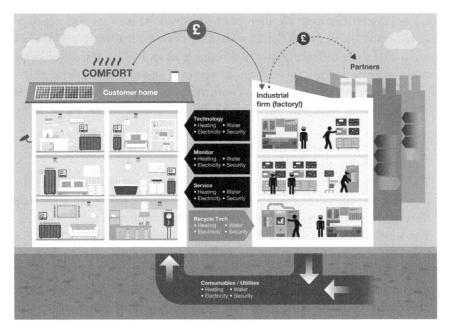

Fig. 2.8 Typical example of outcomes at the level of the business platform (© The Advanced Services Group Ltd)

system could be indicated by faults (or the absence of faults) at the electrical consumer unit/fuse box, and alarms could be checked as being on and receiving power.

A B2B example here is from Tetra Pak, the well-known Swedish-Swiss multinational packaging and processing firm that operates, primarily, in the food sector. Tetra Pak produces and sells equipment and spare parts, along with maintenance packages (known as 'Plant Care') [36] and 'Plant Perform' [37], which ultimately provide the guaranteed performance of its assets and processes. The company now plans to go beyond these services and provide 'Full Site' packages (advanced services based around platforms) under their 'Plant Secure' [38] offering, which focuses on improved operations of the entire plant, optimised asset utilisation, digital tools and optimised stock inventory.

Chapter Summary

We introduced servitization and advanced services in this chapter. First, we used a business model framework to unpack servitization and then we described the services staircase which helps in distinguishing different product-service offerings. We then defined advanced services and explained what is meant by the term, outcomes, and dealt with ownership. We also looked at the three different types of advanced services. This forms the beginning of our introduction into advanced services, and in the next chapter, we will delve into the value that can be captured from these. Before doing so, we would like to leave you with these highlights from what we have said so far.

1. Think of servitization as the transformation of a firm to compete through outcomes rather than only outputs.
2. The business model framework will help you in distinguishing the offerings for customers, and how they are paid for and delivered. This helps distinguish product-service and revenue model innovations.
3. The services staircase will help you in understanding the different types of offerings that exist within the broad categories of base, intermediate and advanced services.
4. An advanced service is an integrated products-service system, that when used, delivers outcomes that directly align with value creation and capture processes within a customer's own organisation.
5. Advanced services can be of three forms based around the differing scope of responsibilities for outcomes: outcomes around a product or asset, outcomes around business processes, or outcomes around multiple processes within which a variety of products or assets feature.

References

1 Baines, T., et al., *State-of-the-art in product-service systems.* Proceedings of the Institution of Mechanical Engineers, Part B: Journal of Engineering Manufacture, 2007. **221**(10): p. 1543–1552.
2 Posselt, T., T. Posselt, and Berg, *Organizational Competence for Servitization.* 2018: Springer.
3 Kowalkowski, C. and W. Ulaga, *Service strategy in action: A practical guide for growing your B2B service and solution business.* 2017: Service Strategy Press.
4 Linz, C., G. Müller-Stewens, and A. Zimmermann, *Radical business model transformation: Gaining the competitive edge in a disruptive world.* 2017: Kogan Page Publishers.
5 Vargo, S.L. and R.F. Lusch, *Evolving to a new dominant logic for marketing.* Journal of Marketing, 2004. **68**(1): p. 1–17.
6 Vandermerwe, S. and J. Rada, *Servitization of business: Adding value by adding services.* European Management Journal, 1988. **6**(4): p. 314–324.

7 Serco. 2023; Available from: https://www.serco.com/uk.

8 Brax, S.A., et al., *Explaining the servitization paradox: A configurational theory and a performance measurement framework.* International Journal of Operations & Production Management, 2021. **41**(5): p. 517–546.

9 Oliva, R. and R. Kallenberg, *Managing the transition from products to services.* International journal of Service Industry Management, 2003.

10 Mathieu, V., *Product services: From a service supporting the product to a service supporting the client.* Journal of Business & Industrial Marketing, 2001. **16**(1): p. 39–61.

11 Manzini, E., C. Vezzoli, and G. Clark, *Product-service systems: Using an existing concept as a new approach to sustainability.* Journal of Design Research, 2001. **1**(2): p. 27–40.

12 Annarelli, A., C. Battistella, and F. Nonino, *The road to servitization.* 2019: p. 175–205.

13 Reinartz, W. and W. Ulaga, *How to sell services more profitably.* Harvard Business Review, 2008. **86**(5): p. 90.

14 MAN. *MAN Ecostyle.* 2023 [cited 2023 05/01/2023]; Available from: https://www.manfleetmanagement.co.uk/module/fittogo/ecostyle/.

15 Paschou, T., et al., *Digital servitization in manufacturing as a new stream of research: A review and a further research.* A Research Agenda for Service Innovation, 2018: p. 148–165.

16 Baxter, R.K., *The membership economy find your superusers, master the forever transaction, and build recurring revenue.* 1st edition ed. 2015: McGraw-Hill. 272.

17 Liozu, S.M., *The industrial subscription economy: A practical guide to designing, pricing and scaling your industrial subscription.* 2021: Value Innoruption Advisors Publishing.

18 Osterwalder, A., et al., *The invincible company: How to constantly reinvent your organization with inspiration from the world's best business models.* Vol. 4. 2020: John Wiley & Sons.

19 Hockley, C.J., J.C. Smith, and L.J. Lacey, *Contracting for availability and capability in the defence environment.* Complex Engineering Service Systems: Concepts and Research, 2011: p. 237–256.

20 Schaefers, T., S. Ruffer, and E. Böhm, *Outcome-based contracting from the customers' perspective: A means-end chain analytical exploration.* Industrial Marketing Management, 2021. **93**: p. 466–481.

21 Lah, T. and J. Wood, *Technology-as-a-service playbook: How to grow a profitable subscription business.* 2016: Point B, Inc.

22 Bennett, M. *Great Product Managers are "Outcome Thinkers".* 2017 [cited 2023 05/01/2023]; Available from: https://medium.com/.

23 Christensen, C.M., S. Cook, and T. Hall, *Marketing malpractice.* Make Sure All Your Products Are Profitable, 2005. **2**.

24 Levitt, T., *The marketing mode: Pathways to corporate growth.* 1969: McGraw-Hill.

25 Schmenner, R.W., *Manufacturing, service, and their integration: Some history and theory.* International Journal of Operations & Production Management, 2009. **29**(5): p. 431–443.

26 Baines, T. and H. Lightfoot, *Made to serve.* What it takes for a Manufacturer to Compete, 2013.

27 Schürt, A., *Housing and property markets in Germany 2020.* 2021, Federal Institute for Research on Building, Urban Affairs and Spatial Development (BBSR): Bonn. p. 1–16.

28 Brignall, M. *UK car loans: the little-known clause that means you could walk away from your deal.* 2023 [cited 2023 12/01/2023]; Available from: https://www.theguardian.com/money/2023/jan/09/uk-car-leasing-deal-contract-cost-of-living.

29 Saueressig, T. and P. Maier, *Business as Unusual with SAP: How Leaders Navigate Industry Megatrends.* 2022: SAP Press.

30 Baxter, R.K., *The forever transaction: How to build a subscription model so compelling, your customers will never want to leave.* 2020: McGraw-Hill Education.

31 JCB. *Who are JCB Finance?* 2023 [cited 2023 06/01/2023]; Available from: https://www.jcb-finance.co.uk/faq.

32 EdenSprings. *Fully Managed Service KLIX.* 2023; Available from: https://www.edensprings.co.uk/vending-machines.

33 Baines, T., *Servitization impact study: How UK based manufacturing organisations are transforming themselves to compete through advanced services.* 2013: Aston Centre for Servitization Research and Practice.

34 Xerox. 2022; Available from: https://www.xerox.co.uk/en-gb/connectkey/document-workflow-solutions.

35 Schneider. *EcoStruxure Outcomes: Secure Power as a Service.* 2023 [cited 2023 05/01/2023]; Available from: https://www.se.com/au/en/work/services/field-services/ecostruxure-outcomes-spaas.jsp.

36 TetraPak. *Tetra Pak Plant Care. Proactive Maintenance—Predictable Cost.* 2023 [cited 2023 06/01/2023]; Available from: https://www.tetrapak.com/en-gb/solutions/services/service-portfolio/services-solutions/plant-care.

37 TetraPak. *Tetra Pak Plant Perform. Improved performance with a guarantee.* 2023 [cited 2023 06/01/2023]; Available from: https://www.tetrapak.com/en-gb/solutions/services/service-portfolio/services-solutions/plant-perform.

38 TetraPak. *Tetra Pak Plant Secure. Optimised plant operations for a guaranteed cost.* 2023 [cited 2023 06/01/2023]; Available from: https://www.tetrapak.com/en-gb/solutions/services/service-portfolio/services-solutions/plant-secure.

3

Creating and Capturing Value for Advanced Services

As servitization has gained traction within the industry some technology vendors have seen this as an opportunity to sell more software licences for IT systems. Particularly those systems which enable subscription-based charging. Over recent years, we have seen more and more marketing campaigns stating 'we offer servitization' by such vendors. Partially this has caused some confusion about servitization; subscription-based charging does not itself define servitization. On the other hand, it has helped raise awareness and stimulate the development and adoption of different forms of 'revenue' models that complement advanced services.

The term 'revenue model' is given to one of the ways a provider can capture and channel economic value from an advanced service. These models can take various forms and go by such names as 'pay-per-use' or 'pay-per-outcome'. Apart from economic value, there are other three types of values that can be created and (potentially) captured by the providers, namely strategic, knowledge, and relational values (Table 3.1). Understanding these different values and associated processes for their creation and capture is foundational to defining, evaluating and implementing an advanced service business model. However, we should note that the value capture processes and mechanisms for the strategic, knowledge, and relational values are not as formalised as the ones available for capturing the economic values (i.e., revenue model).

T. Baines et al., *Servitization Strategy*, Palgrave Executive Essentials, https://doi.org/10.1007/978-3-031-45426-4_3

Table 3.1 Types of value that can be created and captured by advanced services

Types of value	Definition	Examples
Economic	Monetary benefits determined by the quality, availability, and accessibility of the offering, as well as by market demand and competition	Revenue, profit, market share, reduced costs
Strategic	Higher level of competitiveness for both provider and customer	Access to new markets, competitive position in market, risk reduction, increased flexibility, and improved compliance
Knowledge	The innovation opportunities arising from the knowledge and insight of how the product or service is being used in the customer's operation	Market intelligence, asset usage data, product and service innovation, operational information, and insight
Relational	Benefits deriving from long-term relationship between the customer and provider	Customer relationships, customer retention, customer referral, improved communication, and increased trust

Foundations of Value Creation

First, let us explore the fundamentals. The business model framework (Fig. 2.1) has helped to provide an inclusive picture of an advanced service: a value proposition focused on delivering outcomes for the customer, which are then paid for as those results are realised. *But why do these business models work so well? What are the fundamental mechanisms that enable value creation over that associated with the more conventional transactional sale/purchase of a product?*

In other words, what changes have occurred in the relationship between the provider and customer that result in greater benefits compared to a conventional product sale? We appreciate that this is a more theoretical discussion and that most practitioners are interested in the benefits of offering/sourcing one customer value proposition over another. However, understanding why these benefits occur can help explain how the revenue model and delivery system should be configured to maximise the value potential of advanced services (as explained further in Chapter 4).

Many people in the industry view value creation as occurring mainly during the design and production processes, while value capture happens when a product is sold (value in exchange). In recent decades, however, there has been a growing emphasis on the role of the customer in this process. The ideas about industrial value systems (for instance, those that were suggested by Michael Porter; see [1]) are giving way to more systemic and symbiotic ecosystem concepts, where mutual learning and trust building play an important part. More emphasis is on value co-creation. The aim of value co-creation is to create outcomes that the individual parties could not achieve on their own, by working together to design and deliver products or services that meet the specific needs and preferences of the customer.

Value co-creation is a collaborative process between providers, customers, and potentially other partners, where interaction through the exchange of data, information, and knowledge plays a crucial role. This interaction takes place throughout the product-service lifecycle, from design to delivery, in order to achieve outcomes that the individual parties could not achieve on their own. To illustrate, KONE, a leading lift manufacturer, demonstrates this approach by using service design and design-thinking methods to drive a collaborative approach to innovation [2]. By holding co-creation sessions with customers and visiting their sites, KONE works collaboratively with its own research and development teams, architects, and other partners to develop bespoke solutions for customers' buildings.

So how does value co-creation occur with an advanced service? Our work with businesses has suggested that this is achieved by improved customer-provider alignment, such that the integrated product-service offered by the provider performs in a way that directly complements the value creation and capture processes of the customer themselves. The customer gets these benefits when the advanced service is used (value-in-use). We see that there are three principal mechanisms that enabling this co-creation of value and so deliver benefits to all stakeholders. These illustrated in Fig. 3.1 and set out below.

- Incentives to deliver value are better aligned across customers, providers and partners.
- Responsibilities for risks are better aligned with the core competencies of organisations.
- Innovation processes are more open and better aligned between the providers and customers.

Done well, this alignment helps to explain why advanced services benefit both customers and providers, over and above the benefits achieved through the more conventional transactional sale and exchange of products. A summary

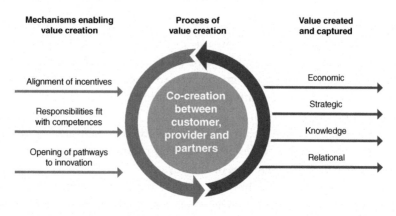

Fig. 3.1 Summarising value creation and capture through advanced services (© The Advanced Services Group Ltd)

of how these three mechanisms play out in practice is given in Table 3.2. This shows how attitudes and behaviours of both customers and providers differ between a conventional product (output) and an advanced service (outcome) orientated business model. We will now explain each of these mechanisms in more detail in the following sections.

Alignment of Incentives

In conventional product-centric firms the underlying attitude amongst executives is 'we make money by selling it', and our customers 'make money by using it'. This means, for example, when a customer has purchased a machine and, later, there is a long-term deterioration in performance then this is seen as the customer's problem. The provider's incentives are principally around the sale of machines with little beyond; indeed for some, a deterioration might be seen as an opportunity for the sale of spare-parts or even a replacement machine. In the meantime, the customer wrestles with an underperforming asset.

With an advanced service, the provider is incentivised to ensure the customer achieves the outcomes they need to be successful in their own business processes. The alignment of incentives improves the outcomes for both parties [3]. This means that a deteriorating machine is a problem shared, and both work together to restore performance. This means that performance is more likely to be restored, more quickly, and this also improves customer satisfaction. This, of course, places a greater burden on the provider, rather than with the output-based business model. However, the burden is offset by

Table 3.2 Contrasting value creation and capture for outputs against outcomes

| Drivers | Product: output orientated business model | | Advanced service: outcome orientated business model | |
| | Best product cost, quality and delivery | | Best total customer experience | |
Host	Customer	Provider	Customer	Provider
Typical approach to incentives	We make money by using it	We make money by selling it	We share our successes and failures	We make money when our customers make money
Typical approach to reponsibilities	We use it, if we break it, we fix it	We make it, we don't own it	We don't make money out of fixing it	We made it and we are best to fix it
Typical approach to innovation	We buy it	We have labs	We do this with our customer	We experience it, so we improve it

improved reputation and customer retention. Also, by aiding the customer to be successful, extra value is captured and additional wealth is created.

DuPont provides a practical example of this alignment in action. DuPont supplied paint to Ford Motor Company and originally this was sold by volume. The sales staff inside DuPont were incentivised to sell as much paint as possible; their bonus schemes were structured to 'sell as much as you can' and if the customer purchased too much and there was waste then this was not a problem. Ford then changed the model to become outcome-oriented: payment-per-painted car. Almost overnight, DuPont had to change its own incentives, aligning them around the production of painted cars with as little waste as possible. Ford's costs were reduced, helping them to be more competitive, and DuPont itself then shared in this improved economic activity.

A similar example is provided by Rolls-Royce in its relationship with its customer, American Airlines, in the 1990s. At that time Rolls-Royce had an output-oriented business model: its gas turbines were competitively priced with the underlying assumption that once sold and 'on the wing', then it would make money through the sales of maintenance and spare parts. Repair and maintenance were charged according to 'time and materials'. In other words, if a turbine developed a fault while in use, any repair costs would be charged to the customer on the basis of 'how long it took to make the repair, and how many spare parts were consumed'. The longer the turbine was in the repair shop, the more money was made by Rolls-Royce; yet, the longer the turbine was 'off the wing', the more money was lost for the customer. American Airlines became very dissatisfied with this model and forced a shift. It insisted on a model where 'when the plane was flying' then Rolls-Royce would benefit, but when it was not, because of a faulty engine, then it would be penalised. The longer the engine was 'off the wing', the greater the cost for Rolls-Royce. Power-by-the-hour was born, and the rest is history.

Responsibilities Fit with Competencies

Visit any traditional factory and you will come across Maintenance Fitters. Blue overalls, toolboxes on wheels, gravitating towards a centrally located workshop, their job is to keep the production running. The attitude amongst senior management in such factories is that these Fitters are the first line of defence. They are there to take care of the machines within the Factory; to keep them operational so that they can be used for production. If a machine breaks down during production, the Fitters repair it; if a machine needs an oil change or greasing, this is done by Fitters on the night shift or at the weekend; if it needs an overhaul, then it's put in the workshop and becomes an in-fill job when the factory is not so busy. These in-house teams of maintenance Fitter tend to exist because managers believe that this is the most cost-effective and responsive solution to keeping the factory running. And the same thinking occurs across organisations, from transport and logistics firms, through to universities and hospitals.

Modern management practice however emphasises the importance of core competencies as the basis of competitive advantage. The idea of core competencies was first proposed in the 1990s as a new way to judge business managers compared to how they were judged in the 1980s. Firms that define, cultivate and exploit core competencies are more likely to succeed against the competition. Given this understanding, the question is: *Which organisation is likely to have competencies best aligned with the responsibility to fix a machine – those who use it or those who made it?* Advanced services argue for the latter.

MAN Truck & Bus UK help to illustrate this in practice. During the early 2000s, the regulations on diesel engine technology changed from Euro 5 to Euro 6. To comply, MAN incorporated more digital technologies into their engines. This meant that Fitters who were only skilled in mechanical systems needed to be retrained and acquire new toolsets to be able to maintain these new engines. Acquiring these was prohibitively expensive for many customers. MAN was of course able to take on such maintenance as it had both the people and know-how, creating a new revenue stream and helping to overcome barriers to adoption of the new engines.

Opening of Pathways to Innovation

In output-orientated business models, providers have limited opportunities to co-develop innovations with their customers, whereas in outcome-orientated models these are more prevalent. The providers retain access to the products or assets they have produced, and there are both incentives and opportunities for innovations to improve performance. As captured in Table 3.2, because providers have direct experience of how their products or assets perform, they have greater insights into what could be changed and improved.

Alstom's Train Life Services serves as an example of this concept in action. In the past, it provided services that other businesses, particularly logistics providers, sought to take over. Alstom maintained that it was an expert in the supply chain and could more quickly source replacement parts for trains. For example, if a train's air conditioning unit failed, and it was a unit sourced from Austria, Alstom was better equipped to arrange repairs and transport.

Alstom could defend its position through design authority and manufacturing capability. In the case of the air conditioning unit, Alstom could not only complete the repairs but also modify the design to reduce the likelihood of recurrence. As a result, the product was improved to better suit the application.

This example begins to explain why manufacturers are well suited to servitization. Rolls-Royce has the design authority and manufacturing capability to make changes to its product so, it can increase its differentiation as well as enhance its service offering and improve its customers' experience. In contrast, Air France KLM is a business that is not an Original Equipment Manufacturer (OEM) but offers an outcome-based contract on gas turbines it has refurbished. It does not have the design authority, know-how or manufacturing capability to the same extent as Rolls-Royce. This limits how much it can modify the design of a gas turbine to suit an application.

Capturing Economic Value

Different forms of revenue models can be used with servitization. In this section we will first explore popular revenue models (ways in which customers might pay and the provider might benefit), and then draw these together as a consolidated model to reflect what we find in practice for an advanced service. Figure 3.2 illustrates these popular models and how they typically relate to the activity cycle of an asset.

Flat-Rate Subscription

Subscription has become a broad topic of discussion. Most executives that we come across see subscription as a transactional process extended over time: regular payments (for example, monthly) at a flat rate over an extended time period (Fig. 3.2e). Gym membership is a typical example: you make payments irrespective of whether you attend or not, and how long you spend there. In industry, longer-term rental, leasing and hire purchase are all examples of subscription models. In its simplest form there are no upfront payments, no tie-in period, and the contract can be cancelled at any time. Spotify, the music-streaming service is another example of a service tied to a subscription revenue model. Here, customers pay the same fee every month for the facility to listen to music, and this is irrespective of the extent to which they use the service or the consistency with which the service is delivered. There is a regular fee to gain access to a product or service.

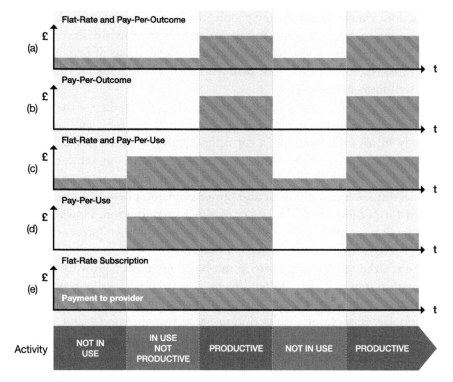

Fig. 3.2 Popular revenue models and their relationship with the activity and outcomes (© The Advanced Services Group Ltd)

Subscription-based models are popular in the automotive industry. These include hire purchase (HP), personal contract plans (PCP) and personal contract ire (PCH). Sometimes these models have usage limits; for instance, with HP there is no mileage limit, whereas there is with PCP or PCH. Typically, customers pay an initial deposit and then monthly instalments to gain 'access' to the car for a pre-determined period of time. When all the payments are made, the contract terminates, and the customer might have the choice to own the car (maybe for an additional fee termed a balloon payment) or enter into another plan. There is a final balloon payment that must be made if they want to keep the car. It is possible, though, to view subscription models in broader terms. Some authors see subscription models to also include pay-per-use, pay-per-additional-use, pay-pre-outcome (see, for examples, the work of Stephan Liozu [3]). We discuss these revenue models separately below.

Other researchers and authors see the topic of subscription to be even broader. Extending well beyond the revenue model and as being intrinsically coupled to concepts such as the 'membership economy'. This is reflected in the work of authors such as Robbie Kellman [4], in there book the Forever

Transaction, which discussed how people may choose to engage with a group or organisation and (in some instances) paying for this privilege through subscription. People choose to engage so as to satisfy needs of belonging and esteem (see Maslow in [5]), with platforms such as Facebook and Instagram being well-known examples.

The concept of a membership economy [5] also links to the sharing economy. A model based on sharing (or renting) products and assets not currently in use—for example, a car or an apartment when not being used by the owner. Interestingly, some areas of the research on product-service systems deal directly with the sharing economy from the perspective of sustainability—community heat and power generation being examples—and so draw further links with the bigger picture of servitization. However, most of our focus is on services in a B2B context and we will, therefore, concentrate mainly on subscription as a financial arrangement.

Finally, although flat-rate subscription-based models are growing in popularity within industry, they do tend to be associated with value-propositions on the lower half of the services staircase. For example, Software-as-a-Service is a popular example of a subscription-based revenue model and refers to software being provided to a customer in return for a defined monthly fee. More advanced services might have some element of flat-rate subscription, but this is then combined with another revenue model that reflects the desired outcome being experienced by the customer.

Pay-Per-Use

Pay-per-use is a model where payments for a product or service are made according to availability and extent of usage. This is illustrated in Fig. 3.2d where the payment is aligned with the service activity. Returning to the gym membership, as an example, this form of revenue model means that the fee reflects the time you actually spend at the gym. In the case of the excavator example, a fee might only be generated when the engine is running, and the bill to the customer is calculated from the recorded engine hours.

Often there are both upper and lower boundaries on the use of a advanced service. Quite often these are for practical reasons to help ensure that the service can be sustained by the provider. An upper boundary or 'ceiling' on the level of activity might exist to discourage overuse of the product or asset on which the service is based. For example, an upper boundary might be set on an excavator to ensure there is a downtime and so an opportunity for service technicians to carry out regular maintenance on the machine. In such a case, if the customer continues to use the excavator beyond the upper boundary, then they could be financially penalised.

A lower boundary on usage is more common than an upper and is often referred to as a payment 'floor'. It is again a more likely occurrence where physical assets are involved, when below certain levels of activity only 'floor payments' are made. Hence a combination of flat-rate and pay-per-use and is illustrated in Fig. 3.2c. An example of this form of revenue model is domestic electrical power supply: customers are attached to the power grid and charged according to their electricity use, but there is also a standing charge which has to be paid, whether or not the service is used.

There are, though, instances where a model of pay-per- 'not'-use is actually advantageous, with payments being reduced during usage. We came across this model with Wastespectrum [6], a small business which manufactures incineration equipment for poultry farmers. Farmers acquire this equipment in the hope of never having to use it, as its purpose is to incinerate the carcases of dead animals, should the farm be hit by a disease. Avian Flu, for instance, is deadly to chickens, highly contagious, and can wipe out a farm's population in just a few days. Should this occur, farmers need to appropriately dispose of the carcases, sterilise their facility, and buy in new stock. A distressing and expensive time for them, and so the manufacturer wanted to avoid adding to their misery with payments for the use of the incinerator. To achieve this, they explored a revenue model based on the principle of pay-per-(not)-use, and this was structured very similarly to the payments associated with a more conventional insurance policy.

In general, pay-per-use models tend to be associated with the lower—mid part of the services staircase. However, usage can be a component of more advanced services business models as we will describe shortly.

Pay-Per-Outcome

With pay-per-outcome the fee reflects the results of the service. With this model customers pay for outcomes; for example, pay-per-mile, pay-per-page, or pay-per-gigabyte. Returning to the gym membership, as our example, this type of model would mean that you only pay when actually exercising and burning calories, rather than just attending the facility. Similarly, a large quarry truck might clock up many engine hours idling, perhaps queuing to be loaded or unloaded with rock. If this was charged using a pay-per-use model, the customer will be charged a fee irrespective of whether or not the truck had moved any rock; whereas with a pay-per-outcome model, the customer will pay on the basis of productivity in rock transportation (Fig. 3.2b).

This form of revenue model is intrinsic to more advanced services where an outcome could be considered at the level of an asset (a printer or photocopier), process (a print room) or a platform (document management). Xerox Corporation offered 'pay-per-copy' business models over 40 years ago. The examples often necessitated service innovation to enable an outcome to be delivered (i.e., the bundling together of the asset, condition monitoring and maintenance) and on the basis of which the revenue model was constructed. Again, in practice, a flat-rate and pay-per-outcome model are often combined (Fig. 3.2a) to introduce a floor to the payment value.

The notion of 'outcomes' is the basis of these models and can take various forms. Take the example of a food packaging line, an outcome could be thought of as an item of packaged food. Here, payments to the equipment supplier could be based on the number of items packed (payment-per-pack). Value creation in the supply chain is well aligned; the greater the demand, the more food the customer packs, the more revenue is received by the equipment provider. If, however, the customer can only sell products that meet particular specifications of packaging (for example, packaged in an inert atmosphere), then a better outcome on which to focus would be pay-per-good-pack.

Finally, proxy-indicators of outcome (as mentioned earlier) might be used as practical substitutes for measures of the actual desired outcome. Returning to the gym membership example, the desired outcome from using an exercise machine might be weight loss and improved fitness. In practice, these are too difficult to attribute to the use of a specific exercise machine, so a substitute may be calories burned (though on reflection, a more appropriate revenue model for a gym might be pay-per-calories 'not' burned!).

Penalties and Risk-Sharing

Flat-rate subscription, pay-per-use and pay-per-outcome can all be coupled to penalties to incentivise the desired behaviours. For example, if a product or service is 'unavailable', cannot be 'used' or does not provide the 'outcomes' then clauses may be included in the contract to reimburse the customer.

Alstom's train-life operations [7], for example, have experience of putting in place penalty clauses as a contingency and reassurance that a transport system should perform as expected. These can be setup against metrics for train performance, its availability for use, and reliability against unpredicted failures. An Alstom advanced service for a transport system can be assessed against these measures. Should there be a variance from these agreed targets, then Alstom may take on the responsibility for any corrective action, along with some compensation for any disruption caused. These penalties are designed not as a punishment, but rather to help incentivise and ensure the desired behaviours.

There are two ways in which penalties can be added to the process. Customers can draw back payments if the manufacturer's product does not perform as expected. Similarly, the manufacturer can be entitled to compensation if the customers do not use the product as agreed. To illustrate, Rolls-Royce may adjust the fee structure for gas turbines on an advanced service in accordance with which routes in the world the aircraft will be used. Different routes impact the fundamental rate of wear and tear the engines experience and the amount of maintenance they need as a result. For example, an airport in the Middle East is likely to be sandier, increasing wear rates on blades. Long flights need more fuel to be carried, require higher take-off thrust and see greater deterioration of hot components in the engine per flight. Conversely, short flights, whilst individually less damaging, accumulate fewer operating hours per flight and can see higher deterioration per hour (rather than per flight) of operation. If the customer decides to change the route, such as moving from long-distance to regional travel, then a premium may be charged.

In situations where there is a raft of uncertainties and limited control over costs and performance, then there may be a risk-sharing agreement between the service provider and the customer. This is usually a provision in the contract which allows the provider and customer to agree on an adjustment to the fee charged for a service if something goes wrong during execution. For example, in our heat-as-a-service example (discussed in Chapter 2) we were careful to point out that we would not debate the 'energy consumption'. Yet, ideally, energy consumption should be bundled into the service offering, the problem is that these costs can be volatile. They are subject to variances outside the influence of most industrial firms and their customers. However, this can be dealt with by a risk-sharing agreement, within the service contract, where there are thresholds above which energy costs are partially passed on to the customer. This allows a more granular description of the specific risks taken on by the service provider, and the rewards (and possibly penalties) for these being successfully managed and protecting the customer from these.

Composite Revenue Model

In practice, a typical revenue model for an advanced service will have various components. To the customer, it may appear as a flat-rate fee, on top of which there are additional charges to reflect the outcome of the service (or proxy indicators for this outcome). In addition to the flat-rate fee providing a floor to the payment, there is also likely to be a ceiling to disincentivise the overuse of the service (especially where there is an asset which requires regular maintenance). There may also be penalties to incentivise outcomes being achieved, over possibly three to five years, and some risk-sharing over factors where both the customer and provider have limited control.

To the customer, it will appear as an integrated model provided by one organisation (typically the manufacturer), but behind the scenes, the revenue flows and organisations are more complex. Figure 3.3 summarises the typical revenue flows for a power-by-the-hour type contract. As mentioned earlier, the notion of 'ownership' is somewhat contentious and can muddy conversations about advanced services. In practice, this is usually taken on by an independent financial leasing company or a financial business unit within the corporation of the industrial firm. Here, the industrial firm is providing the asset, and the financial partner takes the responsibility of providing the resources for the customer to be able to complete the purchase. The customer then commits to a regular payment schedule. A part of these payments goes to the financial partner to cover the purchase and interest charges. The other part is paid to the industrial firm for their services package.

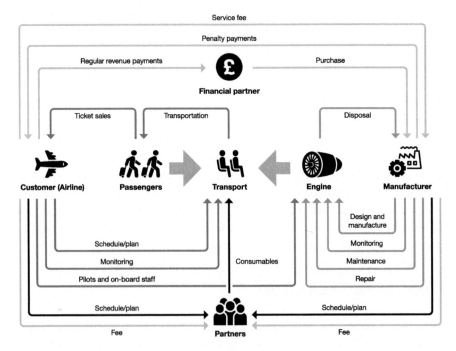

Fig. 3.3 Generalised revenue flow for advanced services (© The Advanced Services Group Ltd)

The element of the economic model which deals with the service component then, itself, usually consists of several sub-components. Often the revenue flows have contingencies and penalties to assure desired performance. In practice, the structure of the revenue model varies to reflect different forms of outcomes. To illustrate, Table 3.3 provides examples of three types of customer value propositions—at the level of the asset, the customer's process, and the customer's business model in three different industries, along with the revenue models that might be associated with them.

Capturing Strategic Value

There are forms of value, in addition to economic value, that can be created and captured from offering advanced services. However, both in research and practice, the capturing mechanisms for these values (i.e., strategic, knowledge, and relational) are not yet fully developed or formalised, often remaining fragmented or unrecognised. Our goal here is to foster understanding and realisation of these three types of values, which have the potential to be created and captured alongside economic values.

Strategic value refers to the boost in competitiveness for both the provider and its customers. For the provider, a key driver of competitiveness is market differentiation. This is achieved by offering tailor-made and distinctive products and services that are deemed more valuable by customers as they meet their needs. Meanwhile, customers benefit from (i) reduction of asset failure or downtime (ensured through improved reliability), (ii) cost structures around assets that are better aligned to their own business model (ensured through different revenue payment regimes), and (iii) improved compliance (ensured through regular updates and maintenance).

Another strategic value advanced service business models often offer is scalability and flexibility since they are not limited by physical product constraints. Organisations can expand their services without necessarily needing to increase production capacity. An example of this is demonstrated by Volvo Construction Equipment, a global manufacturer of construction machinery. Instead of solely focusing on selling construction equipment, Volvo Construction Equipment provides a range of value-added services, including equipment maintenance, operator training, fleet management, and productivity optimisation. By adopting service-led business models, the company has expanded its services without needing to increase its production capacity. They leverage their existing fleet of machines and expertise to offer enhanced support and solutions to their customers. This enables them

Table 3.3 Examples of different forms of direct revenue models and customer value propositions

	Value proposition—what the company will do for the customer and the outcome they will get	Revenue model—how the company can capture the value
Packco: A producer of equipment for the weighing and packaging of foods		
A proposition at the level of the asset	'Guaranteed packed product'. Ensuring for the customer that food products are reliably sealed within a package which has a preserving gaseous atmosphere. Results in regulatory compliance, predictable costs, dependable machine uptime	Pay-per-good-pack (payment for each correctly sealed pack produced by the machine) coupled with a monthly flat fee, and combined with penalties if issues occur with food packaging
A proposition at the level of the customer's process	'Production assurance'. Capability to know that food production line is fully operational. Results in reduced production disruptions, simplifies production management, improves awareness of issues, and waste through production disruption	Pay-per-pack (payment for each pack produced by the production line) coupled with a monthly flat fee, and combined with penalties and incentives for production availability and reliability within specified limits
A proposition at the level of the customer's business model	'Flexible production facility'. Offering a production capability with a capacity to deal with increasingly varied customer demands. Results in potential to increase revenue, reduces risk of overly constrained production envelope, improves integration with customers, reduces time and costs associated with production changeover and expansion	Pay-per-production (payment based on an algorithm of available production time, product produced, and variety) coupled with a monthly flat fee, and combined with incentives based on profit share with customers

Value proposition—what the company will do for the customer and the outcome they will get	Revenue model—how the company can capture the value
Filtrationco: A manufacturer of industrial air filtration equipment	
A proposition at the level of the asset	'Guaranteed dust collection'. Ensuring for the customer that the dust collection machinery operates effectively whenever needed. Results in regulatory compliance, predictable costs, dependable machine uptime	Pay-for-use (based on hours used) coupled with monthly flat fee, and combined with penalties for poor availability, reliability or failure to conform as specified
A proposition at the level of the customer's process	'Worry-free air quality'. Providing the customer with clean, safe air in the factory and surrounding environment. Result is assured regulatory compliance, occupational safety, reducing risk of litigation	Pay-for-dust extract (based on volume of dust extracted), coupled with monthly flat fee, and combined with penalties for failure to comply with air quality regulations
A proposition at the level of the customer's business model	'Emissions management'. Providing optimised air filtration to enable a reduction in airborne emissions. Results in increased output and revenues and assured regulatory compliance	Pay-per-clean-air (payment based on an algorithm of air quality measures, volume of dust collected, and operating hours) coupled with monthly flat fee, and combined with incentives based on profit share with customers
Measureco: A manufacturer of equipment that measures the chemical, physical and biological composition of materials	
A proposition at the level of the asset	'Hassle-free testing'. Providing for the customer an assured capability to reliably evaluate the chemical composition of substances. Resulting in reduced risk of lack of test compliance, assured asset availability, and saving time on maintenance and repair	Pay-per-test (payment for each test performed) coupled with a monthly flat fee, and combined with penalties if issues occur with test accuracy

(continued)

Table 3.3 (continued)

	Value proposition—what the company will do for the customer and the outcome they will get	Revenue model—how the company can capture the value
A proposition at the level of the customer's process	'Hassle-free compliancy checking'. Providing evaluation of production process compliance against necessary regulatory and best in class standards. Results in saving analysis time, reducing risk of non-compliance, and reduces analytical effort	Pay-for-use (based on hours of production monitored) coupled with monthly flat fee, and combined with penalties for failure to comply with associated quality measures
A proposition at the level of the customer's business model	'Recipe innovation support'. Evaluation, insight and innovation into the taste, quality and likely appeal of beverages. Results in greater variety of product line and increased revenue potential, and informs research and development	Pay-per-innovation (payment based on an algorithm of involvement with recipe innovation) coupled with monthly flat fee, and combined with incentives based on profit share with customers

to provide a complete package that includes not only the machinery but also ongoing support and optimisation services. By leveraging their existing resources, expertise, and equipment, they can provide value-added services and solutions that meet customer needs.

Advanced service business models can also help firms become more resilient to market fluctuations and economic uncertainties. By diversifying revenue sources, organisations can reduce their dependence on product sales and better withstand market disruptions. As an example, by shifting the focus to service-led business models, leading telecommunications equipment manufacturers such as Cisco and Verizon are now offering managed services that include network uptime, network monitoring, maintenance, and upgrades. By diversifying their revenue sources beyond equipment sales, the companies now generate recurring revenue through service contracts, ensuring a stable income regardless of the product sales.

Lastly, offering advanced services can help businesses to overcome market resistance to their new technology. By shifting the focus from upfront costs to measurable outcomes, businesses provide customers with greater confidence and assurance that the technology or product will deliver the expected benefits. This lowers the financial risk and initial cost burden for customers, making it more attractive for them to embrace and invest in innovative technologies.

An example of this in action can be seen in Rolls-Royce's well-known power-by-the-hour concept. Although this business model is commonly associated with Rolls-Royce, its origins can be traced back to Bristol Siddeley, an aircraft manufacturer. In the 1960s, Bristol Siddeley introduced a new executive jet called the Viper, which was equipped with a ground-breaking gas turbine engine [8]. However, the jet initially struggled to gain traction in the North American market. One of the main obstacles was the reluctance of existing repair and maintenance facilities to stock spare parts for the Viper engine, as they awaited substantial sales to justify the investment. On the other hand, there was hesitation from potential buyers to buy the aircraft without the assurance of readily available maintenance support. To overcome this deadlock, Bristol Siddeley devised a solution known as the power-by-the-hour contract [9].

Essentially, Bristol Siddeley utilised an advanced services contract to overcome market resistance and gain acceptance for their new technology. The power-by-the-hour contract provided a comprehensive maintenance and support package, giving buyers confidence in the long-term viability of the Viper engine. This strategic approach ultimately proved successful in breaking the stalemate and establishing the Viper as a viable choice in the market.

Advanced services can, therefore, provide a low-risk route for customers to adopt new technologies. By coupling the introduction of new technology with an advanced services contract that guarantees performance, reliability, and availability, the risk for the customers is significantly reduced. This lowers the barrier to early adoption of new products. Additionally, the manufacturer gains a chance to increase competitiveness by introducing new products into the market, gathering feedback on their performance, and subsequently creating a new revenue stream.

Capturing Valuable Knowledge

Advanced service business models provide greater insight into what customers are consuming and what they value [10]. Knowledge and insight into how products or services are being used in customers' operations can generate significant opportunities for both the provider and customers. From the provider's perspective, such intelligence can support it in designing better service offerings that will address its customers' requirements more effectively. In addition, the data from the assets in the customers' operations could significantly assist the provider in optimising their site visits for repair and maintenance activities.

Such knowledge and insight can also provide huge value to customers too, as they are able to become more efficient in their operations through optimising their assets' performance, identifying areas for improvement, and making more informed decisions such as those related to their inventory management, production scheduling, and resource allocation.

An example of knowledge capture is provided by the equipment manufacturer, JCB. It provides customers with the function to create geofences—a geographic zone within which the equipment should be operated. JCB LiveLink sends geofencing alerts to the customer if a machine moves out of its permitted operating zone [11]. The value to the customer is clear (maybe it has been stolen), and the manufacturer can gain through knowing the precise location of the machine, including information on how it is being treated, and identifying any at-risk machines. It also sends curfew alerts if a machine is switched on when it shouldn't be. This can significantly improve the efficiency of field service technicians when they come to carry out scheduled maintenance programmes (time is not wasted attempting to locate equipment).

Another example of how knowledge and insight can generate significant opportunities for both the provider and customers is demonstrated by

Nicklin Transit Packaging, a UK-based manufacturer and provider of bespoke timber and corrugated transit packaging products. The company's packaging products include timber cases and crates, plywood cases, glass stillages, timber pallets and corrugated cases. Many of its customers are within the automotive, glass and construction sectors. By adding a remote asset monitoring service to its packaging, Nicklin allows customers to monitor their packed products in real-time through all stages of transport, giving insight into shock, drop and tilt, humidity levels and temperature, as well as location. This gives customers real-time information on the whereabouts, safety and security of their products, hence greater peace of mind. By offering such a solution, the company also help customers comply with local regulations through, for example, using the least amount of material necessary in their packages, which is a requirement for manufacturers in Britain.

Capturing Relational Value

Advanced service offerings shift the relationship dynamics between providers and customers. They inspire long-term relationships (as opposed to the one-time transaction) in which the customers become collaborators and co-creators with their providers. These new relationships can also lead to improved communication and a better understanding of customer needs and increased trust, customer loyalty, and experience.

A prime example of this is the Alstom and Virgin contract. For almost two decades (up until early 2019 when the UK's Department of Transport barred Virgin from bidding to keep hold of the West Coast Main Line route due to problems with pension contracts), Alstom provided Pendolino trains to Virgin Trains under availability contracts and, in return, got paid based on the miles travelled or the number of passengers moved [12]. This outcome-based contract transformed the relationship between the two parties, where Virgin became a collaborator rather than being just a customer. The success of this long-term contract enabled Virgin to greatly increase its operational performance and enhance its customer satisfaction level. In turn, Alstom was able to better grasp its customer's requirements and fine-tune its offerings on a regular basis, which subsequently helped the company to offer similar contracts to a wider range of customers (including London Underground).

This benefit was also demonstrated by a Caterpillar dealership that would carry out scheduled maintenance on quarry trucks. The field technicians always arrived slightly ahead of time to discuss the equipment's performance with the operators. As a result, the technicians got early insights into any issues and potential faults with the equipment. This practice also allowed the technicians to show the operators all the resources they were using to support the services contract. Without this practice, the efforts of the field technicians would have gone unnoticed by the equipment operators.

In addition, advanced service offerings enable companies to incorporate ethical and social responsibility into their offerings. By considering sustainability, environmental impact, and social welfare in the services they provide, companies demonstrate a commitment to shared values and societal well-being. This ethical stance resonates with customers, strengthens the relationship, and captures relational values centred around social consciousness.

To exemplify this, consider Patagonia, an outdoor clothing and gear company. Patagonia has adopted servitization by offering a "Worn Wear" program. Instead of solely focusing on selling new products, they encourage customers to repair, reuse, and recycle their existing Patagonia gear. Through their "Worn Wear" program, the company provides repair services, guides customers on how to maintain their gear, and even offers trade-in options for used items. By promoting the longevity and sustainability of its products, Patagonia demonstrates a commitment to reducing waste and environmental impact. This approach aligns with their core values of environmental stewardship and social responsibility, capturing relational values centred around ethical consumption and sustainability. The program has garnered positive customer feedback and loyalty, strengthening the relationship between Patagonia and their customers based on shared values and a sense of social responsibility.

Pricing, Cost Drivers and Contract Duration

In this chapter we have focused on process of value capture. We believe it is essential to understand this process in order to explain advanced services effectively and lay a solid foundation for innovating these within a business. When we talk to executives about value capture, we often find that the conversation includes a discussion about cost drivers and pricing. Therefore, we will touch upon this subject briefly. However, it is important to note that since business models tend to vary across organisations, approaches to determining costs and establishing prices also differ. Nonetheless, we have identified some commonalities, which we will now outline.

Various pricing approaches exist to pricing, including: (i) Skim pricing, which targets situations where customers are relatively insensitive to price, allowing for premium pricing, (ii) Penetration pricing, which a aims to grow the customer base by setting a low price, and Neutral pricing, to minimize the impact of price on the buying decision [13]. The most common approach to pricing is a cost-based method that involves adding a mark-up to cover expenses and making adjustments by benchmarking against any competitors. Unfortunately, early adopters may face challenges in this regard, as customers might not fully comprehend the costs associated with carrying out a particular activity.

In such cases, a value-based approach to pricing becomes appealing. This approach emphasizes the customers' perception of value, including their willingness to pay [3]. Pricing structures typically reflect the cost drivers involved in successfully delivering advanced services, such as field service, maintenance, consumables, and decommissioning [14]. To adjust prices, several strategies can be employed. For instance, grandfathering can be used to keep existing customers at their current price while raising it for new customers. Another approach is to introduce price tiers by adding benefits and raising prices accordingly [5]. To gauge price sensitivity, targeted customers can be asked questions such as: What price would make you question the quality of the offering? At what price does it start to seem like a bargain? When does it begin to appear expensive, and at what price does it become too expensive? [3].

We should mention that sometimes at conferences and workshop we will hear executives talk about 'customer lock-in' as a perceived benefit of servitization. They take this to mean tying customers to a contract, as part of the pricing model, which makes it difficult for them to leave. This is not a view we share. The harder you make it for customers to leave, the less likely they are to come back [5]. Our argument is that done well, a services contract should strengthen the customer relationship such that they don't want to change providers. 'Stickiness' should be through the benefits of the value proposition itself rather than an obstinate pricing model.

Advanced services are likely to require a longer contracted period from the outset than other forms of service. This period is largely determined by the cost of setting up the service, the initial asset value and rate in which this deteriorates when in use. In other words, the potential resale value. This value helps to explain why financiers are attracted to working with OEMs to deliver advanced services: 'Who better to maintain the condition of the asset than the original manufacturer'. We see this ourselves if we purchase a second-hand car; those with a main dealer service history fetch the higher prices.

In situations where there is no asset involved, for example, Spotify's music streaming, then the contract duration can be short—weeks or months—and flexible. Whereas with an asset, such as a car, it might be three years, or with a production machine three-five, and a locomotive 15–25 years. These durations are necessary for the provider and financier to recoup their initial investment. If a customer chooses to exit early then typically there are financial penalties, and there may also be penalties if the provider seeks to exit. Don't forget that, with an advanced service, the provider is contracting to deliver business outcomes for the customer, and these may be more onerous than anticipated. In the early days of the Alstom/Virgin contract on the Pendolino trains in the UK, performance was disappointing, but both businesses chose to make additional investments rather than face the financial and reputational costs of exiting early.

Chapter Summary

In this chapter we explained different revenue models and how they may be blended to enable their application in practice. In the following chapters, we will explore the business practices and technologies that make these services deliverable. Before doing so, we would like to leave you with these highlights from what we have said so far.

1. Value is created by advanced services because:
   - Incentives to deliver value are better aligned across customers, providers and partners.
   - Responsibilities for risk are better aligned with the core competencies of organisations.
   - Innovation processes are more open and better aligned between the providers and customers.
2. Economic value for advanced services is typically captured through a composition of a flat-rate subscription fee over a predetermined term, on top of which there are additional charges to reflect the outcome of the service (or proxy-indicators for this outcome). There may also be penalties to incentivise outcomes being achieved and risk-sharing over factors where both the customer and provider have limited control.
3. Strategic value can be realised and captured by both the provider and the customer. For the provider, such values can be created and captured through differentiation; for the customer, these will then be achieved through the reduction of asset failure or downtime, increased flexibility and improved compliance.

4. Knowledge value arises from insights into how a product or service is being used in the customers' operations. Such intelligence can support the provider in designing better service offerings that will address their customers' requirements more effectively. Customers are able to become more efficient in their operations through optimising the asset's performance and identifying areas for improvement.
5. Relational value is in improved communication, intelligence, and the better understanding of customer needs, and increased trust, customer loyalty and experience.

References

1 Porter, M.E., *The competitive advantage: creating and sustaining superior performance*. 1985: NY: Free Press. 60–78.
2 KONE. *Design in its truest form: Why service design matters*. 2023 [cited 2023 06/01/2023]; Available from: https://www.kone.com/en/news-and-insights/stories/design-in-its-truest-form.aspx.
3 Liozu, S.M., *The industrial subscription economy: A practical guide to designing, pricing and scaling your industrial subscription*. 2021: Value Innoruption Advisors Publishing.
4 Baxter, R.K., *The forever transaction: How to build a subscription model so compelling, your customers will never want to leave*. 2020: McGraw-Hill Education.
5 Baxter, R.K., *The membership economy find your superusers, master the forever transaction, and build recurring revenue*. 1st edition ed. 2015: McGraw-Hill. 272.
6 Laurent Probst, L.F., Benoît Cambier, PwC Luxembourg & Jesper Ankeraa, Sarah Lidé, PwC Sweden., *Servitisation: service and predictive maintenance contracts. Business Innovation Observatory*. 2016.
7 Alstom. *Train operations & System maintenance: Increased value and performance*. 2023 [cited 2023 12/01/2023]; Available from: https://www.alstom.com/solutions/services/train-operations-system-maintenance-increased-value-and-performance.
8 Ramirez, R., et al., *Using scenario planning to reshape strategy*. MIT Sloan Management Review, 2017. **58**(4).
9 Parker, R. and G. Fedder, *Aircraft engines: A proud heritage and an exciting future*. The Aeronautical Journal, 2016. **120**(1223): p. 131–169.
10 Lah, T. and J. Wood, *Technology-as-a-service playbook: How to grow a profitable subscription business*. 2016: Point B, Inc.

11 JCBLiveLink. *JCB livelink—Security*. 2023; Available from: https://www.jcb.com/en-gb/customer-support/livelink/security.

12 Baines, T. and H. Lightfoot, *Made to serve*. What it takes for a Manufacturer to Compete, 2013.

13 Dunn, P. and R.J. Baker, *Time's up!: The subscription business model for professional firms*. 2022: John Wiley & Sons.

14 Brignall, M. *UK car loans: The little-known clause that means you could walk away from your deal*. 2023 [cited 2023 12/01/2023]; Available from: https://www.theguardian.com/money/2023/jan/09/uk-car-leasing-deal-contract-cost-of-living.

4

Delivering Advanced Services

Two hundred and fifty years of industrialisation have profoundly shaped our ideas of how products are made, and services provided. Around the mid-1700s, the factory-based production system was pioneered by industrialists such as Matthew Boulton at the Soho Manufactory in Birmingham, Great Britain [1]. Although this system has evolved, many of the underpinning principles are today still evident in the operations of a wide range of successful firms worldwide. Whether it's the way Toyota produces cars or McDonald's prepares hamburgers. Consequently, the fields of management and engineering possess a wealth of knowledge about designing and operating production systems. However, what happens when a company shifts its focus away from simply producing products and starts competing based on the outcomes enabled by those products?

We originally suggested how the more successful firms organised themselves in our earlier book, *Made to Serve*. Our research since then (see Table 1.1) has helped us to refine and reinforce our knowledge, and so in this chapter, we summarise eight lessons that characterise the operations that industrial firms use for delivering advanced services. These lessons help to highlight the differences between the 'operations' of industrial firms that are customer-centric from those that are solely product-centric.

Our focus is on what some researchers refer to as the "operating model" or "organisational backend" of the business model, though we generally consider this as the "service enabling system". We do so to emphasise the importance of treating this as a 'system'. *Why is this important?* In the 1980s, when Japanese production methods were recognised as superior to those in the West, many books were published on Just-in-Time techniques. These books discussed

© The Author(s), under exclusive license to Springer Nature
Switzerland AG 2024
T. Baines et al., *Servitization Strategy*, Palgrave Executive Essentials,
https://doi.org/10.1007/978-3-031-45426-4_4

practices like Kanban, single-minute exchange of die (SMED), quality circles, and more. Manufacturers outside Japan tended to adopt these practices piece-meal, and the impact on firm performance was mixed. They failed to realise that success relied on implementing the complete and integrated "system," and that the observed practices were most effective when implemented holis-tically. The same holds true for the successful delivery of advanced services; we will now share with you a series of lessons that we found characterise the operations of firms; just keep in mind that these come together as an integrated system to deliver advanced services.

Strategic Orientation

> *Lesson 1: Successful providers of advanced services are customer-centric and align incentives, responsibilities and innovation processes to deliver the desired customer outcomes cost-effectively.*

Quite simply with advanced services, it all starts with the customer. Execu-tives with a background in the world of production can struggle to appreciate how this orientation is subtly different to their own, how it influences their thinking about the operations of the firm, and indeed the extent to which a 'production' convention is ingrained in how they see the world. Ask any manager from a production-based firm to illustrate a supply chain and they will produce a drawing like Fig. 4.1. It starts with supply and shows the flow of materials (from the left) through processes to customers (on the right). First comes the materials, last comes the customer.

Similarly, take an experienced manager to a factory. Ask them to make an evaluation and they will most likely want to 'walk the process' to understand what's going on in the firm—and do so following a particular convention. To illustrate, in the early 2000s, I was delivering a course on Operations Strategy to master's students at Cranfield University, one of the UK's premier institutions for studying manufacturing. This was a multi-year programme

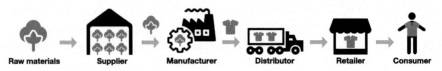

Raw materials   Supplier   Manufacturer   Distributor   Retailer   Consumer

Fig. 4.1 Illustrating how mangers with a production mindset tend to think of the world: it all starts with supply

that had been commissioned by Rolls-Royce in their pursuit of Operations Excellence and the students were senior managers from across a range of functions. I took these executives to a wide range of production facilities to help them appreciate what elements of World Class could look like, Ford, Airbus, and Nissan. Every time I would cause them a little anxiety because I would always 'walk the process' in reverse, starting at the customer, and I would illustrate a supply chain with the customer on the left side of the diagram rather than the right. In their minds, this was wrong—but they couldn't say why. I, however, had a clear objective, and that was to demonstrate a sense of customer-centricity.

When we began to research servitization, we became aware that firms differed in terms of where their leaders mainly focused their attention; what issues were prioritised and in turn where effort and resources were invested. Sometimes, we felt these differences reflected contrasting cultures, while in other instances, it appeared that firms were demonstrating distinct competitive priorities. However, none of these terms adequately described what we were seeing, and so we began to use the term 'strategic orientation' to represent these differences. What we saw were three different strategic orientations; production-centric (supporting a base services value proposition), servicing-centric (supporting an intermediate services value proposition) or customer-centric (supporting an advanced services value proposition). The characteristics we associate with each can be summarised as follows, and ultimately, we were interested in the difference between a product-centric and customer-centric organisation, and how these influenced the firms' operations.

Product (or production)-centric: This is an archetypical manufacturing organisation, focusing on product design, the supply of materials and components, production, and sales. The culture is typically technocratic with an engineering bias. Facilities tend to be centralised and positioned to exploit resource availability and market access. The priorities within such organisations are production volume, cost, quality and delivery and the core competencies of staff are in product design and innovation and smooth operation of the production system.

Servicing-centric: This organisation excels at supporting the maintenance of a product in the field, providing the technicians, parts, and consumables to maintain product functionality. Services in this type of organisation are often thought of as an adjunct to production, perhaps outsourced to partners, dealers, and distributors. The focus here is on maintaining the condition of products in such a way as to encourage repeat product sales. Facilities tend to be decoupled from manufacturing operations, with a stronger footprint in the market region. Priorities are customer satisfaction with responsiveness and efficiency, which are enabled by innovation in field service practices, technologies, and supply chain performance.

Customer-centric: This organisation supports the customer directly and works to deliver outcomes either at the level of the customers' assets, business processes or business platform. This type of organisation fosters a strong and ongoing collaboration and intimacy with the customer, with a focus on the alignment of incentives, responsibilities, and innovation processes. Facilities tend to be co-located with those of the customer to ensure high levels of intimacy. The priorities of these firms are the customer achieving the outcomes they need to be successful themselves.

Performance Measures and Processes

Lesson 2: Successful providers of advanced services develop performance measures that are aligned with the desired customer outcomes and demonstrate their fulfilment. These then cascade throughout the service delivery system to orchestrate activities.

A Product-centric organisation will focus on the delivery of products and prioritise cost, quality and delivery. From one factory to the next, these are prominent measures that feature strongly in conversations, performance charts and overall reporting procedures. These measures have a broad influence, ranging from the choice of practices and technologies in operations to product design and the skill sets of people.

With advanced services, the measures change and become much more customer-centric. Performance measures are chosen to directly reflect the desired customer outcomes or the proxy indicators for these. These measures then form the basis of the management reporting systems used by providers. They are also cascaded throughout the providers' operations, characterising what and how things are done, and influencing the form of relationships with partners and suppliers. As we mentioned earlier, Alstom trains used train availability, reliability and performance as proxy indicators of passenger mobility. These were broken down into more localised performance measures, such as 'variance against standard times for repair'.

There is also a need to demonstrate performance fulfilment. In a production setting, customers experience order fulfilment when a product is delivered, whereas, for advanced services, this might be more difficult to demonstrate. This opens up the possibility that customers will undervalue the outcome: if customers do not see what they are getting, they may believe they are getting nothing. To address this issue, for higher-value products or assets, providers may set up operations, war rooms and training rooms, to show how they are delivering outcomes, and/or well-presented and organised maintenance facilities, to demonstrate their expertise and capability.

Product and Service Design

Lesson 3: Successful providers of advanced services design products that can withstand as much use as possible without intervention from the outset, are easy to maintain, and can be modified as easily as possible during the life of the services contract.

In a product-centric organisation, design is usually considered in terms of product features, aesthetic qualities and costs. In the automotive industry, for example, a car design is largely considered a success if the car appears to be faster, more economical, and has a more attractive style than those of the competitors. The designers, processes, tools, and culture within the car manufacturer are aligned to deliver products with these qualities. However, as the focus moves to 'delivering mobility' rather than 'selling a car', the product designs need to evolve, and priorities need to extend to include maintainability, repairability, upgradability and recycling.

In a customer-centric organisation, cost considerations extend beyond those associated with production to include the whole lifecycle of the product. In the product-centric world, when customers buy a product, they provide cash up front and are then responsible for maintaining and monitoring its capability. Even during a warranty period, providers are not normally responsible for monitoring whether the product is working or not. Customers are usually responsible for letting manufacturers know if there is a problem, and for negotiating when and if a repair or replacement is required, and how much will be paid.

When customers buy an advanced service, however, the providers are responsible for maintaining the capability of the product and ensuring any deviations from the agreed outcomes are dealt with. Typically, providers need to guarantee the uptime of products for many years, monitoring and maintaining the product's capability throughout. If a product forms the basis of a long-term contract to deliver outcomes, then any intervention with the product is a cost to the service providers. Consequently, a product design should withstand as much use as possible without intervention. Also, not only must the product deliver customer outcomes from the outset, it must also be designed so that modifications can be made as easily as possible throughout the life of the services contract. The picture that emerges is one where design becomes all about developing a product that can deliver outcomes for as long as possible.

Business Processes

Lesson 4: Successful providers of advanced services develop business processes that extend across a wide range of customer 'touchpoints' and sustain ongoing value creation and capture.

Business systems and digital innovations are so intertwined that most executives won't necessarily distinguish between them. Many production systems, for example, are reliant on computer-based Enterprise Resource Planning (ERP) systems, which have modules dedicated to managing the flow of materials and scheduling the activities of machines and people. In a product-centric environment, these systems pull together the information, people and facilities that are essential to build and deliver products. A principal difference between this and a customer-centric organisation is the type and frequency of 'touchpoints' with the customer, and as a consequence, the business processes that facilitate and respond to these.

In a product-centric organisation there are various touchpoints with the customer. For example, in sales and marketing activities where the customer explores product information and negotiates terms. Should a customer decide to make a purchase, they engage with the factory to place the order by providing specific details and configurations. Throughout the manufacturing process, the factory may provide production updates and communicate performance against milestones or any changes.

The touchpoints between a provider of an advanced service and the customer require different interactions. These begins with contract negotiation, where the terms and conditions of the contract are discussed and agreed upon. The provider and the customer collaboratively define the desired outcomes and establish performance measurement methods. Regular reporting and communication channels are established to share performance results and address any issues that may arise during the contract execution. Additionally, touchpoints are utilised to drive continuous improvement and optimize the contract for better outcomes. At the end of the contract term, touchpoints occur for contract renewal discussions or closure procedures based on the evaluation of achieved outcomes and overall contract performance.

These touchpoints facilitate effective collaboration, performance management, and evaluation throughout the duration of the outcome-based contract. Traditional processes primarily focus on post-sale services such as spare parts provision and repairs. However, there are numerous customer touchpoints beyond product sales that require additional processes to handle interactions. These systems are designed to be highly responsive, prioritising the customer experience.

Many of the touchpoints between the customer and provider are then around communication rather that negotiating an action. For example, should a quarry truck on an advanced services contract become available earlier on an occasion, the manufacturer will be informed so that they can use any extra time to execute more lengthy repairs. Alternatively, the manufacturer might, on occasion, struggle with a repair, meaning that the truck is unavailable. Here, the customer will be informed so that contingencies can be executed. The outcome of the whole process is that the product is returned to be available for use rather than simply repaired. The manufacturer is incentivised to achieve the outcome because there are penalties associated with the customer-facing performance measures. In the example above, where the truck is not available for use, the manufacturer will be penalised.

Facilities and Locations

Lesson 5: Successful providers of advanced services develop facilities which foster customer collaboration by being co-located or distributed throughout their operations.

In product-centric organisation, efficiency necessitates scale: large, centralised factories, often located to give favourable access to markets and resources. This situation changes in a customer-centric organisation, especially where a higher-value asset is concerned. Providers need to be on hand, either in or next to their customers' operations. They need to be able to respond quickly to help, diagnose and rectify a problem, or perhaps even witness an incident and take corrective action immediately and with precision. Proximity to customers also helps to foster closer relationships, leading to a better understanding of their desired outcomes and how products and services can be further innovated to achieve these.

Rolls-Royce, Caterpillar, and MAN Truck & Bus exemplify the practice of strategically locating their facilities to cater to their customer base. Rolls-Royce has expanded its operations by engaging in joint ventures in the civil aerospace sector to provide power-by-the-hour contracts. This endeavour has led to the establishment of repair and maintenance facilities in Singapore, Hong Kong, and Texas, with each location strategically important to a key customer. Caterpillar, similarly, has developed an extensive network of dealers and strategically placed depots in proximity to its customer base.

MAN Truck & Bus follows a similar approach by carefully situating its facilities geographically to be closer to its primary customer base. For example, in regions such as London, the facilities are located within a ten-mile radius of the customer. These distributed facilities support advanced services that complement the centralised production facilities responsible for product design and manufacture. Thus, a complex picture emerges of one where conventionally sold products are produced in centralised production facilities, while advanced services, which encompass products, are delivered through facilities co-located with customer operations.

Suppliers and Partnerships

> *Lesson 6: Successful providers of advanced services integrate into customers' operations and form key partnerships, where necessary, to ensure responsiveness and innovation.*

The concept of a supply chain is powerful for expressing the structure of suppliers, manufacturers, wholesalers, distributors and customers to show the flow from raw material to semi-finished goods and then on to finished products. In the very early part of the twentieth century, Henry Ford made history with the production of his Model T, which was produced at Highland Park in Detroit [2]. Many publications described and celebrated the characteristics of the car's production process—'you can have any colour as long as its black' [3, 4]—and underpinning each was strong business logic. In the case of the one colour choice, it enabled consistency and repeatability, which enabled painting at scale, which enabled low-cost production, and which enabled customer affordability. This also explains why Ford developed vertically integrated processes so control could be exhibited.

Customer-centric organisations integrate forwards in their supply chain to adopt a wide range of customer activities while retaining any capabilities essential to delivering the desired customer outcomes. For example, in Alstom's case, they sourced components such as coffee machines and door actuators from external suppliers during the original manufacture of the trains. The air conditioning units were also initially sourced from suppliers overseas, but during the deployment of the services contract, the overhaul of these large and complex units was carried out by Alstom itself within its maintenance facilities. Alstom retained the production of the air conditioning units to retain the responsiveness and innovation of the product design. This helped to ensure the units were brought back into commission as quickly as possible and also enabled design improvements.

Indeed, within a customer-centric organisation the thinking shifts from 'supply chains' to 'value networks'. Moving from a single firm following linear logic for creating value, to multiple firms participating in networked business operations to co-create value. A value network consists of stakeholders collaborating on key activities and sharing resources to achieve shared goals. An example here is the IT supplier, Fujitsu in Sweden. It is partnering with Volvo to trial the weather-tracking and reporting technology for Volvo drivers [5]. It is also collaborating with Microsoft and Intel, which will allow Fujitsu to manage the connected car data that can be passed across the connected cars and their systems. Through such partnerships, they are working together as a value-creating network with a shared vision of offering integrated transport services.

Digital Technologies and Systems

> *Lesson 7: Successful providers of advanced services develop digital technologies and systems that provide real-time insight to the location, condition, performance and use of products and the fulfilment of outcomes.*

Product-centric organisations invest in digital technologies and systems to improve the efficiency of the factory, helping to bring about the innovation of new processes and coordinate their activities. Customer-centric organisations invest in these technologies and systems to provide 'visibility' of products 'beyond the factory gate', and to enable the 'intelligence' that can be used to help ensure the desired customer outcome is achieved. Indeed, Industry 4.0, the Internet-of-things (IoT), and the accompanying digital technologies are key drivers of servitization in manufacturing [6–8].

Digital information can be stored, processed, and transmitted to any digital device [9], making it possible to monitor customers' usage processes in real time. Collecting and analysing this data can help in understanding how customers use their products, enabling providers to offer value-creating services, such as advice on improving their business processes. Analysis of usage patterns and insights into customer processes can also empower providers to intervene and ensure the delivery of outcomes for customers [10, 11]. They are also key to automating processes which enable the innovation and scaling of services [12, 13].

Figure 4.2 illustrates the typical arrangement of technologies and systems that enable the insights and intelligence for successfully delivering an advanced service. This architecture consists of five key functions. The first function, 'Monitor,' involves capturing data from sensors placed on product components or subsystems. The second function, 'Transmit,' involves sending either basic data (e.g., temperature, pressure, run time) or fault codes (e.g., overheating, pump failure, scheduled maintenance required). The third, 'Store,' is responsible for maintaining records of the transmitted data. The fourth function, 'Analyse,' focuses on translating the data into meaningful information. Finally, the fifth function, 'Report,' provides information on various factors, such as the current status (e.g., location, busy, idle), historical changes in status (e.g., periods of inactivity, energy consumption rates), predicted changes in future status (e.g., degradation, likely breakdowns), and recommended interventions (e.g., adjustments, repair, shutdown).

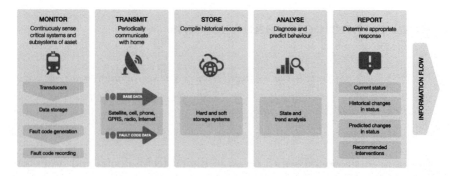

Fig. 4.2 Architecture of digital innovations that combine to give visibility of products within customers' operations (*Source* Baines et al. [14] © The Advanced Services Group Ltd)

This visibility and intelligence empower the provider to effectively manage assets. Taking a photocopier as an example, the provider can install sensors that send alerts regarding paper and toner levels, belt tracking, and cleanliness. This intelligence can be shared with the customer, enabling them to improve their management of paper and toner inventory while minimising the risk of breakdowns and subsequent service disruptions. By leveraging this information, the provider can proactively maintain their equipment and ensure uninterrupted operations.

People, Skills and Culture

Lesson 8: Successful providers of advanced services encourage staff to demonstrate flexibility and resilience, and foster customer intimacy through strong relational skills.

The evolution of the manufacturing industry has led to significant changes in the location, organisation, and skill sets of its employees, and the move to a customer-centric organisation demands even further innovations. People working in services behave quite differently compared to those working in production. If you would like to reflect on what it means to work in production then read Ben Hamper's book, *Rivethead* [15]. In a customer-centric organisation, people have to facilitate the delivery of outcomes and sustain positive relationships with customers.

The extent to which these skills are demanded of individual staff will vary according to the role. For example, a Condition Monitoring Technician tend to have stronger technical skills than an Account Sales Manager, who correspondingly are stronger at relationship building. The necessary skills can, of course, be identified and developed: recruitment processes can test for important skills, worker selection can be carried out, and developmental training can be given. The picture that emerges is of people who are characteristically flexible and resilient in how they work, are relationship builders, customer-centric, authentic, and technically adept (see Fig. 4.3). This is especially the case with staff who are in the front-line of delivering an advanced service.

Frontline employees act as advocates for customers, building relationships with them, understanding their business, and identifying their concerns. Additionally, they cultivate strong relationships with colleagues within the organisation and leverage these connections to address customer issues. They are technically proficient and prioritise customer matters over their own

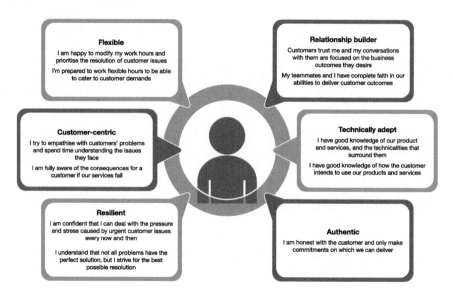

Flexible
I am happy to modify my work hours and prioritise the resolution of customer issues
I'm prepared to work flexible hours to be able to cater to customer demands

Relationship builder
Customers trust me and my conversations with them are focused on the business outcomes they desire
My teammates and I have complete faith in our abilities to deliver customer outcomes

Customer-centric
I try to empathise with customers' problems and spend time understanding the issues they face
I am fully aware of the consequences for a customer if our services fail

Technically adept
I have good knowledge of our product and services, and the technicalities that surround them
I have good knowledge of how the customer intends to use our products and services

Resilient
I am confident that I can deal with the pressure and stress caused by urgent customer issues every now and then
I understand that not all problems have the perfect solution, but I strive for the best possible resolution

Authentic
I am honest with the customer and only make commitments on which we can deliver

Fig. 4.3 Skill sets and behaviours of front-line staff in the delivery of an advanced service (*Source* Adapted from Baines and Lightfoot [16] © The Advanced Services Group Ltd)

schedules and commitments. They have a good understanding of the systems and technologies that comprise their offerings to the customers, and they make realistic commitments related to these technologies. They recognise that both customers and providers are imperfect and there are factors beyond their control, and they are sufficiently resilient not to take these as personal failures.

Salespeople in particular, differ in their approach within a customer-centric organisation. They are motivated by different priorities to those who sell products, communicate differently, and exhibit distinct behavioural patterns when interacting with customers. These salespeople have a relational rather than transactional approach to engaging with customers. Selling a service requires intimate knowledge of the customer's business, including their facilities, workflows, metrics, and overall business model [17].

Chapter Summary

In this chapter, we have focused on the key technologies and practices supporting the delivery of advanced services, and we have captured these as the following eight lessons.

Lesson 1: Successful providers of advanced services are customer-centric and align incentives, responsibilities and innovation processes to deliver the desired customer outcomes cost-effectively.

Lesson 2: Successful providers of advanced services develop performance measures that are aligned with the desired customer outcomes and demonstrate their fulfilment. These then cascade throughout the service delivery system to orchestrate activities.

Lesson 3: Successful providers of advanced services design products that can withstand as much use as possible without intervention from the outset, are easy to maintain, and can be modified as easily as possible during the life of the services contract.

Lesson 4: Successful providers of advanced services develop business processes that extend across a wide range of customer 'touchpoints' and sustain ongoing value creation and capture.

Lesson 5: Successful providers of advanced services develop facilities which foster customer collaboration by being co-located or distributed throughout their operations.

Lesson 6: Successful providers of advanced services integrate into customers' operations and form key partnerships, where necessary, to ensure responsiveness and innovation.

Lesson 7: Successful providers of advanced services develop digital technologies and systems that provide real-time insight to the location, condition, performance and use of products and the fulfilment of outcomes.

Lesson 8: Successful providers of advanced services encourage staff to demonstrate flexibility and resilience, and foster customer intimacy through strong relational skills.

References

1 Craig, W. and A. Leonard, *Manufacturing engineering and technology*. 2019, United Kingdom: ED-Tech Press.

2 Hounshell, D., *From the American system to mass production, 1800–1932: The development of manufacturing technology in the United States*. 1984: JHU Press.

3 Duncan, J., *Any colour-so long as it's black: Designing the Model T Ford, 1906–1908*. 2011: Exisle Publishing.

4 Ford, H., *Today and tomorrow: Commemorative edition of Ford's 1926 Classic*. 2019: Routledge.

5 Livesey, N., *How collaboration is changing the manufacturing sector*. 2020.

6 Kohtamäki, M., et al., *Digital servitization business models in ecosystems: A theory of the firm*. Journal of Business Research, 2019. **104**: p. 380–392.

7 Coreynen, W., P. Matthyssens, and W. Van Bockhaven, *Boosting servitization through digitization: Pathways and dynamic resource configurations for manufacturers.* Industrial marketing management, 2017. **60**: p. 42–53.

8 Vendrell-Herrero, F., et al., *Servitization, digitization and supply chain interdependency.* Industrial Marketing Management, 2017. **60**: p. 69–81.

9 Waltermann, H.M.L. and T. Hess, *Competitive recombination of digital technologies in the tv-media industry.* 2020.

10 Belvedere, V., A. Grando, and P. Bielli, *A quantitative investigation of the role of information and communication technologies in the implementation of a product-service system.* International Journal of Production Research, 2013. **51**(2): p. 410–426.

11 Martínez-Caro, E., J.G. Cegarra-Navarro, and F.J. Alfonso-Ruiz, *Digital technologies and firm performance: The role of digital organisational culture.* Technological Forecasting and Social Change, 2020. **154**: p. 119962.

12 Barrett, M., et al., *Service innovation in the digital age.* MIS Quarterly, 2015. **39**(1): p. 135–154.

13 Münch, C., et al., *Capabilities of digital servitization: Evidence from the sociotechnical systems theory.* Technological Forecasting and Social Change, 2022. **176**: p. 121361.

14 Baines, T., et al., *Performance advisory services: A pathway to creating value through digital technologies and servitization.* 2020: The Advanced Services Group. Aston Business School.

15 Hamper, B., *Rivethead: Tales from the assembly line.* 2008: Hachette UK.

16 Baines, T. and H. Lightfoot, *Made to serve.* What it takes for a Manufacturer to Compete, 2013.

17 Kowalkowski, C. and W. Ulaga, *Service strategy in action: A practical guide for growing your B2B service and solution business.* 2017: Service Strategy Press.

Part II

Why Servitization and Advanced Services Are Important

#servitization => Improved economics, resilience and environmental sustainability

5

Economic Performance and Growth of the Firm

Why give attention to servitization? Organising an industrial firm to compete with services, alongside products, can be challenging and demanding of resources. Chief Executives looking into servitization for their businesses need 'proof' that it is a 'good idea': that it is going to be both feasible and financially rewarding. So, in these chapters, we explore the evidence that exists, largely drawn from independent research studies, about the impact that servitization has had on firms that have traditionally competed through products (or outputs) and have subsequently developed services strategies.

In this chapter, we focus on the commercial results experienced through servitization. This is an arduous task and there are a few caveats to keep in mind. It would be foolhardy to take the insights we share as forecasts of how servitization will precisely impact an individual business. Situations vary from one firm to the next. Instead, we examine the available evidence to establish the key arguments linking servitization with firm performance. Think of these as hypotheses about the likely effect of servitization. We flesh out these arguments by identifying the factors which appear to have the more significant influence on performance results. Our intention is to both succinctly summarise what is known about servitization, and also create the foundations for an analysis of the likely effect of servitization on firms.

To complement our focus here on the commercial performance of the firms, in the next chapter (Chapter 6), we explore how servitization can affect the resilience and sustainability of firms. First, though, we explore the actual status of the knowledge the world currently has about servitization.

© The Author(s), under exclusive license to Springer Nature Switzerland AG 2024
T. Baines et al., *Servitization Strategy*, Palgrave Executive Essentials, https://doi.org/10.1007/978-3-031-45426-4_5

Reflecting on the Knowledge Base About Servitization

There is now a vast wealth of articles that have been written debating the benefits of servitization, yet teasing out eligible and relevant insights is challenging. Some articles are loose predictions, such as, 'Nine out of ten executives say much more of their future revenues will come from services.' Others are broad generalisations, for example: 'Services are more profitable than products.' A few, rather unhelpfully, give a one-sided message: 'Services lock out competitors and lock in customers.' And finally, some ignore the specific context of the firm and make unreliable predictions, such as: 'Services will increase your firms' revenues by 25–30%'. To overcome these limitations, we have adopted the following policies in our review of the evidence. '

First, we do not consider that servitization and advanced services are always 'best practices' and will not refer to them in this way. This term is used frequently in industry, and almost always without statistical backup. While there are practices that are commonly adopted by the better performing companies, only a thorough appreciation of context and a broad statistical sample could evidence a specific practice as 'best'. This very rarely happens, no exhaustive studies exist, and there are circumstances where servitization should not be prioritised, for example, in a firm that has an ongoing problem with product reliability.

Second, we do not accept that all types of services share the same impact on firm performance. Few studies have distinguished between service types when reviewing economic impact. To illustrate, Bernard Hoekman and Ben Shephard examined manufacturing firms, and in particular, those that sell services. They then drew on OECD (Organisation for Economic Co-operation and Development) data from over 100 developing countries and concluded that a 10% improvement in services productivity is linked to an increase in manufacturing productivity of 0.3% [1]. The breadth of this study is admirable, but the downside is that its insight is limited because it has not distinguished between differing types of services. We know from our work with firms that selling advanced services (such as outcome-based contracts) will bear very different results on firm performance than just selling more spare parts (base services). So, where the evidence allows, we will strive to examine the impact of service types rather than servitization as a collective.

Third, we recognise and embrace that terminology in the research and industrial community continues to evolve. To illustrate, the terms 'green servitization' and 'digital servitization' have become popular recently to emphasize different types of services, particular motives and technology enablers. Therefore, we have sought to include and learn from such contributions, even if the terminology isn't exactly the same as we have used in this book.

Fourth, the main interest is in industrial firms with a heritage in products and production and their adoption of servitization. However, as we highlighted earlier, servitization is not exclusive to such firms, and not all studies take this as the unit of analysis. And so, we also take insights from firms which might conventionally be recognised as service providers and are bringing products into their portfolio of offerings. Such as the 'utility' businesses in the energy sector that are currently buying up 'heat-pump manufacturers'. Similarly, we also attempt to reach beyond the firm offering services, and where possible investigate the wider external impact on customers, suppliers and other stakeholders in the value network.

These summaries illustrate how we have approached our review of evidence about servitization and advanced services. We now begin by examining the topics of economic performance and then economic growth.

Economic Performance

In the early days of researching servitization, publications would often focus on the economic and financial benefits of offering services rather than selling products alone. This is still a common theme at many field service conferences and articles, and it's quite usual for Service Executives to exalt the revenues and profits that they have witnessed arising from increased sales of spare parts or maintenance programmes. Professional research, though, has moved on and there are now clearer insights into how servitization can (if done well) impact revenue, profit and the overall productivity of an industrial firm. To sum this up, servitization is likely to benefit the financial performance of firms in the following ways.

Servitization as an Aid to Revenue Generation

> *The revenue argument:* As a firm progressively adopts servitization and effectively expands its service offerings, the total value of revenues earned (i.e., the combined total of both product and service revenues) is most likely to increase linearly and significantly.

Worldwide surveys of manufacturing firms have consistently reported servitization as a new and significant revenue stream. Survey results of 4,762 firms from as early as 2004 [2] found that manufacturers diversifying into services achieved higher financial performances (measured by financial/accounting indexes, such as returns on investment/asset, sales growths and profit margins) than those that are focused just on product sales. Studies from 2008 reported an increasing interest within manufacturing firms for services; some impressive numbers from back then show between the years 1990 and 2005, the average proportion of service revenue increased significantly. In 1990, services accounted for 8.9% of total revenue, but by 2005, the share of service revenue had risen to 42.2% [3, 4].

Reports of such upward trend in service revenue have continued to emerge over the years [5, 6]. For instance, an analysis of publicly listed annual reports of 57 UK manufacturing firms from 2016 found that 75% of those firms were demonstrating growing revenues from services [7]. More recent surveys from 2021, such as the one of 185 American and European manufacturing firms evidences that servitization has both grown and had a direct positive effect on firms' revenue generation [6]. Another recent survey of 200 commercial function leaders from B2B industries [8] revealed some interesting figures—about 75% of the manufacturers said they expected service delivery to become a prominent part of their business, with 21% already delivering outcome-based services. And 57% of these businesses anticipated delivering them in the next three to five years, with nearly 61% saying they were already delivering output-based services.

Higher revenue potential often exists in industries with an extensively installed product base (e.g., aerospace, locomotive and automotive industries), as service revenues can be one or two orders of magnitude greater than new product sales (see [9–11]). With OEMs, typically 70% of new equipment sales are to existing customers, with 90% of returning customers having had frequent aftermarket interactions with the OEM, in other words, the installed base is a gift that keeps giving [12].

Global industrial firms, such as GE, Rolls-Royce, Schneider Electric, and Siemens have all reportedly earned additional revenues from delivering outcome-based services to their customers. According to the numbers reported in Rolls-Royce's annual report from 2022, around half of the company's total revenue was generated from the long-term service agreements and maintenance of its engine products [13]. Other firms have also reported significant increases in revenue from services. For instance, in 2021, GE Power generated a total of £12.6 billion in revenue, of which £5.9 billion (accounting for 48% of total revenue) came from services such as maintenance contracts, equipment upgrades, and software solutions [14]. Similarly, Johnson Controls, a multinational manufacturer providing maintenance services for HVAC (Heating, ventilation, and air conditioning) systems, security systems, and fire protection systems generated over 40% of its revenue through its services portfolio in 2021 [15].

Services are considered a steadier source of revenue and increasing service revenues can compensate for declining revenues in equipment sales (see [16–18]). The overwhelming message over the last two decades has been that manufacturers can increase revenue by adding services.

Servitization as an Aid to Profitability

> *The profitability argument:* As a firm progressively adopts servitization and effectively expands its service offerings, the total value of profits earned by firms providing these services is most likely to increase, though not necessarily linearly.

While firms providing services can expect to generate higher revenues through services, profits do not necessarily follow. We find mixed evidence for the effect of servitization on firms' profitability [19]. While some studies make standard claims about the potential of services to generate higher profits for manufacturing firms, others have empirical evidence suggesting that this is not always the case. One of the key reasons for these inconsistent results about the link between servitization and profitability is related to how firms' performance is measured and then reported [19, 20]. Many times, studies discuss the financial performance of firms using a range of indicators, such as returns on sales, market shares, profits and returns on investment, and as a consequence, it can be difficult to tease out exactly what this means in terms of the profitability of firms.

These limitations aside, the general message is that the total value of net profits is likely to increase with servitization, but as a 'percentage' of total revenues, that in some circumstances can be lower than for pure product sales. Heiko Gebauer et al. [9] called this the concept of 'service paradox' and argued that, '[W]here there is such a paradox, substantial investment in extending the service business leads to increased service offerings and higher costs but does not generate the expected correspondingly higher returns.' A few other studies also discuss the notion of the service paradox by providing evidence on the challenges of deriving profits from base and intermediate services [21]. A firm can increase its profit margins through advanced service offerings, but not at the same rate for its intermediate service offerings. In addition, several studies have reported a U-shaped non-linear relationship between services and the financial performance of firms [6, 22, 23]. One such study of 477 publicly traded American manufacturers from 2008 [3] found that only after a firm reaches a critical mass of service sales, which is around 20–30%, will it see a positive impact from services on firm value [3, 17].

Reasons given for the service paradox are varied. Servitized firms can have higher-than-average labour costs, working capital and net assets and there comes a point when the costs of resources for supporting a new strategy, like the one for services, can initially outweigh the benefits [24, 25]. Similar challenges are associated with changing organisational direction and focus [26]. When products themselves are offered as a service and customers pay for specific outcomes, then more radical transformation efforts are required. Some studies find that there are cultural issues which can contradict traditional manufacturing practices which are pivoted around standardisation and efficiency [27]. Other reasons include insufficient attention from top management, deficiencies in organisational design and information technology, and insufficient capabilities for service management [28–30].

A variety of studies report on how this lull in profitability can be mitigated. For example, studies show that manufacturers who leverage their service supplier networks tend to increase the financial return [23]. Many have also argued about the importance of a separate service business/unit and managerial orientation towards services as the two critical conditions for improving service sales [31–34]. Despite the significant investments required to build, for example, a separate service business, the net sales margins will be greater due to the higher volume of customer value proposition attached with the provision of services, and more specifically, advanced services [32].

While the paradox suggests that some firms will initially experience a reduction in profitability with services, once a critical mass has been reached then profitability significantly improves. Annual reports from 2016 show how evidence of improved profitability is a principal motive for UK manufacturers (46% of the respondents) to transition to services [35]. A further survey, this one from 2018, questioned 200 industrial executives whose companies were on the servitization journey. It reported that manufacturers with higher service maturity can turn up to three times more profits than those focused on only products [36]. Those offering annual contracts with planned maintenance or guaranteed Service Level Agreements were 24% more likely to be profitable with their services. A more recent survey, in 2021, of 120 manufacturers indicated when manufacturers grow their service business and capabilities, customer business-related services become the majority (53%)

of their total service revenue, leading to profitable growth; firms offering proactive services reported gross margins of 60% [37]. Another survey of 200 commercial function leaders from B2B industries revealed the average growth margin from services varied between 15 and 35%, much more than the growth margin from products [8].

Servitization as an Aid to Productivity

> ***The productivity argument:*** *As a firm progressively adopts servitization and effectively expands its service offerings, the productivity of both the firms providing and consuming these services is most likely to increase.*

Productivity is especially valuable as a benchmark to indicate how hard and smart a firm needs to work to reap the benefits of servitization. It is the measure of the combined or integrated efficiency of employees, machines and other devices and equipment, raw material inputs, and management performance. Productivity is reliant on resources; if these are unavailable or inefficiently used, productivity is lower. Productivity isn't everything but, in the long run, it is almost everything.

Like profitability, increased productivity is another motive for manufacturers to servitize. A survey from 2021 found that firms offering more advanced services such as proactive solutions had 27% higher productivity levels than firms which only provided services on the lower steps of the staircase. This difference was seen to exist because the revenue per fulltime employee is higher for those services which are knowledge-intensive, than it is for more conventional services [37]. Also, customers adopting and using advanced service offerings can also experience greater productivity, mostly because the provider has greater knowledge of the asset and can maximise its operational performance in line with what the customer values [38].

Other studies have reported similar findings. A survey of more than 4,000 German manufacturing and non-manufacturing SMEs found that firms selling bundled products and services are more productive than those selling products and services separately [39]. A similar study of French firms in 2017 found that those with increased servitization intensity saw their profit margin rise relative to pure product firms. Their number of employees increased between 2.1% and 4.2%, and their turnover rose between 0.6% and 3% [40]. A text-mining and econometric analysis of secondary data from across 258

UK book publishers found that servitized firms, despite the service paradox, are more productive relative to pure product firms [5].

Some research has looked at specific approaches to servitization and also reported a positive impact on productivity, for example digital-servitization has indicated higher productivity levels than pure product firms [5]. Digital servitization is seen to help dampen supply chain uncertainties and manage demand to improve efficiency, and so increased productivity [41]. While much research has confirmed the positive link between servitization and higher productivity, whether this relationship is linear or not remains unclear [42]. There are studies that examine the factors affecting this relationship. For instance, a study of French firms found that those with increased servitization intensity saw their profit margin rise relative to pure product firms, and employed around 2.1% and 4.2% more employees, and reported a higher turnover of between 0.6% and 3% [40].

There is also research suggesting that the position of a firm in the value chain can alter the rate of productivity caused by servitization. A study using the WIOD database (World Input–Output Database) and relevant statistical yearbooks from 2000–2014 found that for industries at a higher position in the global value chain, servitization yielded higher productivity [43]. Similarly, productivity seems to improve particularly in smaller firms. Our own study of 77 small- and medium-sized manufacturing firms based in the central region of the UK saw that services-based business models stimulated growth in Gross Value Added (GVA) of £7,500/employee and productivity improvements by 16% [44].

Economic Growth

So far, we have considered the economic performance of a firm, and in particular revenue, profitability, and productivity. The economic growth of a firm, on the other hand, specifically measures the expansion and increase in the firm's market presence and channels to growth. In this section, we present evidence that servitization is likely to benefit the economic growth of firms in the following ways.

Servitization as a New Channel to Market

> ***The new market argument:*** *As a firm progressively adopts servitization and effectively expands its service offerings, this unlocks new opportunities in global markets that are greater than for products alone.*

The contribution of manufacturing production to the global economy, as a percentage of global Gross Domestic Product (GDP), has decreased significantly compared to the contribution of services. In other words, the share of economic activity related to manufacturing has declined relative to the share attributed to services (for a comparison of GDP derived from products and services see the World Bank 2018 [45]). In 2020, services accounted for an average of 65.7% of the GDP across world economies by (Fig. 1.1). Generating about two-thirds of the world's GDP, services are a significant part of the world economy.

Over the years, the services sector has experienced fast growth and has become a more dominant force in driving the economic activity. This is reflected in the increasing number of firms with a well-established manufacturing core in countries like the United States, the United Kingdom, Sweden, France and China moving quickly towards services [46]. Recent surveys suggest that about 95% of B2B manufacturing companies plan to increase their service revenues, and 75% of those based in Europe expect delivering services to become a significantly bigger part of their business over the next few years [47]. More focused numbers project the growth of the global Everything-as-a-Service (XaaS) market from £457.51 billion in 2022 to £1,995.03 billion by 2029 [48]. This does not mean the manufacturing sector is shrinking or will be less important to the global economy. Instead, it highlights the complementarity of the manufacturing and services sectors.

The boundaries between these two sectors are diminishing, and the influence of services on national economies is increasing, creating a prominent, more opportunistic market for outcome-based services. A study puts together examples of firms from various sectors that have embarked on servitization journeys to tap into new markets with service business opportunities [49]. One of those firm is IBM - following significant losses in the personal computer market, IBM divested its personal computer division to Lenovo and changed its registration as a service company to embrace services for reshaping its business. Magna Steyr is another firm that primarily produces automotive components, but also offers assembly services for entire cars. This expansion into providing assembly services represents a new channel to market. Xerox, a prominent player in the document technology industry moved to bundling contracted services, equipment maintenance, consumable supplies, and financing, and created a new channel to market focused on recurring revenue. Other sectors have also embraced servitization, like Michelin which with its price-per-mile contract for tires, and Swiss Fresh Water with its water-as-a-service instead of selling and maintaining water treatment equipment, particularly in regions like Africa where access to potable water is limited [49].

Another example here is of Apple and its strategy to unlock new opportunities in global markets that go beyond the products. Traditionally, Apple's success is attributed to its innovative product design, software, and marketing, which led to its valuation at $2.3 trillion in 2020, surpassing the entire value of FTSE 100 companies [50]. However, as the market dynamics changed and iPhone sales revenue declined, Apple recognised the need to diversify its income streams [51]. Apple realised that focusing on the 'user experience and 'outcomes' enabled using apps on its products could drive its growth in the long run [52]. The services business, including the App Store, Apple Music, and licensing deals, has emerged as the next big frontier for generating revenue. By transitioning into a firm that relies not as much on physical products and more on services, Apple is addressing changing customer preferences who want outcomes such as access to music, efficient navigation, and health monitoring, rather than simply purchasing expensive devices with limited updates.

More evidence is captured in studies like this one from the Waste-to-Energy (W2E) industry in the European region [53]. It discusses the new demand for W2E technologies from independent power producers (IPPs), utilities, and fast-growing countries such as Brazil, India, and China. Wind turbine manufacturers and component suppliers have embraced servitization to cater to these new markets. They have intensified services to ensure turbine availability, productivity, and customer-specific solutions for entire wind parks. Co-specialised service competencies developed along the value chain have strengthened the collaboration between component suppliers and turbine manufacturers. These servitization processes have opened up new markets, including utilities and IPPs, who require long-term service-level agreements to guarantee the availability and performance of wind turbines and components. The expansion into new markets, facilitated by service competencies, represents a significant portion of the total W2E revenue, contributing to industry growth.

Servitization as an Aid to International Trade

> *The export argument*: As a firm progressively adopts servitization and effectively expands its service offerings, it is exposed to export barriers that are different to products and often easier to overcome.

International trade refers to the exchange of goods and services between different countries. Statistics over the years suggest that the proportion of international trade in the global GDP has witnessed a substantial rise, climbing from 16.71% in 1960 to 46.14% in 2018 [54, 55]. International trading patterns used to be dominated by goods, but now we are seeing a rise in the services share, which has increased from only 9% in 1970 to over 20% in 2019 [56]. The World Trade Report estimates that services will make up for nearly one third of the world's trade by 2040, which is a 50% rise in services share in the next 17 years [56]. More focused global export data shows a rise in the number of manufacturers exporting both goods and services. Recent OECD figures also reveal that services represent more than 50% of value added in such exports [55]. Overall, the share of service exports globally has increased from 17% in 1980 to over 24% in 2016 [57].

It is important to understand that the balance of trade, and particularly whether there are any surpluses or deficits, is especially important to an economy and those managing it [58]. This means the use of tariffs, regulations and quotas by countries to protect domestic industries from imports, which then present barriers to international trade. Advanced services business models can help navigate these barriers because revenue generation is from a service and, so, not subject to tariffs in the same way as it would be for products [59–61]. MAN, for instance, uses a range of organisational approaches to navigate the regulatory environments across the many countries where it operates. Recognising the value of advanced services in gaining a competitive edge, MAN developed MAN Fleet Management, a comprehensive solution that offers services focused on optimising vehicle performance. In some countries like Germany, it internally develops the technological solution, while in other markets, such as the UK, MAN collaborates with a specialised software provider to offer the system, to ensure compliance with regulations [62].

Import tariffs are outdated in their treatment of goods and services, and there is a clear distinction between tariffs imposed on goods versus those imposed on services [63]. The business community has long recognised the artificial nature of this distinction. Take, for instance, the case of Rolls-Royce's power-by-the-hour offering. Is it appropriate to classify this as a good or a service? Furthermore, what transpires when the end customer is not purchasing ownership of the asset but rather the utilisation or desired outcome derived from it? Regulations and tariffs are just one set of concerns for businesses, especially when trying to sell products. Manufacturers are also frequently anxious about protecting their intellectual property, being concerned that exporting to some regions of the world opens them up to local competitors who might appropriate their technology (See Trade related aspects of Intellectual Property Rights [64]). In addition, they worry that exporting, even to reliable customers, might leave them exposed if their machines are inappropriately used or maintained, perhaps resulting in premature failure or poor performance, and so damaging relationships and reputation. In contrast, there is also a possibility that customers might be reluctant to consider buying manufacturers' machines, simply because they are concerned that they won't be able to get the necessary spare parts and maintenance support [65].

Furthermore, where ownership is not transferred to customers, and so third-party suppliers are prevented from maintaining the equipment, there is less likelihood of the intellectual property being stolen (See The General Agreement on Trade in Services [66]). Indeed, one of the principles of advanced services contracts is that customers need not concern themselves with the maintenance of the equipment whatsoever, which helps to alleviate their concerns about support [67, 68]. Quite simply, if the machine is not working, customers don't pay, rather than paying and then hoping that suppliers will make good on maintenance and spare parts. There are still risks, of course, for customers, but in this new relationship the manufacturers are taking a greater slice of them. Manufacturers have to put in place local field support, and to do so need their customers to ensure access to their facilities for maintenance operations [69]. To help make this affordable, the manufacturers need digital connectivity, so that their machines can be remotely monitored and visits by field technicians kept to a minimum. All this localised activity impacts the profitability of a contract; but this needs to be seen in the light of much greater value creation afforded by the new business model.

The example of Koolmill Systems [70] helps to illustrate that this opportunity can be taken even by small businesses. Koolmill is an SME which was incorporated in 1988 in Solihull (the UK's West Midlands) by founder engineer Alec Anderson. The company designs and builds high-speed rice-milling machines with pioneering technology. The Koolmill rice-milling processes are a significant improvement over traditional methods and offer much less energy consumption and much greater production efficiencies than its competitors' machines. Although based in the UK, the market for rice-milling equipment is centred around Asia and is very traditional in its adoption of new technologies. In terms of metric tonnes milled, India and China are the biggest producers and processers, followed by Indonesia and Bangladesh. These are, therefore, the target markets for KoolMill; however, they share a range of characteristics that are potential concerns for a small UK- based manufacturer.

Firstly, the target markets are relatively low-income economies with poor access to capital expenditure revenues. Secondly, the rice producers are typically state-owned cooperatives, often wary of new technologies, and tending to purchase machinery and then take care of all the maintenance themselves. As a consequence, they favour technologies with which they are familiar, and which if a spare part is required, they can remanufacture themselves, and indeed on occasion even set about building a new machine taking the purchased machine as a pattern. Thirdly, the markets are protected by import tariffs, which can be complex and costly to navigate for a manufacturer simply seeking to sell equipment. On a more positive note, however, these producers are searching for new ways to improve efficiencies and reduce waste.

The characteristics of the incumbent markets are worrying, practically because the rice producers tend to favour equipment with which they are familiar and, also, there are risks of the equipment breaking down. Therefore, rather than selling it machines, Koolmill has set out to compete through offering advanced services—rice-milling-by-the-hour. The company offers rice production output, based on a service of guaranteed number of hours of high-performance cereal milling to customers for an agreed monthly or quarterly fee. The benefits to customers have principally been achieved through both the capabilities of the new technology over the old, but also, because this technology has been offered as an advanced service. This has allowed Koolmill to enter a market that would have been problematic if they had used a more traditional transactional sales model.

Koolmill is still early in its development cycle as a business, but the impact so far of offering its production process as an advanced service has been very promising. The opportunity is now for Koolmill to increase its export market by opening up new markets, where access to capital is scarce to small- and medium-sized cereal millers. Its goal is to make its high-performance technology accessible to 1.5 million SME millers and 200 million smallholder growers/potential millers globally. Its technology reduces the cost per tonne milled by up to 63% and drastically cuts processing losses. Koolmill is also a very good example for the new product introduction argument that we are next going to elaborate on.

Servitization as an Aid to New Product Introduction

> *The new product introduction argument:* As a firm progressively adopts servitization and effectively expands its service offerings, this can smooth the introduction of new products with disruptive technologies into the marketplace.

Offering a new product as a service can help firms overcome barriers associated with product adoption and address any market resistance to their new technologies. With advanced services, firms can reduce the financial risk and initial cost burden for customers, making it more appealing for them to embrace and invest in innovative technologies.

Leading organisations in the healthcare industry, such as GE Healthcare, Siemens, and Fresenius, are embracing servitization to facilitate the adoption of new products and technologies [71]. They are shifting from traditional models of equipment ownership to pay-per-outcome models. For instance, GE's TruPay offering provides comprehensive care for medical equipment ensuring high equipment uptime, complete care for a specified duration, and remote services. The pricing is based on the outcomes delivered. This approach reduces the upfront costs and risks associated with adopting new equipment, making it more attractive and accessible to healthcare providers. It exemplifies how servitization helps in overcoming barriers to adoption and enables organisations to offer value-based care.

More evidence suggests that firms can overcome customer resistance to new products by introducing service offerings that provide extra support and minimise any perceived adoption risks. For instance, using data from 12 different industries, a study found that firms implementing servitization strategies are in a better position to prioritise and address customer concerns about reducing the cost of owning products and other financial commitments, including managing risks associated with product use [72]. One example is the shift from capital expenditure, which involves purchasing IT equipment, to operational expenditure through service-based contracts.

Evidence of this can also be found in the very well-known power-by-the-hour programme that we referred to earlier. While often associated with Rolls-Royce, its origins can be traced back to Bristol Siddeley, an aircraft manufacturer. In the 1960s, Bristol Siddeley introduced the Viper, a groundbreaking executive jet equipped with a gas turbine engine [73]. One of the main obstacles was the reluctance of existing maintenance and repair facilities to stock spare parts for the Viper engine. They hesitated to make the investment without significant sales to justify it. Conversely, potential buyers were hesitant to purchase the aircraft without the assurance of readily available maintenance support. Bristol Siddeley that later became Rolls-Royce introduced power-by-the-hour programme to overcome market resistance. For a fixed operating fee per hour, the programme guaranteed engine availability and absorbed the maintenance costs [74]. The firm aligned its commercial incentives with its customers, who in turn benefitted from predictable operating costs and lower risks. This programme embodies the first industry-wide shift from the traditional time-and-material type contracts to those focused on performance.

A further example of how advanced services can help with new technology introduction is offered by Baxi. Baxi is one of the largest suppliers of heating and hot water solutions for domestic and commercial markets in the UK. Around 15% of total UK greenhouse gas emissions and 25% of total energy use comes from heating. To achieve net zero by 2050, UK households need to adopt new low-carbon heat solutions. One critical component of this transformation requires that consumers move from gas central heating to systems such as solar water heating or air and ground source heat pumps and, indeed, regulations in the UK have recently changed to favour their installation (see [75]). Currently, among the country's 29 million, less than a quarter of a million households use heat pumps.

Yet, heat pumps require a significant initial financial outlay by the homeowner, and despite government incentives, this is inhibiting adoption. The heat pumps also require installation technicians to have a different set of skills to those needed to install a gas heating system. Consequently, at the current rate of adoption, it is likely to take between 1,500 and 2,000 years for the heating systems in the UK to be replaced by heat pump technologies. Even then, once installed, heat pumps require some adjustments to the heating curve so that their performance matches the fabric of the property and energy consumption is optimised. All these factors combine to slow the adoption and effectiveness of the technology and, therefore, the realisation of an energy decarbonation.

Servitization allows customers to transfer certain risks associated with product ownership to the service provider. For example, maintenance, repairs, and upgrades are typically handled by the service provider, relieving the customer of potential uncertainties and costs related to product reliability. Baxi has set out to accelerate the adoption of new technologies by selling 'heat-as-a-service'. Rather than buying a boiler or heat pump, the company is exploring the opportunity to offer customers the outcome of 'Warm Hours', with Baxi taking responsibility for the new technology installation along with its maintenance, efficient operation, financing and electricity consumption.

These changes alone can significantly reduce reliance on fossil fuels and CO_2 reduction.

Chapter Summary

In this chapter, we focused on how servitization affects firms' commercial performance. Our intention has been to summarise what is known about servitization and then create the foundations for analysing the likely effects of servitization for individual firms. In the next chapter, we will look at the evidence from the perspective of resilience and sustainability and then draw together a complete picture about the likely impact of servitization.

References

1 Hoekman, B. and B. Shepherd, *Services productivity, trade policy and manufacturing exports.* The World Economy, 2017. **40**(3): p. 499–516.

2 Skaggs, B.C. and S.B. Droege, *The performance effects of service diversification by manufacturing firms.* Journal of Managerial Issues, 2004: p. 396–407.

3 Fang, E., R.W. Palmatier, and J.-B.E. Steenkamp, *Effect of service transition strategies on firm value.* Journal of Marketing, 2008. **72**(5): p. 1–14.

4 Böhm, E., A. Eggert, and C. Thiesbrummel, *Service transition: A viable option for manufacturing companies with deteriorating financial performance?* Industrial Marketing Management, 2017. **60**: p. 101–111.

5 Kharlamov, A.A. and G. Parry, *The impact of servitization and digitization on productivity and profitability of the firm: A systematic approach.* Production Planning & Control, 2021. **32**(3): p. 185–197.

6 Abou-Foul, M., J.L. Ruiz-Alba, and A. Soares, *The impact of digitalization and servitization on the financial performance of a firm: An empirical analysis.* Production Planning & Control, 2021. **32**(12): p. 975–989.

7 Huxtable, J. and D. Schaefer, *On servitization of the manufacturing industry in the UK.* Procedia Cirp, 2016. **52**: p. 46–51.

8 PA-Consulting. *From products to services: Creating sustainable growth in industrial manufacturing through servitization.* [cited 2021 15/10/2021]; Available from: http://www2.paconsulting.com/rs/526-HZE-833/images/PA%20Servitization%20Report.pdf.

9 Gebauer, H., E. Fleisch, and T. Friedli, *Overcoming the service paradox in manufacturing companies.* European Management Journal, 2005. **23**(1): p. 14–26.

10 Wise, R. and P. Baumgartner, *Go downstream.* Harvard Business Review, 1999. **77**(5): p. 133–133.

11 Ambroise, L., I. Prim-Allaz, and C. Teyssier, *Financial performance of servitized manufacturing firms: A configuration issue between servitization strategies and customer-oriented organizational design.* Industrial Marketing Management, 2018. **71**: p. 54–68.

12 Liozu, S.M., *The industrial subscription economy: A practical guide to designing, pricing and scaling your industrial subscription.* 2021: Value Innoruption Advisors Publishing

13 Rolls-Royce, *ROLLS-ROYCE PLC ANNUAL REPORT AND AUDITED FINANCIAL STATEMENTS* 2022.

14 GE, *General electric company: Form 10-K*. 2021.

15 Johnson, *Johnson controls international plc annual report.* 2021.

16 Eggert, A., et al., *Industrial services, product innovations, and firm profitability: A multiple-group latent growth curve analysis.* Industrial Marketing Management, 2011. **40**(5): p. 661–670.

17 Suarez, F.F., M.A. Cusumano, and S.J. Kahl, *Services and the business models of product firms: An empirical analysis of the software industry.* Management Science, 2013. **59**(2): p. 420–435.

18 Raddats, C., et al., *Servitization: A contemporary thematic review of four major research streams.* Industrial Marketing Management, 2019. **83**: p. 207–223.

19 Wang, W., K.-H. Lai, and Y. Shou, *The impact of servitization on firm performance: A meta-analysis.* International Journal of Operations & Production Management, 2018.

20 Bustinza, O.F., et al., *Product-service innovation and performance: Unveiling the complexities.* International Journal of Business Environment, 2018. **10**(2): p. 95–111.

21 Kastalli, I.V., B. Van Looy, and A. Neely, *Steering manufacturing firms towards service business model innovation.* California Management Review, 2013. **56**(1): p. 100–123.

22 Kohtamäki, M., et al., *Non-linear relationship between industrial service offering and sales growth: The moderating role of network capabilities.* Industrial Marketing Management, 2013. **42**(8): p. 1374–1385.

23 Zhou, D., et al., *Performance implications of servitization: Does a Manufacturer's service supply network matter?* International Journal of Production Economics, 2020. **219**: p. 31–42.

24 Benedettini, O., A. Neely, and M. Swink, *Why do servitized firms fail? A risk-based explanation.* International Journal of Operations & Production Management, 2015.

25 Neu, W.A. and S.W. Brown, *Forming successful business-to-business services in goods-dominant firms.* Journal of Service Research, 2005. **8**(1): p. 3–17.

26 Bowen, D.E., C. Siehl, and B. Schneider, *A framework for analyzing customer service orientations in manufacturing.* Academy of Management Review, 1989. **14**(1): p. 75–95.

27 Gebauer, H., et al., *Innovation of product-related services.* Managing Service Quality: An International Journal, 2008. **18**(4): p. 387–404.

28 Brax, S.A., et al., *Explaining the servitization paradox: A configurational theory and a performance measurement framework.* International Journal of Operations & Production Management, 2021. **41**(5): p. 517–546.

29 Oliva, R. and R. Kallenberg, *Managing the transition from products to services.* International Journal of Service Industry Management, 2003.

30 Neu, W.A. and S.W. Brown, *Manufacturers forming successful complex business services: Designing an organization to fit the market.* International Journal of Service Industry Management, 2008. **19**(2): p. 232–251.

31 Li, H., G. Tian, and Y. Tian, *Servitization: Its preferred organization and impact on firm performance.* Human Systems Management, 2018. **37**(2): p. 181–193.

32 Sousa, R. and G.J. da Silveira, *The relationship between servitization and product customization strategies.* International Journal of Operations & Production Management, 2019. **39**(3): p. 454–474.

33 Yan, K., et al., *Overcoming the service paradox by leveraging organizational design and cultural factors: A combined configuration and contingency approach.* IEEE Transactions on Engineering Management, 2019. **68**(2): p. 498–512.

34 Lexutt, E., *Different roads to servitization success–A configurational analysis of financial and non-financial service performance.* Industrial Marketing Management, 2020. **84**: p. 105–125.

35 McCallion, R., *The manufacturer: Annual manufacturing report 2016.* 2016.

36 Rathmann, C., *Industrial Servitization and Field Service Technology.* 2018, IFS.

37 Noventum and IFS, *The Service Business Growth Model for B2B Manufacturers. Benchmark Report. .* 2021.

38 Aquilante, T. and F. Vendrell-Herrero, *Bundling and exporting: Evidence from German SMEs.* Journal of Business Research, 2021. **132**: p. 32-44.

39 Crozet, M. and E. Milet, *Should everybody be in services? The effect of servitization on manufacturing firm performance.* Journal of Economics & Management Strategy, 2017. **26**(4): p. 820–841.

40 Opazo-Basáez, M., F. Vendrell-Herrero, and O.F. Bustinza, *Uncovering productivity gains of digital and green servitization: Implications from the automotive industry.* Sustainability, 2018. **10**(5): p. 1524.

41 Zhang, J., *Impact of manufacturing servitization on factor productivity of industrial sector using global value chain.* Sustainability, 2022. **14**(9): p. 5354.

42 Baines, T. and H. Lightfoot, *Made to serve. What it takes for a Manufacturer to Compete,* 2013.

43 Vargo, S.L. and R.F. Lusch, *Evolving to a new dominant logic for marketing.* Journal of Marketing, 2004. **68**(1): p. 1–17.

44 Baines, T., et al., *Servitization applied, an insight into small and medium-sized businesses innovating their service strategies.* The Advanced Services Group. Birmingham: Aston Business School, 2019.

45 TheWorldBank. *Manufacturing and service value added indicators.* 2021.

46 Nayyar, G., M. Hallward-Driemeier, and E. Davies, *At your service?: The promise of services-led development.* 2021: World Bank Publications.

47 Benedettini, O., *Structuring servitization-related capabilities: A data-driven analysis*. Sustainability, 2022. **14**(9): p. 5478.

48 Insights, F.B., *Everything-as-a-service (XaaS) Market: Market Research Report*. 2022.

49 Kowalkowski, C., et al., *Servitization and deservitization: Overview, concepts, and definitions*. Industrial Marketing Management, 2017. **60**: p. 4–10.

50 BBC, *Apple more valuable than the entire FTSE 100*. 2020.

51 Singh, V. *Apple business strategy: Plans that made it a Multi-Trillion dollar Company*. 2023.

52 Delventhal, S. *Apple's 5 Most Profitable Lines of Business*. 2022.

53 Gebauer, H. and C. Binz, *Regional benefits of servitization processes: Evidence from the wind-to-energy industry*. Regional Studies, 2019. **53**(3): p. 366–375.

54 Nanfosso, R.T. and J. Hadjitchoneva, *THE EUROPEAN UNION FACING THE CHALLENGES OF GLOBALISATION*. Economic Studies, 2021. **30**(5).

55 OECD, *Services trade in the global economy*. 2022.

56 WorldTradeReport, *The future of service trade*. 2019.

57 Buckley, P. and D.R. Majumdar, *The services powerhouse: Increasingly vital to world economic growth*. 2018.

58 Torkington, S. *What is a trade deficit and how does it affect the economy?* 2022.

59 Francois, J. and B. Hoekman, *Services trade and policy*. Journal of Economic Literature, 2010. **48**(3): p. 642–692.

60 Copeland, B., *The Basic Economics of Services Trade, w: A Handbook of International Trade in Services, red. A. Mattoo, RM Stern, G. Zanini*. 2008, Oxford Press, Oxford.

61 Ingo, B. and M. Aaditya, *The crisis-resilience of services trade*. The Service Industries Journal, 2010. **30**(14): p. 1–20.

62 Bustinza, O.F., et al., *Servitization and competitive advantage: The importance of organizational structure and value chain position*. Research-Technology Management, 2015. **58**(5): p. 53–60.

63 Zimmerman, C. and J.W. Enell, *Service industries*. Juran's Quality Control Handbook, 1988: p. 33.1–33.72.

64 WTO, *TRIPS — Trade-Related Aspects of Intellectual Property Rights*. 2023.

65 Boddin, D. and P. Henze, *International trade and the servitization of manufacturing: Evidence from German micro data*. ETSG, München, Germany, 2014.

66 WTOGATS, *The General Agreement on Trade in Services (GATS): Objectives, coverage and disciplines*. 2023.

67 Arup, C., *The new World Trade Organization agreements: Globalizing law through services and intellectual property*. 2000: Cambridge University Press.

68 Bradley, A.J., *Intellectual property rights, investment, and trade in services in the Uruguay Round: Laying the foundations*. Stanford Journal of International Law, 1987. **23**: p. 57.

69 Peng, S.-y., *A new trade regime for the servitization of manufacturing: Rethinking the goods-services dichotomy*. Journal of World Trade, 2020. **54**(5).

70 Koolmill. *About Koolmill*. 2023; Available from: https://www.koolmill.com/.

71 Maxence Tilliette, A.B., Shalini Gopikumar, Brett Humphrey, *Servitization as a product strategy*, in *The industry X magazine*. 2021.

72 Raddats, C., et al., *Motivations for servitization: The impact of product complexity.* International Journal of Operations & Production Management, 2016. **36**(5): p. 572–591.

73 BEIS *Heat and Buildings Strategy*. 2021.

74 Ramirez, R., et al., *Using scenario planning to reshape strategy.* MIT Sloan Management Review, 2017. **58**(4).

75 Parker, R. and G. Fedder, *Aircraft engines: A proud heritage and an exciting future.* The Aeronautical Journal, 2016. **120**(1223): p. 131–169.

6

Strategic Resilience and Sustainability of the Firm

The economic arguments in favour of servitization are compelling. Executives may look at these alone and seek to progress with servitization because of the potential impact on the revenue, profitability and productivity of their own firm. Yet, there are other arguments in favour of servitization that may be even more compelling, and these are about the impact on the strategic resilience and sustainability of the firm. It is these arguments that we explore here.

In this chapter, we again largely focus on the results that servitization has had on the performance of businesses with a heritage in selling products. Unfortunately, an extensive knowledge base about this impact is still developing. However, don't be put off by this, the same is true for a variety of management topics, large international research studies take time and funds. However, there is clear evidence at the level of the experiences of individual firms, and so in this section we draw more heavily on reasoning and case studies to present as clear a picture as possible.

Finally, we should just mention that sometimes studies in this area, can tangle together three topics. They might appear to be investigating 'what are the results of servitization' but they can easily morph into articles trying to answer the question, 'Why do servitization?' Such articles can themselves become confused with 'Why is servitization happening?' These questions are clearly linked, but our interest is in the first and we have sought to disentangle the available research to summarise what is known about the effect of servitization on the resilience and sustainability of the firm. Armed with such knowledge, executives themselves can decide whether or not to engage with a servitization programme.

© The Author(s), under exclusive license to Springer Nature
Switzerland AG 2024
T. Baines et al., *Servitization Strategy*, Palgrave Executive Essentials,
https://doi.org/10.1007/978-3-031-45426-4_6

Resilience

Resilience means the ability of a business to adapt and function at desired levels in the presence of adversities, internal and external to the firm, including financial crises, supply chain disruptions, natural disasters and pandemics. Resilient organisations are those that can withstand and recover to achieve their core objectives in the face of adversity. Servitization can help to make companies more resilient in the following ways.

Servitization as an Aid During Economic Disruptions

> *The mitigating business disruption argument:* As a firm progressively adopts servitization and effectively expands its service offerings, this portfolio of offerings can help the firm become more resilient to economic disruptions.

In 2020, the COVID-19 pandemic brought the concept of organisational resilience to the forefront of nearly every industry. Businesses suddenly had to figure out how they could continue to function in a world in which employees were largely unable to enter the workplace for an undetermined length of time. Manufacturers across all sectors need to be able to radically innovate their business models, or design new ones, to manage uncertainty [1].

The evidence that is now available indicates that those manufacturing firms with service-led business models can be more resilient to external disruptions than those that are purely product-based. Reasoning given for this is that servitization can broaden information sharing, which can enable firms to anticipate and react to disruptions more effectively. And that servitization motivates firms to engage with their stakeholders, such as suppliers and customers, and stronger relationships are built across the network. In turn, there are then increasing levels of trust between companies [2], which is a strong factor in times of need, and partners are more likely to share critical information and key resources with the firms they trust the most [3].

In addition, there are arguments that firms with diversified business models are in a better position to cope with changes, because the diversification of their revenue streams leads them to be less reliant on the sale of products alone. Even if one or more of their sources of revenue are negatively affected by disruptive events, these firms can still gain revenues from their other streams [4, 5]. In contrast, firms with less diversified business models tend to depend on limited business lines for revenue. When disruptive events occur, firms with a small number of revenue sources tend to be worse affected [6]. The direct result of diversified revenue streams is a significant increase in firms' organisational resilience, much higher than those with purely product-based business models.

An example that helps to illustrate this is the experiences of Rolls-Royce during the pandemic. During and immediately after this period, there was a wealth of speculations, usually given in online posts and blogs, that 'power-by-the-hour' was the reason that Rolls-Royce was so adversely affected by the pandemic. In reality, the reverse is true. Due to the COVID-19 pandemic in 2020, there was a significant decline in air travel. Given the structure of its TotalCare contracts, a proportion of Rolls-Royce's revenues is directly linked to the flight hours of its airline customers (often referred to as power-by-the-hour). Therefore, the reduced flight hours in 2020 inevitably affected the firm's revenue. Towards the end of November, Rolls-Royce disclosed that the flying hours covered under TotalCare for the period spanning from January to November were only 42% of the 2019 figures, so their annual revenue was also approximately 42% of the 2019 figures [7]. This was undoubtedly an extremely challenging position for any firm to be in.

In the aviation industry, however, customers manage a large proportion of the older engines on a break-fix basis, with operators either maintaining and repairing engines themselves or paying for the OEM to do so on the basis of time and materials. When the pandemic hit, and flight hours were reduced, operators set out to cut all possible costs. This includes reducing planned or event-based maintenance and preferring to just use a different aircraft rather than repair an engine. In doing so, operators took the risk of devaluing their assets once the market reopened, exposing themselves to costs to make engines serviceable and reinstate them into the fleet.

Aircraft on TotalCare contracts were treated differently. First, these contracts featured mainly on the newer engine models, enabling a high payload capability, improved fuel efficiency, and the utilisation of the most advanced gas turbine technology. In addition, airline operators needed to know their costs per hour with a high level of certainty to make reliable decisions about when and where to fly aircraft. TotalCare facilitated predictable cost modelling and forecasts. In contrast, there was a substantial decline in revenue for its product business because customers started cancelling and deferring their orders for new equipment. With the aircraft mostly grounded and no demand for expanding the fleet capacity, the customers had to make critical cost-cutting exercises. Also, when the flight hours increased slowly, the initial demand was for spares (i.e., the services) rather than new production.

In summary, the aviation industry was severely disrupted by the market downturn in 2020. Firms like Rolls-Royce faced significant short-term difficulties. Within Rolls-Royce, there were several redundancies, which had a distressing impact on its workforce and the city of Derby, UK, where its headquarters are located. However, this is not a story of a failed services-focused business model. Contrary to all speculations, TotalCare was crucial in preventing a much graver outcome for the civil aerospace business. Services have been the driving force behind its recovery and have proved to be the most resilient part of its business.

Servitization as a Response to Competitors

> *The competitive barriers argument:* As a firm progressively adopts servitization and effectively expands its service offerings, it cultivates longer-term relationships with the customers that are more resilient to low-cost competition.

Firms operating in developed economies are exposed to competitors from lower cost economies like never before. There is evidence that suggests servitization can be an effective strategy for firms to deal with their competitive landscape [8, 9]. A variety of reasons are given for it, one of which is differentiation [10]. For example, by offering a broader portfolio of services that go beyond just selling products, firms can differentiate themselves from their competitors. Offering simple product-related services (e.g., spare parts and maintenance) alone might not be enough to warrant a high level of differentiation, and we know there should be diversification in offering services supporting products, as well as services supporting the customers' operations [11, 12].

Another reason discussed by studies is that servitization within the high-tech manufacturing industry typically requires a significant amount of knowledge and technological expertise [13]. Such high levels of expertise can be difficult for competitors to quickly replicate. This not only creates barriers to competition, but also enables a sustainable competitive advantage with cost reductions from the spillover effect of such knowledge and technology across the business, and also across the industry in some cases.

Furthermore, servitization is seen to support firms in building longer and stronger relationships with their customers, which help to establish a loyal customer base that is less likely to switch to a competitor. By developing a strong reputation for expertise, like with a data-driven approach, for instance, manufacturers can capture data that can be leveraged to enhance product design, customer satisfaction, and service provision. The firm can develop customised services that align with individual customer requirements and offer personalised customer experiences. This can foster greater customer loyalty, satisfaction, and profitability for the manufacturer that encourages customer retention [14]. In addition, such insights create opportunities for firms to develop and protect intellectual property, leading to further barriers to entry for other competitors.

A fitting example here is of MAN Truck & Bus, UK. In the early to mid-2000s, the company was struggling to differentiate its products from those of similar truck producers, such as Scania and DAF. They all shared similar products, features and performance levels. The CEO of MAN at the time, Des Evans, tells how he and others invested a great deal of time in understanding the company's customers, analysing their cost structures, and how through this, they fully appreciated that the biggest cost for customers operating a truck fleet was fuel consumption—and that there was little difference between the fuel consumption of one manufacturer's truck to another. Innovations in engine technology would, of course, improve the efficiencies of MAN trucks over time, but their competitors' trucks would also be improved. Could there be another way to achieve differentiation?

MAN recognised that fuel consumption was heavily dependent on the way that a truck was driven; a driver who drove erratically, braked heavily, and accelerated hard, would burn more diesel than an equivalent truck driven smoothly. It explored how they might influence driver behaviour, and this led to the development of its Trucknology service, and more latterly the FittoGo fleet management system. It encourages economical driving with 'MAN | Ecostyle A–G performance bands' which translates into financial impacts. MAN uses digital technologies to monitor how a truck is being driven, generates a ranking of drivers, and then offers incentives and training to bring about improvements in driving style [15]. These improvements deliver reductions in fuel consumption. This service, when coupled with MAN's truck, provides a proposition which helps its customers to the outcomes needed to make their own businesses succeed—efficient truck operation. This service innovation helped MAN to achieve differentiation in the marketplace and win market share from its rivals [16]. Additionally, it helped to bring about a significant reduction in fuel consumption by trucks and reduced CO_2 omissions.

Sustainability

Research on servitization is partly rooted in the work on product-service systems (PSS) which was initiated in Scandinavia in the late 1990s (see Goedkoop et al. [17]). PSS seeks to understand, explain, develop and promote the environmental advantages of selling Products-as-a-Service over the traditional production-consumption business models. Although research on the effect of servitization on the environmental performance of firms is limited, the general message is that there is a positive impact [18]. The available evidence supports the idea that servitization can effectively reduce carbon emissions. For example, recent research shows that servitization led to carbon emission reductions in China. The study showed that, for every 1% increase in the level of servitization, there was a decrease of 1–2% in carbon emissions related to the manufacturing export trade [19]. In this section we explore reasoning and arguments explaining how servitization can achieve this effect.

Servitization as an Aid to Resource Efficiency

The resource efficiency argument: As a firm progressively adopts servitization and effectively expands its service offerings, it facilitates the introduction of new products with improved technologies that run longer and are more efficient.

Resource efficiency is a broad concept that encompasses the optimal and sustainable use of all resources, including materials, energy, water, land, and other natural resources. It focuses on maximising the value derived from resources and the output of services or user satisfaction while minimising material consumption in the economy, waste and any harmful environmental impact [20, 21].

There is evidence to suggest that implementing servitization strategies and practices can enhance resource efficiency within manufacturing firms. One survey of multiple manufacturing firms found that by shifting from a product-centric approach to a more service-oriented one, firms can optimise the utilisation of resources, reduce waste, and improve overall efficiency in delivering value to customers [22]. Another comprehensive review of servitization studies finds that an integrated product-service approach incentivises the reduction of material costs and encourages innovative approaches that differ from traditional product sales [21]. With outcome-based models, the use of materials is merely a cost, and increasing material usage does not lead to increased revenues. Therefore, there is an inherent incentive for manufacturers to reduce material costs by using fewer materials or extending their lifespan.

Another aspect of resource efficiency is revealed by a study of B2B manufacturing firms [22]. It finds that servitization facilitates information sharing, and this allows firms to enhance their resource efficiency, because they can make informed decisions using such information and optimise their operations based on a deeper understanding of the process. More evidence suggests that servitization can aid in addressing climate change by facilitating the adoption of advanced and relevant technologies while incentivising their optimal use. By investing in expanding their technological innovation capabilities, firms can increase the lifespan of products by reducing defects and lowering energy consumption [23, 24]. Overall, focus on resource efficiency contributes to the broader goal of sustainability by minimising resource consumption and environmental impact, and two fitting examples in this context are of Signify and Danfoss.

Signify, a market leader in lighting-as-a-service, helps to illustrate the role of servitization in promoting resource efficiency and addressing climate change [25]. By offering lighting solutions as a service, Signify takes on the responsibility of selecting, implementing, operating, and managing the technology for their customers. This approach relieves customers of the burden of managing the lighting infrastructure, allowing them to focus on their core business activities. As a result, Signify's services have led to tangible resource efficiency improvements, such as a 50% reduction in electricity consumption at Schiphol Airport through digitalisation and the implementation of appropriate technological platforms. This highlights the potential for significant results when technologies are managed holistically by providers who have a comprehensive understanding of their customers' operations, ultimately contributing to sustainability and energy conservation.

Danfoss is another example demonstrating resource efficiency in its solutions that enable effective energy management, waste reduction, and cost savings within the supermarket industry. Danfoss has played a crucial role in the context of supermarkets, which account for 2–4% of energy consumption in real estate, with 40% of that energy consumption attributed to refrigeration. Through the implementation of smart connectivity and servitization, they have successfully achieved a reduction of over 20% in banana waste for one of their clients. Servitization allows for holistic system optimisation, and this involves various energy storage solutions including utilising technologies such as solar panels for energy production. Consequently, supermarkets can effectively redistribute energy within the building or even to surrounding buildings. This optimised energy distribution has the potential to lower heating costs by as much as 45%. Danfoss has been able to seamlessly implement all these improvements without causing any inconvenience to the end customer.

Servitization as an Aid to a Circular Economy

> *The circular economy argument: As a firm progressively adopts servitization and effectively expands its services offerings, it leads to better tracking and control of materials, and this increases the likelihood of recycling and reuse.*

Circular economy aims to create a sustainable and efficient economic system that maximises resource utilisation, reduces environmental impact, and supports long-term resilience. In such a system, efforts are made to reduce the number of resources used, minimise the generation of waste, and prevent any energy leakage or loss [26]. This means effectively managing material and energy loops through strategies such as prolonging product lifecycles, implementing maintenance, repair, reuse, remanufacturing, refurbishing, and recycling practices.

Servitization is argued to support circularity [27]. Circular economy approaches look beyond the traditional relationship between the manufacturer and the customer to focus on exploring different business models through servitization [28]. By adopting servitized business models, firms can form networks that have a positive impact on the reverse flow of items (movement of products or materials back through the supply chain once they have reached the end of their useful life) [29]. By integrating services and activities related to the reverse flow of items, organisations can enhance their ability to reuse, recycle, and recover materials, thereby closing the loop and reducing waste in the overall system.

In offering outcome-based services, manufacturers retain product ownership and this motivates them to develop products with extended work life and reduced wastage [30, 31]. The ownership retention that comes with the advanced services business models promotes stewardship, where there is a transition taking place from product sales to overall performance, guaranteed reliability, longevity and product reuse [32]. Closely associated with the product reuse is an ongoing debate regarding some tough choices manufacturers must make in vertically integrating into the product recovery chain to recover their own products. Manufacturers often leverage the practices and technologies of the salvage industry for product recovery. On one hand, vertical integration into the recovery chain may provide better control over the recovery process, quality assurance, and potentially cost savings. On the other hand, it can require significant investments, specialised knowledge, resources, and operational considerations. Caterpillar, for example, has had some success with its engine remanufacturing services, where it has control of collection, recovery and reuse of its products [33].

Available evidence also suggests that by promoting the reuse and remanufacturing of products, circular models contribute to climate mitigation by reducing the need for primary material production [27]. A study comparing three industries (construction, papermill and cleaning) that offered integrated products and services with businesses focused solely on product sales, revealed significant environmental and economic benefits associated with the integrated approach [34]. These industries had lower environmental impacts throughout the lifecycle of their offerings because they employed engineering activities aligned with circularity. They implemented strategies such as recycling, reuse, remanufacturing, maintenance, holistic planning and operation, all of which contributed to resource efficiency and reduced waste generation.

Another case study focused on a prominent Chinese elevator firm reports how the firm achieved operational flexibility and made significant strides in environmental sustainability by adopting a Product Service System approach [35]. This firm transitioned from being a simple elevator manufacturer to an elevator solution provider. It implemented modular design to enhance reusability which enabled each elevator to save approximately 10,800 kWh of energy per year, resulting in a power saving rate of around 30%, contributing to a reduction in the environmental impact associated with elevator operations.

Yet another example is of Renault. Its circular economy practices, specifically the establishment of a remanufacturing plant and integration of remanufactured parts into their supply network, demonstrate how servitization can extend the value and lifespan of products, enhance customer experience, and optimise resource utilisation. This plant implements product designs that prioritise reuse and remanufacturing from the outset, including increased use of standardised components to make sorting and reuse easier. It also enables altering material specifications to ensure recovered materials retain a grade suitable for manufacturing new vehicles, rather than being downgraded. Collaborative efforts with recyclers and waste management companies have been instrumental for the firm in conducting this redesign work. Renault has also realigned and reconfigured its supply network. Recovery of subassemblies for repair and remanufacturing has been seamlessly integrated into the return trips of delivery vehicles used to distribute replacement parts to dealers [29]. This integration optimises the supply chain by minimising empty trips and maximising resource utilisation, underscoring the commitment to efficiency and sustainability.

Overall, firms have to strike a balance between the profit-driven development that they are used to with the new mindset of sustainable development [36]. The alignment of the circular economy principles with servitization, makes the latter a valuable strategy for sustainable business practices.

Servitization as an Aid to Dematerialisation

The dematerialisation argument: As a firm progressively adopts servitization and effectively expands its service offerings, these services have the potential to reduce product consumption and even enable substitutions.

Dematerialisation is a specific aspect of resource efficiency that focuses on reducing material consumption and environmental impact associated with the extraction, production, transportation, and disposal of materials. Based on the definition provided by the United Nations Environment Program, we understand it to be a process of decreasing the overall material and energy usage associated with a product or service, that results in a reduced environmental impact. This involves reducing the amount of raw materials used during production, lowering energy and material inputs during use, and minimising waste during disposal [37]. Dematerialisation also means that data and information are becoming more important than physical products and equipment [38].

Current data suggests that global economic activity relies heavily on the production and transportation of raw materials and manufactured goods along global supply chains, which is a significant contributor to environmental pollution. According to the OECD, materials management currently accounts for almost two-thirds of global greenhouse gas emissions, and this figure is expected to increase by two-thirds by 2060 if current trends continue. Could services be the answer? A 2022 study looking into carbon emissions and the role of global value chains from an input–output perspective (flow of inputs, such as raw materials, energy, labour and services and outputs, such as products and emissions between different sectors of the economy) found that servitization in manufacturing industries can lead to a significant reduction in carbon emission intensity [39].

Furthermore, services can play a crucial role in reducing material usage, and in some cases, they can even replace the need for certain products altogether [27]. A relevant example here is of Dupont, a major paint supplier to Ford in the 1990s. At the time, Dupont's sales team incentives were based on the volume of paint sold to Ford, which encouraged higher paint consumption. However, Dupont decided to change its business model to receive payment based on the number of painted cars. By transitioning to a payment-per-painted car model, its paint consumption turned from a source of profit into a cost. This change in incentives prompted the firm to invest significantly in reducing the amount of paint required to paint a car. The objective was to achieve the desired outcome of having a painted car with the minimum amount of materials [40]. This shift in business model led to a change in behaviour and decision-making that took away the focus from maximising paint sales to optimising paint usage and reducing material requirements. As a result, the firm actively pursued dematerialisation by finding innovative ways to achieve the desired outcome with minimal material inputs.

Also relevant here is one of our earlier examples of Renault [29]. It has a remanufacturing plant set up near Paris that employs a workforce of 325 people for examining, testing, and recovering mechanical subassemblies (like water pumps, for example). The remanufactured parts are sold at a reduced price (50–70% of their original price). With this pricing strategy, the firm is providing an alternative to purchasing new spare parts, which are often more expensive. More importantly, it is now economically viable to repair cars that might otherwise be considered write-offs due to the cost of purchasing new spare parts. By extending the lifespan and value of vehicles, the firm contributes to dematerialisation by reducing the need for new car production and helps minimise resource consumption. This price is accompanied by a one-year warranty, which instils confidence in the quality and reliability of the parts. This encourages customers to opt for repaired parts rather than purchasing new ones, further supporting the dematerialisation goal by minimising the need for new material production and reducing waste generation.

In addition, by pooling resources, sharing expertise, and optimising processes through collaboration and integration, industries can potentially reduce their material usage. A study finds that the integrated product-service approach often promotes collaboration and integration of stakeholders in similar industries which leads to a mutualised network that reduces material needs [41]. The knowledge of sustainability-related issues plays a crucial role in encouraging collaboration and mutual comprehension among stakeholders in the fields of economic, environmental, and social sustainability.

A well-structured and coordinated network created through Product-Service Systems can clarify how the network operates and the roles of each stakeholder. This can contribute to dematerialisation efforts by promoting more sustainable resource utilisation and minimise waste generation.

We also find evidence of dematerialisation in lesser reliance on products. For instance, a recent case study of a leading provider of maritime solutions shares that the provider's transformation to digital servitization is very much conditioned by dematerialisation [42]. Amidst growing concerns within the maritime industry regarding data-related issues, the provider's efforts involved detaching data from the physical world to focus on data that underpins digital services. The provider reduced its dependence on physical materials and resources and embraced digital servitization to pay attention to data-related opportunities and issues. Such heightened awareness of data-related challenges can potentially lead to more effective resource optimisation, aligned with the principles of dematerialisation.

Chapter Summary: The Impact of Servitization

In this and the preceding chapter, we explored the evidence that exists about the potential impacts of servitization for firms that have traditionally competed through products (or outputs) and, have subsequently, developed services strategies. We have addressed the main question: *Why give attention to servitization?* We have taken the position of an industrial firm seeking to compete through services, alongside products, and set out to summarise the evidence the arguments and results that currently are available.

As we mentioned at the beginning of Chapter 5, we don't claim these as forecasts of how servitization will impact a specific business as situations vary between firms. Instead, we put forward a series of arguments as hypotheses about the likely effects of servitization. Our intention is to both succinctly summarise what is known about servitization, and also create the foundations for an analysis of likely effect of servitization on individual firms. We capture all these arguments in Fig. 6.1.

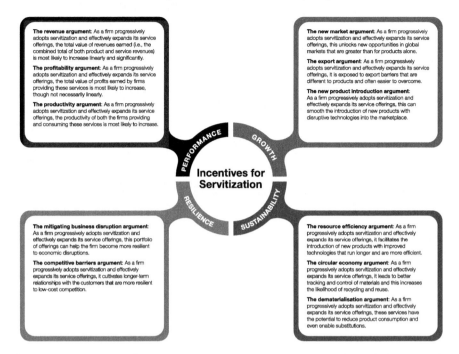

Fig. 6.1 Summarising how servitization can impact an industrial firm © The Advanced Services Group Ltd

References

1 Karamitsos, D., et al., *What is servitization, and how can it help save the planet?* In *World Economic Forum*. 2020.

2 Saueressig, T. and P. Maier, *business as unusual with SAP: How leaders navigate industry megatrends*. 2022: SAP Press.

3 Baxter, R.K., *The forever transaction: How to build a subscription model so compelling, your customers will never want to leave*. 2020: McGraw-Hill Education.

4 JCB, *Who are JCB Finance?* 2023 [cited 2023 06/01/2023]; Available from: https://www.jcb-finance.co.uk/faq.

5 EdenSprings, *Fully Managed Service KLIX*. 2023; Available from: https://www.edensprings.co.uk/vending-machines.

6 Goodyear, *Goodyear launches end-to-end fleet offer, Goodyear total mobility*. 2019 [cited 2023 04/01/2023]; Available from: https://news.goodyear.eu/goodyear-launches-new-end-to-end-fleet-offer-goodyear-total-mobility/.

7 Rolls-Royce, *ROLLS-ROYCE HOLDINGS PLC TRADING UPDATE*. News Release, 2020.

8 Kastalli, I.V., B. Van Looy, and A. Neely, *Steering manufacturing firms towards service business model innovation.* California Management Review, 2013. **56**(1): p. 100–123.

9 Feng, C., et al., *Servitization strategy, manufacturing organizations and firm performance: A theoretical framework.* Journal of Business & Industrial Marketing, 2021. **36**(10): p. 1909–1928.

10 Martín-Peña, M.L., et al., *The innovation antecedents behind the servitization–performance relationship.* R&D Management, 2023.

11 Kharlamov, A.A. and G. Parry, *The impact of servitization and digitization on productivity and profitability of the firm: A systematic approach.* Production Planning & Control, 2021. **32**(3): p. 185–197.

12 Benedettini, O., M. Swink, and A. Neely, *Examining the influence of service additions on manufacturing firms' bankruptcy likelihood.* Industrial Marketing Management, 2017. **60**: p. 112–125.

13 Zhang, W. and Y. Zhao, *Do manufacturing firms benefit from service innovation? An empirical study of high-tech manufacturing firms in China.* In *2012 International Joint Conference on Service Sciences.* 2012. IEEE.

14 Jerry, C., *Servitization: The key to competitive advantage in manufacturing.* Industry Outlook Manufacturing, 2023.

15 Kapoor, K., et al., *A platform ecosystem view of servitization in manufacturing.* Technovation, 2022. **118**: p. 102248.

16 Microlise, *Case Studies: MAN TRUCK & BUS UK. Powering MAN Fleet Management.* 2022.

17 Goedkoop, M.J., et al., *Product service systems, ecological and economic basics.* 1999.

18 Huang, Q. and J. Huo, *The development of manufacturing servitization industry under the strategy of "Made in China 2025".* China Comput. Users, 2015. **11**: p. 46–55.

19 Li, X., et al., *Spatial differences in emission reduction effect of servitization of manufacturing industry export in China.* Emerging Markets Finance and Trade, 2021. **57**(8): p. 2331–2355.

20 EUCommission. *Resource efficiency.* 2023; Available from: https://ec.europa.eu/environment/resource_efficiency/.

21 Tukker, A., *Product services for a resource-efficient and circular economy–a review.* Journal of cleaner production, 2015. **97**: p. 76–91.

22 Pan, J.-N. and H.T.N. Nguyen, *Achieving customer satisfaction through product–service systems.* European Journal of Operational Research, 2015. **247**(1): p. 179–190.

23 Cenamor, J., D.R. Sjödin, and V. Parida, *Adopting a platform approach in servitization: Leveraging the value of digitalization.* International Journal of Production Economics, 2017. **192**: p. 54–65.

24 Hao, M., Y. Tang, and S. Zhu, *Effect of input servitization on carbon mitigation: Evidence from China's manufacturing industry.* Environmental Science and Pollution Research, 2022. **29**(19): p. 27819–27831.

25 Zhu, S., Y. Xie, and D. Wu, *A study on the energy-saving effect of manufacturing servitization and its intermediary mechanism.* Finance & Trade Economics, 2020. **41**(11): p. 126–140.

26 CaaS *How servitisation is helping markets transition to a more sustainable future.* 2021.

27 MacArthur, E., *Towards the circular economy.* Journal of Industrial Ecology, 2013. **2**(1): p. 23–44.

28 OECD, *Building back better: A sustainable, resilient recovery after COVID-19.* 2020.

29 Insanic, I. and L.-E. Gadde, *Organizing product recovery in industrial networks.* International Journal of Physical Distribution & Logistics Management, 2014.

30 Spring, M. and L. Araujo, *Product biographies in servitization and the circular economy.* Industrial Marketing Management, 2017. **60**: p. 126–137.

31 Kjaer, L.L., et al., *Product/service-systems for a circular economy: The route to decoupling economic growth from resource consumption?* Journal of Industrial Ecology, 2019. **23**(1): p. 22–35.

32 Doni, F., A. Corvino, and S.B. Martini, *Servitization and sustainability actions. Evidence from European manufacturing companies.* Journal of Environmental Management, 2019. **234**: p. 367–378.

33 Ritchie, N.H., *Leadership for a climate resilient, net-zero health system: Transforming supply chains to the circular economy.* In *Healthcare management forum.* 2021. SAGE Publications Sage CA: Los Angeles, CA.

34 Rahimifard, S., et al., *Barriers, drivers and challenges for sustainable product recovery and recycling.* International Journal of Sustainable Engineering, 2009. **2**(2): p. 80–90.

35 Lindahl, M., E. Sundin, and T. Sakao, *Environmental and economic benefits of integrated product service offerings quantified with real business cases.* Journal of Cleaner Production, 2014. **64**: p. 288–296.

36 Song, W. and T. Sakao, *A customization-oriented framework for design of sustainable product/service system.* Journal of Cleaner Production, 2017. **140**: p. 1672–1685.

37 Ullah, F., et al., *Barriers to the digitalisation and innovation of Australian Smart Real Estate: A managerial perspective on the technology non-adoption.* Environmental Technology & Innovation, 2021. **22**: p. 101527.

38 Kramer, K.-L., *User experience in the age of sustainability: A practitioner's blueprint.* 2012: Elsevier.

39 Tronvoll, B., et al., *Transformational shifts through digital servitization.* Industrial Marketing Management, 2020. **89**: p. 293–305.

40 Tang, Y., et al., *Input servitization, global value chain, and carbon mitigation: An input-output perspective of global manufacturing industry.* Economic Modelling, 2022. **117**: p. 106069.

41 Chen, S.-H., et al., *The servitization of Taiwan's ICT manufacturing and its industrial upgrading,* in *Servitization, IT-ization and Innovation Models.* 2013, Routledge. p. 73–100.

42 Lelah, A., et al., *Collaborative network with SMEs providing a backbone for urban PSS: A model and initial sustainability analysis.* Production Planning & Control, 2012. **23**(4): p. 299–314.

Part III

How to Bring About Servitization Through the Innovation of Advanced Services

#servitization = business model innovation and organisational change

7

Exploring the Process of Servitization

When we began our research, we wanted to clearly distinguish between the *what*, *why* and the *how* of servitization: *What are these advanced service business models that can enable firms to deliver outcomes through a product-service integration? Why are they growing in importance for business?* And *How can firms rooted in production successfully compete through these alternative models?* Our book reflects this structure, and in this part we deal with the transformation; understanding this journey and then setting out the principles to guide firms through this to innovate advanced services.

Understanding the processes of servitization is challenging. Look around: how many businesses do you see that are exemplars in this space? You probably don't see many. If this was a book on Lean production systems in the early 2000s, it would be littered with many more industry cases and benchmarking statistics than we are yet able to give you for servitization. In part, is simply explained. Many managers are not yet fluent in the language and concepts of servitization, and so they struggle to describe and articulate their product-service innovations. Also, servitization is not a quick fix—it takes time for industrial firms to make the transformation. Often, service innovations have to be brought about while the firm is still making money through conventional product sales. These innovations have to be tempered to complement the existing business model portfolio, and have to piggyback and share production resources.

The main reason, however, that most firms struggle to servitize is that executives and senior leadership teams don't understand how to do it. And they are not alone, only recently have researchers disentangled and made sense of this knotty process and, in doing so, they have created a scientific platform

© The Author(s), under exclusive license to Springer Nature
Switzerland AG 2024
T. Baines et al., *Servitization Strategy*, Palgrave Executive Essentials,
https://doi.org/10.1007/978-3-031-45426-4_7

to properly explain and manage servitization in action. In this chapter we describe the process, starting with an explanation of what we did to understand how some of the firms have successfully implemented servitization. This chapter and the following are based on our research programme launched at Aston Business School (Birmingham, UK), in 2014 and drawing in research with academics and business leaders from all over the world. We now share what we discovered.

Research Programme

To tell you how to go about servitization, it was essential to first understand how it is done well. But when we started looking to investigate this as a process there was little to go on. To give you a sense of what we faced, think about attempting to describe how to go about successfully buying a house or apartment. Now imagine nobody has fully documented a process like this before, there are no guidebooks and exceptionally few experienced mentors. You want to know the best way so that you can guide others; but what should you say to do first? Should you say find the house then look to see if you could afford it, or should you first say go to the bank for finance? Should you say use an estate or realty agent? Should you say use a legal firm? Should you say sell your old house first? Should you say use a furniture removal company? How should you say to do it all? What decisions should be made and in what order?

If you have ever experienced or witnessed this process, you will know that there were many unknowns, uncertainties, and anxieties. Having been through it once though, it becomes easier to reflect and sketch out the process. And, if asked, you might be able to embroider the tale with what you did to overcome difficult negotiations and deal with challenging vendors. The more houses bought, the richer and more mature the description of the process becomes, and the greater the confidence. This is the way you become an experienced buyer. Compare, contrast, and refine this process with those followed by other experienced house buyers, and you become an expert authority.

Attempting to understand the processes of servitization is a similar challenge to understanding the house-buying process. Executives want to know how to go about it, what to do first, how much it will cost, how they will justify it, and so on. But knowledge about servitizing is extremely scarce, and much of the material is on generic topics such as how to innovate a business model or bring about organisational change. For our study, we knew that we had to thoroughly understand how firms had been through this process and that just investigating one or two companies, and benchmarking their experiences would not be sufficient.

Benchmarks are invaluable but only within the right context. In 2016, we took a group of services executives on a benchmarking visit to the World Parts Centre at JCB Excavators in the UK. This was part of our research to understand how JCB had gained traction with their Performance Advisory service known as JCB LiveLink. JCB gained considerable market penetration by bundling this service with the excavator at the point of sale, rather than charging separately. We had two guests with particular interests, one an executive from Crown Equipment Corporation and the other from Ishida. Both were keen to learn about LiveLink and JCB's successes at scaling their service. The executive from Crown took what they saw, used this to inform their thinking, and they implemented their innovations and were quickly successful. The executive from Ishida found that adopting the JCB approach was more problematic.

Both executives saw JCB as the benchmark, but their attempts to replicate similar successes in their firms yielded quite different results. Why was this? The circumstances of the two firms and the executives differed significantly. Crown produces materials handling equipment, such as forklifts and pallet trucks. Its products, market and customers were somewhat similar to that of JCB. Ishida, on the other hand, produces high-value weighing and packaging equipment for the food industry. Their products, customers and market are quite different to JCB. For such reasons, the JCB approach failed to gain traction with them.

This experience helps to illustrate that, although benchmarks are helpful, they are most valuable when part of a much broader and structured study. There needs to be an understanding of the circumstances and processes which interplay in a particular organisation to bring about a service innovation. With regards to JCB, a deep understanding of its situation would have revealed that its decision to offer LiveLink came about, in part, because executives understood that its customers were increasingly anxious about excavator security—the machines being stolen from building sites. Such anxieties were influencing equipment buying decisions. JCB's Performance Advisory service (LiveLink) enabled geo-fencing (tracking where a machine was located) and this was seen as a valuable feature at the point of sale. Consider, by contrast, Ishida machines. These are large items of capital equipment which are installed within factories, so security doesn't feature in the buying decision in the same way as for JCB.

We knew that understanding servitization would need an in-depth and lengthy study. Developing a rich picture of the dynamic flow of decisions, actions, and influences, all leading to the birth and nurturing of new services-based business models. But to tease this out from what we saw of industrial practice would need exceptional care. To illustrate, in 2017 we spent many hours with Des Evans, the retired Chief Executive Officer of MAN Truck & Bus UK. We had known Des since 2005 and were (and still are) in awe of what he had achieved with services at MAN: their market share developed from 2% in 1993 to 12% in 2003; the service side of the business grew from c. £25 m p.a. to over £250 m pa. It had 15,000 vehicles under service contracts by 2012, and the largest contract in European truck history, with the supply of 7,415 logistic support vehicles to the British Army, together with a 20-year service contact. Yet, we had never fully captured the process Des had followed, the ins and outs of what he'd done when, and how. If we could do this, we could start to create a transformation roadmap that other executives might follow.

As professional researchers, we followed a semi-structured interview process. We had a series of questions that provided an insightful agenda to our conversation but allowed for an open discussion about each. The interview was recorded and transcribed, points raised were checked and qualified with Des, and over an elapsed period of six weeks, a fuller picture emerged. We had (we thought) captured a complete, reliable and insightful picture of the processes that Des had followed; but unfortunately, we hadn't.

Capturing how Des had gone about servitization was more complex than we had realised at the outset. To illustrate, we've constructed the word cloud in Fig. 7.1 from the interview transcripts. It shows the topics that Des spoke about during this interview process, with the font size and positioning representing the frequency and association. There were lots of interesting and relevant topics—servitization being central. Then we realised we had caused a problem. Des had carried out the service transformation before he was introduced to our team and the term 'servitization', and indeed purposely avoided using this term during our interview and questioning. Yet, as the terms in the word cloud illustrated, our work had clearly influenced his reflections. If we had influenced the terminology, what other bias had we introduced into his recollection of his time at MAN?

There was a second problem we faced as researchers. Over the interview, the transformation narrative continually evolved and went well beyond simply clarifying and confirming what we had been told. Each conversation highlighted a different thread to the process; for instance, when we attempted to clarify how telematics were installed on trucks, we opened up

Fig. 7.1 Word cloud representing a services transformation process

another conversation about incentives and workshop skills in MAN dealerships. Each thread led to another, and it felt like we were dealing with a plate of spaghetti which we would need to disentangle if we were going to rationalise this information into a useful and reliable roadmap for others. In practice, Des was an exceptional leader and had brought about successful servitization within a very complex environment, but we were overwhelmed with all these threads and struggled to rationalise what we were seeing. We would need to be extremely careful in our data collection and analytics.

Our experiences with Des not only caused us to rethink our approach to studying the transformation, but they also helped us to better appreciate the challenges individual executives face with servitization. Back to our benchmarking example for the moment; executives will struggle if simply parachuted into a business in an attempt to understand what to do next to bring about product-service innovation in their own firms. Put bluntly, what they are told will reflect what's current in the minds of the managers at the host organisation, what they hear will be highly influenced by their own recent and particular experiences. As researchers, we have the same challenges.

We completely redesigned our research programme. We needed to be more rigorous, insightful and reliable. To achieve this, we set about a comprehensive study of a select group of international businesses. We carefully considered the right industrial firms to study and how to do so. An ideal firm would be one that has successfully executed a complete transformation process and has a portfolio of well-performing advanced services in place. Yet we knew the timeline would be extensive. Rolls-Royce had started its move to TotalCare in the mid-1990s and the origins of power-by-the-hour itself lay in the 1960s. From our conversations with Des, we knew that executives in such organisations were likely to have their recollections of the past influenced. So, we needed to study firms at different stages on the transformation road; we needed to be careful when interpreting the results; and we also knew that firms would not disclose the contributions made by individual business models in publicly available data. With these constraints in mind, we identified the businesses we wanted to study and made our approach.

We designed our study to cover a wide range of multinational businesses across sectors including defence, health, food and aerospace. Table 1.1 provides an overview of those that have been most influential in our work. Sometimes we have simply observed businesses as they have taken this journey, while other times we have directly informed their decisions to bring about servitization. Some businesses have helped us dive deeper into specific aspects of services, providing a small but essential nugget of knowledge. With others, such as Goodyear, Domino, Omron, Tetra Pak, Thales and Baxi, their executives have helped us gain a complete picture of the transformation process. We have learned about these companies' challenges, helped to inform their decisions, and shared their successes and frustrations.

We also looked again at how we could strengthen the theoretical underpinning for this study. In general, we knew that what we were seeing was businesses attempting to grow through services; build revenues, improve profits and break into new markets. And, so, we armed ourselves with a thorough understanding of the previous management research across the topics of business growth, business model innovation and organisational development. We developed three questions to guide the whole study: *(i) is it possible to break down the servitization process into a series of stages? (ii) What was it about the situation or context of a firm that would determine how that firm progressed through these stages, and (iii) What were the underlying characteristics of the servitization process and the innovation of an advanced services business model?* To strengthen the reliability of our study, we also published our approach and findings in a range of internationally renowned research journals, in particular, the International Journal of Production Economics (see [1]), and the International Journal of Operations and Production Management (see [2]). Insights from these articles have helped us shape some of the content we present here.

We were extremely comprehensive in how we gathered data about the businesses we set out to study. Semi-structured interviews were conducted in person and over the telephone, and a series of workshops and discussion sessions were run with personnel from different levels. The interviews were constructed to guide the conversation around the characterisation of servitization initiatives over time, focusing on the process and contextual forces affecting progress towards servitization maturity. Each interview had at least two researchers present, and they documented responses using audio recordings and written notes. Each interview was one to two hours long, and over 300 interviews were conducted with at least three key stakeholders from each case company. Transcripts, notes, and recordings were prepared for each interview. Triangulation was used to verify responses and included supplementary data such as organisational charts, operating protocols, observation notes, process maps, and crosschecked interviewee responses.

Additionally, the data collection process included informal follow-ups through multiple meetings and workshops, coupled with several rounds of on-site observations. The researchers produced written descriptions of the data collected through these activities (for example, capturing key aspects discussed in a meeting). Archival data was also examined by focusing mainly on the annual reports, business plans, and other internal company documents. All relevant data (aligned with the research questions) was extracted, transcribed, and summarised into text. We also kept a reference to the raw data source.

We looked to test plausibility, identify clusters, draw contrasts, make comparisons, and subsume particulars into the overarching context. We undertook a within-case analysis and started organising data according to the research questions. We coded the data based on these research questions and, at the same time, allowed for new codes and relationships to emerge inductively from the data. To ensure reliability and construct validity, two independent researchers coded the data. They discussed different interpretations of the data (for example, classifying the codes into broader conceptual categories) to arrive at a consensual coding.

A cross-case analysis was also undertaken, whereby we summarised the data from each case to identify cross-case patterns that allowed for comparisons. To further enhance the validity, we identified commonalities across cases and compared the cases with different levels of progression in servitization over time. These findings (stages and the key contextual factors that affect progression) were then shared with the interviewees in each case to assess plausibility.

This scientific research helped us to thoroughly understand servitization within the context of an industrial firm; to describe it as a roadmap, its stages and dynamics, and the factors influencing success. We now know that the process that an industrial firm follows in its servitization journey can be explained as four macro-stages: Exploration, Engagement, Expansion and Exploitation. How a firm progresses between and within these stages is determined by four categories of contextual factors (factors about the customer, technology, value network and organisation). While a firm's progression through these four stages might, on reflection, appear unidirectional and structured, there are subroutines within these stages that are characteristically unstructured, organic, and iterative. The entire transformation can be explained as a business growth model with several tipping points, within which business model innovation and organisational change interplay.

We capture this learning in Fig. 7.2. This presents a roadmap which describes how servitization will appear to unfold, around the innovation of an advanced services business model, within an industrial firm with a heritage of products and production. The stages, contextual factors (or forces) and pathway are illustrated, along with examples of the activities and decisions executives will encounter along the way. Do be aware that these activities are just there to illuminate the pathway, not every firm will need to do them all, and most will do many others as well. Yet, every firm has, and will all go through these stages and face these forces if they go down a servitization route, whether they realise it or not. Understanding these four key stages is the first step to take if you want to know how firms have gone about servitization. The remainder of this chapter delved deeper into what we found and, in doing so, provides the foundation for the servitization process we put forward in Chapter 8.

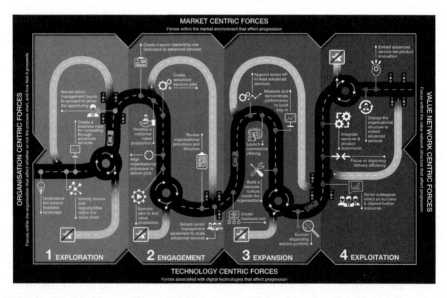

Fig. 7.2 Servitization roadmap (© The Advanced Services Group Ltd)

Stages in the Journey

Just to remind you that our study focused on industrial firms which were product-centric and had or were in the process of innovating new advanced services business models. We expected their journey to go through phases of maturity, but we didn't know what these were, how many, or how they would be characterised. So, we drew together all the data we had across all the firms that we had studied and looked to identify meaningful, distinctive clusters of activities and knowledge amongst the managers who were leading the programme. To illustrate how we did this, take a look at Fig. 7.3. This summarises as a timeline the series of events that Jim Euchner, the Head of Innovation at The Goodyear Tire & Rubber Company, had led his team through to innovate Proactive Services. We carried out similar analysis for all the businesses we studied and so created a very comprehensive picture of the servitization journey businesses had undertaken.

Studying businesses in this way revealed both the stages and also real insights into what was happening within each of these. Since the businesses were at different stages of maturity, their executives were able to give a thorough commentary on the most recent experiences in their particular journey. Jim Euchner had, for instance, led his team at Goodyear through an in-depth analysis of how to create value for the existing and prospective customers and which businesses he could learn from and in what way. Jim told us how: 'Once we understood that we would be building a services-led business, we began benchmarking the practices of manufacturers in other industries to see what we could learn from them and how we should go about building our business.'

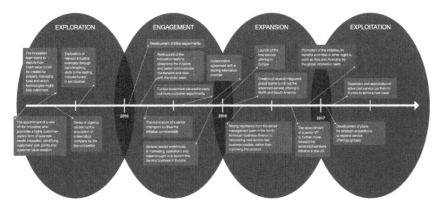

Fig. 7.3 Summary of how the servitization process unfolded for Goodyear (© The Advanced Services Group Ltd)

Likewise, Rolls-Royce and Alstom were also quite developed in their servitization journeys, and their organisational strategies were focused on optimising the delivery of advanced services and exploiting their service-oriented offering portfolios. At these organisations, executives could tell us much more about delivering advanced services at scale, cost effectively, and the changes which were necessary to the firm's operations. We spent much time with Andy Harrison, for example, learning about the work he had led at Rolls-Royce to ensure products were designed to complement TotalCare. In contrast, Yanmar at that time was much earlier in its journey, and we learned from its executives how they struggled to conceptualise what advanced services could look like for their products. They were indeed questioning if selling the data captured about their products directly back to their customers, without any complementary services, might be their most successful option. Other firms, such as Moog Inc. and Genie, operated between these extremes: experimenting with advanced service offerings, holding strong ambition to expand their portfolios, and exploring the potential of these services to their future competitive advantages.

It became apparent from our analysis that the journey a firm takes to servitize could be rationalised into four stages. When we then examined these, we found that our rationalisation reflected theories of business growth postulated by researchers such as Mel Scott and Richard Bruce [3] in the late 1980s. This reassured us that explaining the journey to servitization in this way was appropriate, and we named these four stages as Exploration, Engagement, Expansion and Exploitation. In Table 7.1 we summarise the focus of each stage and illustrate this by giving examples of the types of questions that executives typically ask at each.

The Exploration Stage

The Exploration stage is defined by the activities that executives go through to determine whether servitization is right for their business. They seek to better understand what servitization is, its relevance to their organisation and the market, and how it might help them achieve organisational and personal objectives. They will stay in this stage until, or unless, servitization gains traction as having potential for these.

You can recognise when an organisation is in the Exploration stage because executives ask questions along the lines of: *Is this right for us? How much money could we make? Who does this well? Who will be our customer? What is the cost–benefit ratio? Who is going to lead this? How are we going to bring about organisational change?* And perhaps our favourite question of all: *How do you*

Table 7.1 Characterisation of the four stages in the servitization journey

	Exploration	Engagement	Expansion	Exploitation
Definition	Searching, find out, building a coalition around the possibility of competing through servitization and advanced services	Hypothesising, testing and evaluating new service business models and selecting the most promising	Establishing readiness for scaling and getting in place necessary commitments and resources	Integrating the business model within the existing portfolio and adjusting resourced to achieved efficiencies and economies in service delivery
Typically questions that firms asked at each stage	*Is this right for us?* *How much money could we make?* *Why should we do this?* *Who does this well?* *What is the overall organisational mind-set on services?* *How do we get the board to invest?* *How do we get people to understand the gains from services?*	*How do we educate our customers?* *Why can't we just sell our product monitoring technology?* *What is the right business model?* *How do we assess whether a pilot is successful?* *How do we engage our dealer network?* *How do we go about sharing risk?*	*How do we build our market share?* *How could this become an organisation-wide initiative?* *What acquisitions should we make?* *What skills and competencies will we need?* *What legal, regulatory and financial issues do we face?* *How do we find the right partners?*	*How do we integrate production with service?* *What next, both in terms of the service portfolio and organisation direction?* *How do we improve efficiency of service delivery?* *How do we overcome our production legacy?* *Who are our competitors now?*

spell servitization? Why do you use a 'z'? Quite recently we got drawn into a conversation with a somewhat bombastic consultant from the energy sector, who was adamant that what we were talking about was 'subscription'. Again, this is symptomatic of a person finding their way through the Exploration stage.

James Galloway, the then Head of Product Marketing at Baxi, characterised the Exploration stage wonderfully well: *'I'd heard about servitization, and the need to understand customer challenges, but I was unsure of the potential relevance and importance of advanced services to Baxi.'* Initially feeling his way, his team began to grasp what it meant. James continued: *'I started to really understand servitization, only when we could visualise what a business model might look like, and along with what to expect on the journey.'* And finally, James and his team prepared to exit this stage as they became convinced of the potential He concluded: *"What convinced me most about Servitization was that it was a credible pathway to bringing together customer needs and mobilising new digitally enabled technology.'*

This stage is also characterised by the formation of a coalition within the business. A group of like-minded individuals with shared interests and ambitions for servitization. This group is not necessarily well defined, the individuals might be self-appointed, and there doesn't necessarily need to be formal leadership from senior executives at the outset. Commitment is, though, key to gaining traction for servitization. As a Business Development Manager of Xerox told us, once they understood the basics of the market and their offerings, they built an internal coalition to drive the advanced services initiative forward. This internal team was fully dedicated to advanced services, and their commitment was essential to the success of the initiative. The team was not pressured to support the core business, but rather to focus on making the new venture a success. In other words, the people within Xerox Corporation were convinced that servitization represented a valid opportunity. Once this is achieved then Exploration is complete.

The Engagement Stage

The Engagement stage is characterised by executives within the business seeking to evaluate and demonstrate advanced services. The conversation having moved on from *what is servitization?* to a more precise examination of the form their advanced services might take. Questions typically asked by executives include: *What should be the customer value proposition? Who should we pilot with? Who needs to be involved internally? How do we get people in the organisation to really understand this? How will the customer pay? How much will it cost? How much will we charge? How will we deal with contracts?*

Again, James Galloway, from Baxi, helped to describe the Engagement stage when he said, '*We needed to better understand the form that an advanced services business model takes, and the potential appetite. We developed a pilot where we connected boilers in over 100 homes in the UK and sought to test the payment plans and whether our customers would be interested in buying heat-as-a-service. We were delighted to see that 85% said yes to a form of heat-as-a-service plan, up from 36% before the pilot began*'.

Within this stage there is a much stronger emphasis on organisational commitment. There is a shift towards securing senior leadership sponsorship, a formalisation of the coalition, and wider support from broader business operations. The team at Goodyear experienced this directly. As Jim Euchner stated: '*We started to build alignment with the people inside the organisation for the advanced services initiatives. There was a in one region but other key stakeholders in other regions… so partly it was keeping them in the loop, bringing them up to date with what the global team was doing and building relationships with them.*' This sponsorship was key, as Jim explained: '*We got unlucky, then lucky. The sponsor was moved to another position as we began incubation but had returned to commercial tyres by launch. Without his support, the story would have been different.*'

Jim went on to explain how the breadth of engagement changed across the business: '*Throughout the innovation process, we worked with the leaders of the Commercial Tyre business units in three regions. R&D did the initial experiments to develop the business, and the European business leader sponsored the incubation and launch of the business. Throughout incubation, the progress was reviewed with business leaders in marketing and technology.*'

All this helped Jim and the team at Goodyear to demonstrate the potential of a new business model around advanced services. He was able to show that the service offering the team had innovated would work with a few key customers, that it could be delivered in practice, and that customers were interested and found the idea appealing. Once in place, the process of servitization moved onto scaling the business model.

The Expansion Stage

This Expansion stage is characterised by executives focusing on putting in place the commitments to scale an advanced services business model, making personal commitments and seeking strategic business investment to demonstrate that the new business model represents significant potential value to the firm. Questions that executives ask that typify this stage include: *What is the market we are going to capture? How do we develop a go-to-market plan and a sales strategy? Which customers should we focus on to accelerate growth? How can we build services revenue and not cannibalise our product revenue? What internal changes are we going to need to market? Which of our existing internal processes can we use and where do we need to create new ones?*

The overriding emphasis is on scale. Jim Euchner, from Goodyear, again provided a powerful characterisation of this stage: '*After the success of incubation with the customers in Germany (for nearly 15 months), we launched our first advanced services offering. It was initially called Proactive Services, but the name was later changed to Proactive Solutions. The offering focused on greatly reducing roadside failures for segments of the road haulage companies through the sensor-enabled monitoring of tyre pressure and alerts, based on a proprietary predictive analytics model. The revenue model was a monthly service fee. A leader was hired from outside Goodyear, and a dedicated team from innovation, marketing and sales came together to expand both the core business and other offerings across the continent.*'

The commitments that businesses make to scaling, such as investments in people, processes and technologies, start to become significant at this stage. Greg Parker led the Innovation and Portfolio Management at Johnson Controls. Having experienced this directly, he told us: '*When you want to start delivering services at scale, you need to integrate the processes and structures for designing, building and supporting products. You need to shift your way of thinking and organising, towards managing a product through its life, and have a structure to reflect this.*' Throughout this stage, the pressure is clearly on building scale and demonstrating value. As this is achieved, the firm moves to the final stage of the journey.

The Exploitation Stage

The Exploitation stage is characterised by executives seeking to optimise the innovation and delivery of their advanced services business model. This includes making minor adjustments to the value proposition and how this is presented, integrating the delivery system with other business models in the company portfolio, and ultimately adjusting the organisation to deliver the new business model at scale for the longer term. The questions that executives might ask and which characterise this stage include: *How do we design products to enable services delivery? How do we roll this out across business units in different regions? How do we get the message across the whole organisation? Who is taking responsibility for training? How do we learn from our services in a systematic way? How can we leverage resources to deliver services most cost effectively? Should we centralise and optimise? What is the future vision for our organisation?*

At the Exploitation stage of the journey, efforts will primarily be internally focused, institutionalising the new advanced services business model across different geographies, and across different business units. The firms' vision and strategy may be affected. Product designs will begin to change to complement the new service offering, and there will be pressure on staff to become customer-centric. Andy Harrison led, as an Engineering Fellow from Rolls-Royce, led such changes. As he stated: '*Today, our engines are designed and manufactured in a way that enables us to provide and deliver advanced services more effectively towards our customers.*'

This final stage represents the conclusion of the innovation of a singular advanced services business model, but not necessarily servitization. Invariably, firms support a whole portfolio of business models and, just as the stage is characterised by activities to absorb the new advanced service, simultaneously some legacy models may be decommissioned. And, also invariably, new and as yet unproven business models will perhaps be entering the Engagement stage of their journey.

Forces Influencing the Progress of the Journey

These four stages explain how an industrial firm goes about servitization. Our study also told us how progress through these was determined by the internal and external environment (or context) of the firm. There was a wide range of factors, both within and around the businesses, that impacted the servitization journey. We found that these could be clustered and grouped into four 'forces'. These are explained as follows.

Market-centric forces

These are the conditions in the market environment of firms. They are external to businesses and reflect the 'customer pull'. Customer pull represents the demand, preferences, and expectations of customers that influence businesses' strategies. If a firm has customers demanding service innovations then servitization will move more quickly, or if there are regulatory changes, again a firm might move more quickly. In practice, such 'pull' is apparent when executives make statements such as: *We needed to move towards outcome-based contracts because it was a direct request from two of our largest customers … this did play in our favour later, as we didn't need to engage or persuade them for such offerings.* Many pioneering innovations in advanced services, such as Rolls-Royce's power-by-the-hour, came about because of this force.

James Galloway, in his work on servitization with Baxi, experienced the effect of the customer. He explained:' *We came to realise that there was an increasing customer pull matched with Baxi's existing capabilities to serve in the commercial sector, such as care homes, schools and hospitals, who already have the challenge to decarbonise heat with reducing budgets. HaaS offers a way of consuming heat differently which addresses these pain points.* And James also experienced how regulations were altering the market conditions and affecting customers: '*Most of our income comes from producing and selling gas boilers, and with regulations around decarbonisation and the installation of gas boilers in new build properties changing, our technology had to change, and we had to do something different.*'

These market-centric forces were not only influencing James's work but helping to galvanise the support from the broader organisation. The Managing Director of Baxi, Karen Boswell, was fully committed to the servitization programme that James led. She stated: '*For Baxi, regulation around net zero is fuelling innovation and new business models around services. But we're equally responding to customer demand and the desire from customers to reduce their own carbon footprint, while still maintaining affordable heating. It can be argued that government net zero regulation is also a response to that same shift in consumer awareness and prioritisation, and while we are already embracing that agenda, regulations give us a clear framework in which to fulfil customer demand and meet expectations.*'

Technology-centric forces

Technology push refers to the innovations in technology that support, enable, and even incentivise the development of service offerings. These technological advancements play a crucial role in unlocking numerous new service opportunities. By embracing cutting-edge technologies such as automation, data analytics, artificial intelligence, the Internet of Things (IoT), and other emerging trends, firms can provide innovative and value-added services to customers. Technology push acts as a catalyst for exploring new service concepts, reimagining existing offerings, and delivering enhanced customer experiences. 'Technology push' is implicit in statements such as: *The technology change helped us realise that we could do more.*

MAN demonstrated this technology push in action. Des Evans became aware of the telematic technologies that were capable of recording how the operators were driving their commercial trucks and that such data could be transmitted back to the operating company. This data could then be used to evaluate drivers, which subsequently led to training and incentives to improve their performance. Not only was this a viable Performance Advisory service offering, but it also formed a foundation for further innovations. As Des said: '*The technology change brought about a new realisation that we could do more. It was no longer enough for us to say this is the product, this is the component, these are the features and the benefits, and we were helping to improve the performance. We could move more towards taking care of the total cost of operation rather than cost of the asset.*'

Value network-centric forces

The value network forces reflect the interactions and interdependencies of the firm with other stakeholders. These stakeholders can include customers, distributors, partners and suppliers, and the structure of the relationships with these can directly influence the innovation of a service offering. In MAN, for instance, we saw that the distributors were key stakeholders in accessing customers and also held key resources needed for service delivery. Consequently, their engagement was critical to MAN's success with servitization.

Access to customers is especially influential on the ability to innovate services. It is essential for providers to understand the outcomes their customers value, as without this there is very limited intelligence on which to base the design of a service offering. Rinze van Kammen, a Manager at Yanmar Europe experienced: '*Our position in the value chain meant we were quite far removed from the end-user of our products. This was a barrier to exploring the user's pains in the way we needed to in order to innovate new services.*' This meant that Yanmar, at that time, struggled to move past the Engagement stage, as the direct relationship with customers was largely held by their distributors, and further investment was needed to cultivate better access to their customers.

James Galloway at Baxi was also aware of the need to engage with stakeholders in order to succeed. He told us: '*Our value network is complex, meaning our pathway to the end customer isn't straightforward and involves several other stakeholders: installers, distributors, developers, architects, specifiers and contractors, each holding differing levels of power over the choice of heating systems.*'

The value network forces are broad and extend beyond stakeholders in located between the firm and its customer. A wide range of partnerships are critically important to success. Tom Palmer, former Group Director of Services Strategy, saw this in his work at Rolls-Royce: '*There's a whole number of players that are going to be involved in making an aircraft take off on time, including the customer and many of the customer's other suppliers and partners.'* So significant are such partners at times that they drive the service provider to consider repositioning themselves within the value network. For example, Des Evans, when at MAN, wrestled with the decision of acquiring a technology vendor so the company could have increased access to and control of the information about its truck fleets.

Organisation-centric forces

Organisation-centric forces are about those circumstances, largely internal to a firm, that affect whether or not the servitization journey might start and how well it will progress. In other words, the commitment given from within the organisation to services. These forces, prevalent within the organization, include its culture, leadership, resource allocation, structure, employee skills, information systems, agility, and performance measurement. Many managers might simply recognise these as factors concerned with organisational change. For example, the commitment of everyone involved, not just the leadership and the senior people but also those actively engaged in the effort. These include the strength and support from the wider stakeholder group within the firm. James Galloway, from Baxi, told us how the pace of change is a challenge in a large business that is product-centric and where performance and rewards are based on product sales. Senior management can be committed to change, but trying to bring this about in parallel with business as normal can be a huge hurdle, requiring continuous stakeholder management.

In our research, we found examples where a strong positive commitment from the organisation really helped to accelerate progress. The senior vice president at Nederman was able to lead his team through the Exploration and Engagement stages relatively quickly because he had senior management support. Ben Wilson at Schneider told us how such commitment had really helped him to make progress: *'This all started with the employment of my boss, Howard Bowland, VP, Schneider Services Pacific Zone, who could see our products and solutions were ripe to be servitized. He assembled a team of volunteers to understand what it would take to shift us from transactional hardware sales to a customer-facing business using data and enabling customers to only pay for what they consume.'*

The lack or removal of such commitment can also have a dramatic impact, and we found cases of that in the research, too. Glynn Lloyd, a former Director of Technology at Moog, told us: *'The servitization initiative at Moog was the brainchild and personal passion of a Senior VP who had been in the business for decades. He was very well respected and well connected and had the benefit of years of relationship building and political awareness on his side. His vision was to take services out of the individual product businesses and bring them together for the whole industrial group in one unit. His experience and skills meant he could persuade and influence at the highest level, make things happen in the wider organisation, and build a team of eight passionate and dedicated people to drive the initiative. However, totally unforeseen circumstances took over and we lost his visionary leadership very suddenly. In the short time taken for his highly capable replacement to be in post, momentum had been lost. Despite best efforts from all sides, things unravelled, the new services unit was dissolved and we reverted to individual product businesses handling their own value-added services. Several members of the new services unit also left the business shortly after.'*

Factors Most Influential for Successful Servitization

Although our research showed there to be a range of factors within each of the four forces, all of which influenced the servitization journey, but there were five in particular that stood out. These recurred across the firms we studied and were also factors over which the firms had some influence, and they helped to enable success. Whilst it wasn't necessarily essential for executives to address these factors as part of their servitization programme, if they did, then their progress would be smoother and likely to be more successful. We present these and examine how they influenced the servitization journey.

Leadership Empathy for Services

If the executive leadership of the firm understands services and the opportunities, they represent then servitization is more likely to gain traction and to succeed. As Tom Palmer, the former Group Director of Services Strategy at Rolls-Royce, told us: *'Having senior people in the business with a deep understanding and empathy for services helps to ensure services thinking and business model innovation stay on track.'* James Galloway, at Baxi, shared a similar experience: *'A majority of our senior executive team believes in HaaS but the MD is the most senior sponsor of the new business model. It makes all the difference to making progress, securing resources and investment.'*

This opinion was also endorsed by Kayvan Zadeh, Global Director Product Management Services Solutions at Tetra Pak. Kayvan told us: *'The most important thing in this journey is to ensure that we have the buy in of our executive leadership team. The executive endorsement is critical because the concept is complicated, will create a lot of internal change, and ultimately need significant investment and resources ... We are flipping our business model upside down if you think about it.'* Conversely, if this support is not so strong then progress will slow. This was the experience that Ross Townshend shared about his time at Ishida. He said: *'Services are less tangible than products so it's more difficult to articulate their value. It was difficult for me because the organisational culture didn't see the value in services in the way I did, and had other strategic goals for the business.'*

Support from the leadership can be fostered and encouraged through a number of mechanisms. Our research showed us that good and consistent communication about the value of services was vitally important. Chris Borrill, in his work at Thales, told us how important it was to 'communicate, raise awareness, create and galvanise a community and demonstrate the strategic importance. This was reinforced by Maurizio Poli, General Manager Strategy Implementation at Omron, who told us: *'It helps to anticipate people's concerns that product sales might be affected negatively by services. Let them know that services are good for product sales. We presented this idea at a senior level – that services get you through the door to pick up product sales opportunities.'*

Our research also exposed us to the concept of an 'experience room' which could be used to both foster support with the executive team and also used to engage and co-develop propositions with customers. James Galloway showed us such a room at Baxi. Our earlier research had introduced us to 'operations rooms', which were used to manage large services contracts; we had seen these inside Caterpillar dealerships and Alstom Train Life Services and they contained all sorts of performance charts. The experience room at Baxi differed because it was more of a showroom for the advanced services that James was developing, and contained illustrations, stories and demonstrations supporting his work on heat-as-a-service. James explained this to us in the following way: *'We knew that we needed to educate our people if we were going to progress. So, we created our own HaaS experience room within our building, a physical space where we could explain to our people the concept of servitization, and how critical it is to the future of our business'.*

We also found that structured 'storytelling' was being formally used as an aid to communication and engagement. In particular, carefully constructed and compelling stories about benchmark industries and disruptive technologies. We saw storytelling being used both to create and sustain empathy for services within the leadership team, and also by the firms leaders to foster broader awareness and engagement with services across the wider organisation. So influential is storytelling that Des Evans, the former CEO of MAN, told us he would sometimes refer to himself as the 'Chief Storytelling Officer'. We were intrigued and dug deeper into the research behind storytelling and found that there are formulas for structuring a compelling story, along with a variety of studies confirming the powerful role of storytelling across management [4]. We were intrigued and dug deeper into the research behind storytelling and found that there are formulas for structuring a compelling story, along with a variety of studies confirming the powerful role of storytelling across management [4].

Finally, James Galloway of Baxi told us about the importance of Key Performance Indicators (KPIs) for the executives themselves. And how a senior leader with a vision and passion for services had managed to influence their colleagues at Baxi to adopt KPIs to complement the innovation of services. As James explained: '*Almost every internal stakeholder had something to lose if things went wrong. Key challenge for me was to understand how the KPIs and targets of different teams can be aligned, capability-wise, without putting their departments at risk. For us, it became very important to take everyone together and not move with too much risk at once*'.

Services Function and Partners

If services departments or functions already exist within a firm, or there is a strong relationship with a services partner, then servitization is more likely to gain traction and succeed. Such departments provide a platform in various ways for servitization. It means that servitization is, in effect, already underway and advanced services easier to innovate: there is already a foothold, and some businesses systems, facilities, staff and customer relationships are already in place. Will Edwards, at Domino Printing, explained this value to us: *The company is not new to service – it's our heritage. Our business is built on the back of a heritage of technical support and service. 'We get very good feedback from customers about our technical capability, and this gives us a very good base to build on. So, when it came to getting mindshare and sponsorship within the business, we did this by getting them to recognise the opportunity to build value around our installed base. When you are in a business where the competition is constantly chipping away at your margins, then it's a race to the bottom unless you respond strategically. If you can successfully articulate this within the wider business, then you will get the commitment you seek'*.

Almudena Marcos-Bardera, at Omron, cited for us similar experiences: '*Before moving to the advanced services level, the company must be mature enough in offering and delivering core services (repairs, training, spare parts ... for example). When core services delivered are of high quality, and properly explained within the sales organisation (in terms of value proposition and benefit for customers), the sales organisation starts to believe in services as a facilitator of product sales ... So, at this point, sales are ready to facilitate business discussions with their customers'*.

The services function has to perform well to be credible as a platform. If it doesn't it will undermine any bolder initiatives. To illustrate, in 2015, we accompanied the Service Director of a manufacturer of food processing equipment to one of its customers in the Netherlands. The Director was seeking to engage the customer in conversations around remote condition monitoring with the ambition of innovating an advanced service. We were guests in a conversation with the Site Director and keen to facilitate a good outcome. The meeting was unfortunately disrupted when the Site Facilities Manager joined us and challenged our Service Director over their lacklustre performance in despatching spare parts. The Services Director took on this problem and promised to deal with it urgently, but of course the conversation about advanced services was compromised and did not move on at this meeting.

It is, however, desirable but not essential for a firms to own the services functions. If they don't exist, then servitization can still progress through a strong collaborative relationship with channel partners. James Galloway, at Baxi, explained this to us, saying: '*In residential business our field services activities are relatively mature, we have people and competencies in place to deliver; but this is not yet the case in B2B. So, we know we need to invest here with partners to progress'*. Indeed, if all business goes through distributors, channel partners or other intermediaries, then creating a new services function within the firm, to develop a direct relationship with customers, can be viewed with suspicion and anger. A competitive move.

This situation can be managed, but to do so requires care and understand of the type of leverage or incentives needed for existing partners [5]. Nurturing relationships with channel partners is a task that even well-established firms continue to pursue. Tom Palmer, at Rolls-Royce, brought this to our attention, saying: '*It's vital to understand that the likes of Rolls-Royce are part of an ecosystem; advanced air mobility can't be achieved by one party working alone. Nobody has the capabilities and skills to deliver the full end-to-end solution. So, understanding the ecosystem players and partners and how to contribute value to them is critical. The product needs to fit into the ecosystem seamlessly. There's no point having the best battery technology on a product, for example, if you can never charge It'*.

Finally, the value of a services function to successful servitization, is influenced by the range of offerings that this function provides. In other words, the existing footprint of offerings on the services staircase (Fig. 2.3). If principal offerings are around base services, such as spare parts, then this is a weaker platform than one where Performance Advisory Service (see Chapter 2) are already being delivered. As we explain shortly, such digital connectivity helps to foster customer intimacy, intelligence, and experience to connect well. It also helps if some of the services bring on board distribution partners around simple subscription offers [6]. This opens the door to all kinds of new value-adding opportunities [7].

Customer Relationships and Intelligence

If the firm has strong relationships with customers and intelligence about their operations, then servitization is more likely to gain traction and to succeed. In the research literature this is sometimes referred to as a firm having strong customer intimacy and is based on developing a comprehensive understanding of individual customers' preferences, buying behaviours, and challenges, and then leveraging that knowledge to tailor offerings. A customer-intimate firm makes a business out of knowing the people it sells to, its proposition is that '*We take care of you and all your needs*' [8]. Some executives refer to knowing their customers well as having *heightened customer intelligence*. Whichever way you term it, our research showed that firms that had this strength were more likely to gain traction and succeed. Without it, servitization is difficult because there is insufficient intelligence to innovate a high-value services offering.

Even when customers are demanding services their needs still need to be understood. As our friend and colleague Christian Kowalkowski explains: 'To sell service you need to have an intimate knowledge of the customer (their plant, workflow, metrics, etc.) and the way they operate' [9]. Kayvan Zadeh from Tetra Pak helped us to understand the effect of these close connections: '*We have customers coming to us saying … maybe there's something you can do for us on servitization … And that is telling us we need to accelerate, because that means there is a huge demand*'.

Customer intelligence can reveal how big changes in the customers' business environment are driving them towards consuming more services; for example, how regulation is affecting adoption. Our earlier example of heating-as-a-service is being stimulated by legislation to significantly reduce the consumption of fossil fuels. Similarly, MAN found that, when Euro 6 emission regulations were introduced for trucks and more complex engine management systems had to be installed, then customer appetite for services also increased.

Paul Jennings, the former Managing Director of JCB Finance, explained how something similar was happening with financing. He told us: '*The future of capital investment will increasingly take into account the environmental credentials of such investment. Finance companies, banks and insurance companies are increasingly signing up for the Science Based Targets initiative (SBTi), committing to reduce their portfolio emissions by say, 50% by 2030. To balance their portfolios, they need to finance more green-powered assets, instead of fossil-fuel-powered assets.*' Such regulation will drive technology innovation, and advanced services are of course, the pathway to get these technologies into the market.

In our research we did find firms struggling with customer intimacy. This was particularly the case where relationships and intelligence were held by dealers and distributors. Indeed, some executives struggled to distinguish between their partners, customers and the consumer. To illustrate the issue, consider firm which is a manufacturer of domestic heating boilers. Here, once produced their product might be passed onto distributors, then purchased by builders according to the instructions from architects, delivered by carriers, installed by subcontractors into an apartment block, which has been funded by a mortgage, and where the owner intends to rent out the rooms, with a facilities management company to look after the fabric of the building and an agent to collect rents.

So, in such a situation who here should be the targeted customer for a new service? Even if a suitable candidate were to be identified by the boiler manufacturer, the number of stakeholders that have to be engaged, convinced, trained and equipped to deliver the service can be overwhelming. So arduous the task, that the management team might be excused if they can't yet see servitization as a route to growth and choose instead to focus on product innovation and the provision of spare parts.

This is not to suggest that such a situation will mean that servitization will not occur. It will. The service offering to the customer will inevitably change, but by a different route. In the UK, for instance, the company, British Gas traditionally only supplied gas to households and, in our example above, the tenant renting the room would be its customer and billed monthly. Coincidently it would usually be this tenant that is usually responsible for arranging and paying for boiler repairs. Here, British Gas had strong foundations of customer intimacy and developed boiler maintenance services that have sold well. Today, not only do they specify, supply and fit new boilers but also, through their HomeCare cover [10], they maintain and repair the wider domestic heating system.

Such service innovation cannot be ignored by the boiler manufacturer. A company like British Gas altering its role in the value network means there is another stakeholder to be managed and, also, a customer (such as the tenant) is given greater choice and influence. For the manufacturer this could ultimately mean greater competition and risk of commoditisation. Further still, when there are dramatic changes in the business environment (for example, regulations around climate change) which demand a technology shift, then a supplier like British Gas can disrupt the established network by bringing in a new technology provider to replace the established boiler manufacturer and potentially make them unnecessary.

Our research showed that where there was an extended value-network, as in our boiler example above, then partnering with channel partners is invariably necessary to develop customer intimacy. Caterpillar provides an excellent example of this working in practice. The company is often cited as an exemplar of servitization; yet in practice it is its dealers that deliver the bulk of the services. These are independent businesses, dedicated to Caterpillar and sharing customer insights, and in return Caterpillar acts in the background by providing technical support, spare parts and financing. Services are co-developed, delivery is often partnered, and all parties benefit from the results.

Customer intimacy can also be strengthened by intelligence gained through the Performance Advisory Service we mentioned earlier. Go to any Field Service Conference, and you will hear stories of how firms are remotely monitoring their products in the field, knowing where they are, how they are being used, and their condition. As an example, Yamazaki Mazak Corporation offers MazaCare, which captures information from its assets (machine status log reports, alarm notifications, remote diagnoses, etc.), and uploads it onto its cloud for any following actions on remote services. If done well, this innovation aids in understanding customers and can reveal opportunities in a servitization programme. But be aware, these opportunities are also realised by technology vendors, some of which are predatory in this space. More and more common are digital dashboards and platforms, offered to customers for one-stop asset management by technology companies, disintermediating the value network and causing fostering a transactional relationship with the asset provider. Again, careful partnering is key.

Proficiency in Digital Innovations

If the firm is proficient in the knowledge and application of digital innovations, then servitization is more likely to gain traction and to succeed. Our research showed us that executives didn't necessarily need to be experts in digital technologies and their innovation; what mattered was their proficiency in understanding the opportunity they represented. Coupled with this, executives must also understand the potential threats presented by technology vendors. Jim Euchner at Goodyear shared his thoughts on this topic, saying '*Technology is making services models much more powerful. In almost any industry, there are tech companies trying to displace manufacturers. But the manufacturers are in a much better position to deliver a total solution to the customer.*' Indeed, the business press has many examples of the challenge these firms represent: '*Your margin is my opportunity*' says Jeff Bezos, adding, '*that is why I often advise firms to start and launch their digital innovations without having all their ducks in a row*' [6].

Digital innovations are indeed unlocking the opportunities of advanced services. This was evident across all the firms we studied, and across sectors. For example, in food processing equipment, Marcus Olausson, Senior Product Manager Advanced Solutions at Tetra Pak, told us: '*Data and insights about the different losses that occur along the whole production line are key to make a convincing business case for pay-per-pack services. We knew we had to innovate our digital enablers to give us the confidence required to be able to offer these services to our customers.*' Then, in the construction sector, Matthew Skipworth, Director of Services at Terex said: '*Data is one of the key drivers of a move into servitization. If you make a large investment in IoT and data collection, you then think harder about what to do with this data, and this leads you to the development of enhanced and new services in order to drive value from the data for yourself and your customers*'.

In aerospace, a similar view was held by Tom Palmer, who told us: '*Rolls-Royce has an obligation to put sustainability into the heart of the business and its operations, but that's powered by digital technologies. If Rolls-Royce wants to be relevant in the future, it needs to move with the changes in technology. The technology has advanced around us all, and this is forcing the industry to change how it [we] operates*'. And finally, an as example in industrial systems, Andrew Barrett, Director – Portfolio and Requirements at Domino, said to us: '*The first step within industrial firms is usually to think about digital technologies as providing insight into how a product is being used, its condition and location, so that they can efficiently deliver maintenance programmes, or hopefully unlock more valuable services contracts. But these capabilities are also beginning to enable innovative business models for assets. The insights they provide help to identify and assess the severity of risks, giving confidence to otherwise cautious stakeholders, and so strengthening the platform for more advanced services.'*

Understanding the opportunities that digital technologies offer is a key enabler of making progress with servitization. An example of what we mean by this proficiency was demonstrated extremely well by Chris Borrill and his team at Thales. Chris explained: *'We saw digital trends as a combination of opportunity and threat. An opportunity to digitise how we deliver services. Customers looked to us for innovation. We knew if we didn't seize the opportunity, it could be used against us. We saw digital as a broader opportunity to put services on the agenda. Digital is coming – it's our opportunity because with digital everything is a service. We need to lead this charge rather than follow it. Also using it in a constructive way to convince the group to convince those at the very top level at the company to invest in our services toolkit. To reinforce messaging across the business and within the services community to show that the company was investing in services and give encouragement. Evidence that the message was being heard, that the perceived organisational wisdom about services was changing. We validated the fact that if we didn't respond there was no shortage of other actors both capable of filling our space and aggressively looking to do so. We identified a whole new set of competitors who had had no value proposition until digital came along to enable them. They were creating a lot of noise in the marketplace about how they could sit in front of us, the producers of equipment, to render it more maintainable, less costly, etc. We spent a lot of time on being able to describe the new threats and why what we were planning to do was the right response.'*

Finally, our research showed that that firms that successfully servitize place the emphasis on the analytics and management, rather than the harder technologies of sensors and communication. A common view is that technology side is taking care of itself [6]. Care is needed so that firms don't just drown in data: investing in data collection, monitoring, and data analytics. Dawie Kriel of Energy Partners Refrigeration explained to us the importance of a structured approach which prioritises analytics and management: *'You first need to develop the skills to build digital models, handle large amounts of data and create information based on the data – data and the information it produces are incredibly important enablers of servitization. Modelling is important because before we even contract the customer, we need to be sure how the system will operate throughout the year. This allows us to contract based on accurate efficiency and cooling output, and therefore the contracted tariffs will make sense. The information generated from the data, meanwhile, drives actions. Data must be processed in an intelligent way to turn it into information that drives actions to keep your services on track.'*

Capacity to Innovate

If a firm can demonstrate a capacity to innovate, beyond simply providing incremental improvements to the existing business model portfolio, then servitization is more likely to gain traction and to succeed. Here, we use the term 'capacity to innovate' to refer to the organisation's ability to generate and implement new ideas and business models that create value and drive competitive advantage. It encompasses a combination of factors, including a supportive organisational culture, a skilled and diverse workforce, effective research and development capabilities, access to relevant technology and resources, and the ability to identify and respond to market trends.

A capacity for innovation was a common trait shared by all the firms we researched that had achieved some level of progress with servitization. This ability to innovate played a vital role in their success as they developed and implemented new servitization strategies, business models, and service offerings. These firms demonstrated a strong commitment to fostering a culture of innovation, encouraging creative thinking, and actively seeking out opportunities for improvement and differentiation in the marketplace. This capacity appeared in different ways, ranging from sufficient staff time to work on a services project, or investment in external consultants to execute a project on their behalf. By contrast, we found examples of firms that seemed to be ideal candidates for servitization (for example in the machine tool sector) but that struggled to progress simply because executives and their staff were almost entirely engaged with product design and production.

Our research also revealed a further distinction: executives in industrial firms with a strong capacity for innovation approached products and their performance in a fundamentally different manner compared to firms lacking this capability. They saw that a reliable product as an essential and stable platform for service innovation, whereas those without were tempted to think of servitization as a form of compensation or cushion for a less reliable product. Indeed, some even thought about selling the product cheaply and earning revenue through spare-parts consumption, there thinking being: *The more it breaks and the more time we spend repairing it, the more money we make!* Or, *if it doesn't break how can we sell services?* To illustrate this, Ross Townshend, the then Business Unit Manager for Ishida, told us: '*Unless you manufacture a reliable asset, you will have no place in the advanced services space ... we build a reliable machine, so we can provide a platform of services.'*

Charging customers because of product failure is simply making money out of their misery and needing to repair products stands in the way of firms effectively delivering outcomes. We also come across people saying that 'right-to-repair' legislation can inhibit servitization but this is incorrect. Base services (supplying products and spare parts) are for those customers who 'want to do it themselves'. Rolls-Royce, for example, can still supply spare parts for the Spitfire fighter plane from World War II. Attempting to force customers into managed services (or product replacement) is simply playing games at the lower steps of the services staircase for short-term gain. And the gain is short because in the longer term the firms reputation will suffer.

Examining the Deeper Processes of Servitization

Experiencing Servitization of the Firm

Our research allowed us to understand servitization as a journey and illustrate (Fig. 7.2) how firms with a heritage of producing products had gone about innovating advanced services. It helped us to appreciate that executives such as Des Evans at MAN and Jim Euchner at Goodyear had experienced their initiatives go through four distinctive stages (Exploration, Engagement, Expansion and Exploitation), and that progress had been determined by four sets of forces (market-centric forces, technology-centric forces, value network-centric forces and organisation-centric forces). It also gave us insight into how the journey unfolds in practice: the dynamics, delays and unintentional exits. We strived to really understand this, as we knew that only with this foundational knowledge would we be able to guide others. We needed to understand what it had felt like for those who had succeeded in innovating advanced services.

We learned how the stages play out in practice and that the trigger point for the process is when one or more practitioners in a firm become aware of the servitization and advanced services concepts. Depending on the extent of their firm's commitment, the practitioners begin with the Exploration stage to reflect on the concept. If there is adequate organisational readiness (and no immediate obstacles from other forces), these practitioners seek broader organisational consent to progress to the Engagement stage.

In the Engagement stage, they look for evidence that suggests customer demand (customer pull) and/or test the potential of technologies (technology push). When they find suitable conditions, they move to co-creation, piloting, and incubation of a new advanced service offering. If the resulting outcomes are positive, practitioners use these to demonstrate the value of servitization to the firm. Sometimes, they become particularly delayed because engaging customers means working through the dealerships and the distributors in their value network.

When they move onto the Expansion stage, these pilots are turned into refined commercial offerings. There is an increase in the speed and scale at which advanced services are then taken to market, and as this scale grows, practitioners' attention switches to the Exploitation stage. Here, the emphasis is predominantly on initiatives to improve the reliability and efficiency of service delivery at scale.

We also learned that a range of factors affected the servitization journey and these could be grouped into four categories or forces. We termed these market-centric (the conditions in the market environment of the firm 'pulling' the innovation of services); technology-centric (technologies that support, enable or incentivise the innovation of services), organisation-centric (the commitment given from within the organisation to services), and value-network centric (interactions and interdependencies of the firm with other stakeholders). These forces interplay to determine the speed and success of an industrial firm on its servitization journey.

Within these there are though five particularly influential factors. These are the Leadership empathy for services (executive leadership of the firm understands services and the opportunities), an existing Services function or partners (departments within the firm or a strong relationship with a services partner), strong customer relationships and intelligence (comprehensive understanding of the customers and their needs), a Proficiency in digital innovations (knowledge and application of digital innovations) and a Capacity to innovate (ability to generate and implement new ideas and business models).

From our research, we also learned about the dynamics of the firms' journeys. The four forces interplayed to determine the sequence of decisions and actions in each stage. What executives had to do in each stage was characteristically organic, unstructured, and iterative. A firm's progress from one macro-stage to the next is punctuated by 'tipping points'. These points can be overcome only when the activities of the preceding stage have successfully demonstrated sufficient value for a firm to consent to progression to the following stages. Firms moved from the Exploration stage to the Engagement stage only when the senior management gained confidence that a viable business opportunity existed; from the Engagement stage to the Expansion stage only when the firm accepted the potential of advanced services; and from the

Expansion stage to the Exploitation stage only when a significant value was demonstrated in the firm.

Tipping points are magic moments when the initiatives cross a threshold and begin to spread and become adopted [7]. So significant are they that the servitization journey may halt or even entirely fail under certain conditions. These tipping points can't be skipped; not all companies will immediately (or easily) reach and/or overcome these points. Within the four stages, there are multiple reiterations of actions and decisions that will cycle until specific tipping conditions are met, and then the transformation process will 'tip' and progress onto the next stage. In the case studies, once this process moved onto a new stage, it did not return to the preceding stage unless catastrophic changes occurred within the business.

Unravelling the Firms Experience with Servitization

Our research allowed us to understand and describe how servitization played out in practice. We could make sense of the journey: the stages, forces and dynamics. Indeed, the servitization roadmap (Fig. 7.2) is now being used extensively to help executives to position, explain and benchmark their firms. Yet, we wanted to use this knowledge further—to guide and accelerate the adoption of servitization within product-centric organisations. To achieve this, we had to dig deeper, be more rigorous, and we needed to give a more grounded and theory-informed explanation.

What we discovered is that there are two interdependent and some-what sequential 'mechanisms' that playout when an industrial firm under-takes servitization, these are 'business model innovation' and 'organisational change'. These co-exist and interplay, though the emphasis changes from one to the other as the servitization initiative matures. These mechanisms, and how they relate to each other, explain the stages and activities that appear on the surface of the roadmap shown in Fig. 7.2. In Fig. 7.4 we lay these mechanisms out against the stages in our roadmap, to illustrate how they are positioned and relate to each other. In a successful servitization programme they will typically be played out in the following way.

The characteristics of the Exploration stage is explained by the mechanism of business model innovation gaining traction. Within the firm, a person, or a group of people, will become aware and choose to pay attention to servitization and services innovation. If they have no prior knowledge of servitization, then initially there will be much uncertainty and many unknowns. There will be questioning and debating sessions, and slowly a small coalition of people will emerge who will be interested and committed to exploring the

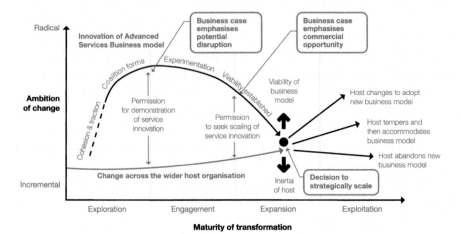

Fig. 7.4 Examining the mechanisms underpinning a servitization journey (© The Advanced Services Group Ltd)

potential of servitization in some depth. They will coalesce around discussions about a new service-led business model, reflecting on what new services might be offered, and strengthening their understanding and ambitions. They may be from a range of different business functions (such as sales, innovation, design and operations), and although they might not be senior executives themselves, they will be valued employees and influential within the organisation.

The coalition will initially focus on exploring innovative opportunities. As the notion of a new services-led business model gains traction, the ideas debated within the coalition are likely to be increasingly radical, exciting and aspirational. Reflecting on what might be possible and taking inspiration from, for example, technology firms operating in B2C (for example, Uber and Airbnb). Ideas will emerge that the coalition is keen to evaluate, and they will want to demonstrate this potential through pilot testing. To do so they will first seek permission from senior executives. At this time there will be very little change across the wider organisation, with these seniors principally focused on the incumbent portfolio of product-centric business models.

The coalition will establish and strengthen this commitment by delivering or reinforcing their business case. This will typically include a reflection on the strategic threats to the established product-centric business model portfolio and will emphasise and embellish how radical change has significantly disrupted other companies and sectors. A little more organisational change will be enacted. Cautiously, they will often cultivate the impression of a 'burning platform'. Executives within the firm will be motivated by this and, with a few caveats, will commission sufficient resources for experimentation. They will then observe and loosely monitor progression, but largely allow the team to be independent and adventurous in exploring their new business model. Organisational change within the wider business will continue to be incremental and focused around improving the established product-centric business model portfolio.

The characteristics of the Engagement stage is explained by the mechanism of business model innovation focusing on developing and experimenting with alternative offerings to targeted customers. As the process moves into the Engagement cycle, the coalition will begin to experiment with new customer value propositions for services. Initially these propositions will be quite adventurous, but then as customers are approached and engaged in testing, the range of potentially viable business models will narrow. Here, viability will be directly influenced by the extent of organisational change the customer themselves is prepared to undergo. Aspirations within the coalition will reduce, though will still be relatively adventurous compared to the wider organisation, which continues to focus on incremental improvements. Executives will continue to monitor this experimentation, and perhaps enjoy the energy and creativity they observe within the coalition.

Only during the Expansion stage do the two mechanisms converge and characteristically tensions arise. The coalition, having identified a viable business model, is motivated to deliver this at scale, and so seeks to understand and then put in place the facilities, people, process, and systems. As the coalition better appreciates that this will require resources and integration from within the wider firm, an inflection in the service innovation pathway occurs.

There will now be increasing emphasis on organisational change. Initially, there will be some minor adjustments to the design of the new business model and, simultaneously, a growing awareness of a potential need to change in the firm. The coalition will take actions to improve visibility and induce commitment, and this will begin to mildly influence actions and investments in the firm. At some point more formal permission will be sought by the coalition to explore the scaling of the new model. A case will be made for business investments supporting a roll-out to a small subset of customers for more extensive market testing. Here, the business case will differ to that made for experimentation, focusing more on commercial evidence and metrics, and if successful will commit the organisation to significantly greater investments.

In the Expansion stage executives within in the firm will pay closer attention to the implications of scaling. Tensions and resistance will increase, especially if the new business model is perceived as a potential distraction or even threat to the existing portfolio. A major decision point will become apparent, whether or not to strategically scale. A range of concerns will arise spanning from investment through to the cultural identity of the organisation. These tensions will reflect the difference between the adventure of the proposed business model and the existing portfolio. They will be less if the organisation already has some services-based models in place, which could potentially be linked and integrated; but more significant if such services are an arm's-length activity delivered by distributors and dealerships.

There are three potential outcomes of this decision point. One possibility is that the integrity of the business model will be preserved, and the firm will undergo a programme of change, so the resources and structures will be put in place for scaling. A second is that both the business model and the organisation will undergo moderate adjustments in an attempt to accommodate the model within the existing portfolio. Or the third possibility is that the new business model might be closed down or spun-off, and the firm will maintain an exclusive focus on those established within its current portfolio. The chosen pathway will be contingent on the viability of the business model and the inertia within the organisation. Much of this inertia will reflect the extent of investments needed in people, facilities, partners, technologies and processes, all of which will be necessary to deliver the new business model at scale. Here, of course, the desired result for advocates of servitization is the first of these three. The characteristics of the Exploitation stage are explained by the mechanism of organisational change. Exploiting the advanced services business model involves optimising its delivery to maximise returns for the business by integrating it into the existing portfolio and adjusting resources for efficient and cost-effective service provision. This task requires recognising, designing, and maintaining a balanced business model portfolio, which involves safeguarding and enhancing existing models, fostering the growth of new ones, and discontinuing unviable ones. Implementing these adjustments necessitates broader organisational changes, and while effective change management principles are valuable, our focus remains on supporting service innovation within the framework of the business model. Once achieved, the cycle completes, and the journey can start again as another opportunity for business model innovation around advanced services is identified and fostered.

Understanding how these two mechanisms interplay is invaluable. As we have just shown, it explains the characteristics of each stage in a servitization journey. The change in emphasis, and timing of this, is crucially important. What our research shows is that successful servitization is usually a process where business model innovation 'pulls' organisational change. This is contrary to many classical management text which treat business model innovation almost as one step in a much broader strategic programme; from the onset there is vision, strategy which then 'pushes' innovation. We are not suggesting that such an approach is not enacted in practice, but rather that this is not the dominant process of servitization that we have witnessed in the firms we have studied,

The forces which affect the servitization journey appear to weigh most heavily on the mechanism of business model innovation. They introduce a bias on the *how* and *when* business model innovation might commence, they shape ambitions and progress, and influence the probability of success. They interplay throughout. For the executive team and leaders, this starts to explain why they feel so stretched and overwhelmed in the Expansion stage. Here, there are tensions between the mechanisms which are potentially unmanageable, especially so for an ambitious innovator in a traditional and long-established industrial firm.

Understanding these two mechanisms also helps to explain why some servitization programmes are slow or stall. In our narrative throughout this part of our book we have focused on the innovation of a single advanced services business model. Indeed, many of the examples we give in this book are about single models and celebrating organisations that create these; for example, the work of Jim Euchner at Goodyear and Tom Palmer at Rolls-Royce. We tease out these specific examples in this way so that we can provide a straightforward commentary. However, throughout our research we came across firms actively attempting to innovate and scale multiple business models simultaneously. All too often executives became overwhelmed, there were conflicting messaging and priorities, and progress stalled.

Multiple business models can be innovated, though this seems to be more likely to be successful when there is a staggered sequence as illustrated in Fig. 7.5. Each innovation is afforded the necessary resources, therefore is more likely to be successful, and so the host firm continues to evolve. Of course, not every innovation will, in practice, be commercially successful. Indeed, the Engagement stage thrives on proposing and testing a range of 'minimum-viable services', but for many firms this stage should coalesce with one innovation prioritised for immediate scaling at that time. Larger firms are more able to accommodate a greater number of business model innovations around the same time, whereas we saw the more successful medium-sized firms dealing with only two or possibly three innovations somewhat sequentially.

All these insights have led us to reflect on how to define servitization such that it best represents what is seen in practice. We can now see it more richly than previously, and so in a firm we see servitization as:

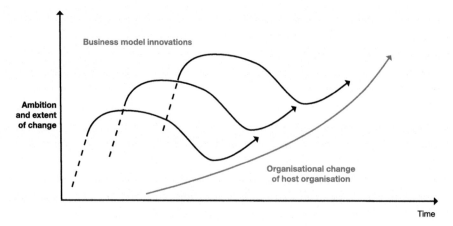

Fig. 7.5 Servitization playing out through multiple business model innovations (© The Advanced Services Group Ltd)

The process where a firm engages with business model innovations and organisational changes, so as to compete through providing business outcomes for customers rather than only producing and selling outputs (products)

This complements and refines our earlier definitions, but the extra precision it incorporates is especially useful for our following chapter.

Chapter Summary

In this chapter we have shared the findings of the international research we carried out to understand, rigorously, how industrial firms have succeeded with servitization and the innovation of advanced service business models. This research established that the journey an organisation takes will consist of the following stages:

- Exploration, searching and finding out about the concept and the implications of competing through advanced services, until there is confidence that the opportunity exists.
- Engagement, seeking to evaluate and demonstrate advanced services, until the potential is accepted within the organisation.
- Expansion, increasing the scale and speed at which advanced services are innovated and implemented until significant value is demonstrated within the organisation.

- Exploitation, seeking to optimise the innovation and delivery of an advanced services portfolio, unless business is adversely disrupted.

Progress through these stages is determined by factors, both internal and external to the firm, and these can be grouped into four sets of forces about the market, technologies, value network and organisation. Progress from one macro-stage to the next may initially appear to be structured and unidirectional but contained within these stages are sub-processes which are characteristically organic, unstructured and iterative.

References

1 Baines, T., et al., *Framing the servitization transformation process: A model to understand and facilitate the servitization journey.* International Journal of Production Economics, 2020. **221**: p. 107463.
2 Baines, T., et al., *Servitization: Revisiting the state-of-the-art and research priorities.* International Journal of Operations & Production Management, 2017. **37**(2): p. 256–278.
3 Scott, M. and R. Bruce, *Five stages of growth in small business.* Long Range Planning, 1987. **20**(3): p. 45–52.
4 Boldosova, V., *Telling stories that sell: The role of storytelling and big data analytics in smart service sales.* Industrial Marketing Management, 2020. **86**: p. 122–134.
5 Baxter, R.K., *The forever transaction: how to build a subscription model so compelling, your customers will never want to leave.* 2020: McGraw-Hill Education.
6 Liozu, S.M., *The industrial subscription economy: a practical guide to designing, pricing and scaling your industrial subscription.* 2021: Value Innoruption Advisors Publishing
7 Lah, T. and J. Wood, *Technology-as-a-service playbook: how to grow a profitable subscription business.* 2016: Point B, Inc.
8 Treacy, M. and F. Wiersema, *Customer intimacy and other value disciplines.* Harvard Business Review, 1993. **71**(1): p. 84–93.
9 Kowalkowski, C., et al., *Servitization and deservitization: Overview, concepts, and definitions.* Industrial Marketing Management, 2017. **60**: p. 4–10.
10 BritishGas. *HomeCare Cover.* 2023; Available from: https://www.britishgas.co.uk/home-services/boilers-and-heating/boiler-and-heating-cover.html?excess=60.

8

Innovation of Advanced Services and Delivering Servitization

People within firms often feel overwhelmed by the prospect of servitization. Once they have started to understand what is meant by servitization, there is an avalanche of questions: How much money will we make? Which department should lead it? What products should we focus on? Which customers? When will we need to partner? What technologies will we need? How do we deal with our distributors? People are consumed with debates around skills for selling services, whether they have the right sales team, incentive programmes, a separate business unit just for services, who should own this, and where it should sit in the broader organisation. All too often they will stall completely around leadership, strategy and vision, as their unanswered questions lead to unyielding textbook-style assumptions about where to begin; We need a leader. We need a vision. We need a strategy. When this happens, the programme fails to progress.

So how should a firm that has traditionally made its way in the world by producing and selling products set about servitization? In this chapter, we provide a generic process we term the 'route planner' to guide a firm through the development and execution of a servitization programme. Our principle (but not exclusive) target is industrial firms with a heritage in products (outputs) and wanting to servitize through the innovation of advanced services. The process we describe is intended to be sufficiently abstract to have relevance to all industrial firms, yet explained in enough detail that managers can readily use this to guide their specific decisions and actions. Our goal is that this process will enable firms to initiate, develop and exploit advanced

© The Author(s), under exclusive license to Springer Nature Switzerland AG 2024
T. Baines et al., *Servitization Strategy*, Palgrave Executive Essentials,
https://doi.org/10.1007/978-3-031-45426-4_8

services business models, and in doing so help to accelerate the exploitation of servitization. We start the chapter by introducing the route planner and its features, and then move onto illustrate how to execute the principal activities within an industrial firm.

Route Planner for Formation of a Servitization Programme

The research described in Chapter 7 provides the foundation on which we have based the route planner that we explain in this section. Our roadmap (Fig. 7.2) embodies much of what we now understand about the servitization journey of a firm; that it plays out through a sequence of four stages, each with a cluster of activities, and progress is determined by four sets of forces. Yet, this roadmap is designed only to 'describe' the journey that firms follow. When used in conjunction with the services staircase it can be a powerful tool to compare and contrast progress, but it only really captures where firms are in their journey, it is not designed to tell them what to do next.

To help executives we need to offer a much more prescriptive set of instructions about what to do and when. For this purpose, we have developed what we have termed the 'route panner' and is intended to guide a firm through the process of servitization. In other words, it is a generic set of instructions for the formation a servitization programme within a firm. The planner reflects the learning embedded in the roadmap, but is designed to give structure and direction and differs in the following ways:

- Rather than 'stages' and 'tipping points' the route planner defines four principal 'tasks' to be executed, each with an associated 'objective' and 'method.'
- Rather than a cluster of 'activities' within each 'stage', the route planner defines a concise 'activity-cycle' to be completed for each task and along with a 'tracker' to aid progress monitoring.
- Rather than 'forces', the route planner defines five key 'enablers' and techniques to strengthen these to help ensure success.

The route planner is drawn together as a complete framework at the end of this section, but to help you appreciate this we first explain the key features in turn.

Tasks

We have defined four tasks for innovating an advanced services business model and driving ahead with a servitization programme. These tasks are: Explore, Engage, Expand and Exploit the innovation of advanced services business models and they reflect the underlying mechanisms of business model innovation and organisational change identified in the previous chapter. Figure 8.1 shows these mechanisms and summarises, fundamentally, the profile of change that the task set out to achieve. This is the approach which was commonly applied by the firms that progressed successfully with their innovation of advanced services and servitization. Later in this chapter we will take you through the execution of these tasks in detail. Each task has a cycle of three activities, and they combine and build on each other as we have shown in Fig. 8.2.

Summarising the four tasks, Explore is where you begin with if you and your firm have no history with servitization. Some people won't need to go through this task because they already have the initial coalition, a compelling argument to Engage with servitization, and the resources committed to move forward with the programme. Be prepared for a period of uncertainty, questioning and consensus building.

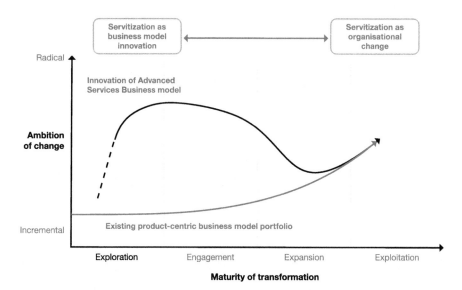

Fig. 8.1 Mechanisms underpinning success with servitization (© The Advanced Services Group Ltd)

Moving onto Engage, you then deal with the task of creating a minimum viable new business model. Sufficient to demonstrate that there is commercial potential for an advanced service. Developing a deep understanding of those customers most likely to embrace advanced services, use these insights to co-create with them a selection of new value propositions. Pilot to test the most promising to demonstrate the value that can be created and captured.

Moving onto Expand, the task is to refine the business model, getting in place all capabilities to deliver commercially, and beginning to enter the market. You are, though, entering a period which is no longer just about business model innovation. Success necessitates strengthening the business model, investing in a service delivery system, and then beginning to roll this out in a select market segment. Expect to cycle around these activities, but here there will be difficult choices and the need for bold decisions.

Finally moving onto Exploit, the task of adjusting the business model portfolio of the firm to optimise the delivery of advanced services business model to maximise the returns to the business. You begin with having in place an advanced services business model that is growing in the market segment. The task now is to Integrate the business model with the existing portfolio and adjust resources to achieve efficiencies and economies in service delivery. Ultimately stepping back to monitor performance and looking out for the next business model opportunity.

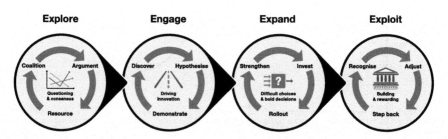

Fig. 8.2 Tasks in the formation of a servitization programme (© The Advanced Services Group Ltd)

Objectives and Methods

Each task has a defined objective and method (Table 8.1). These objectives need to be achieved in sequence, from one to the next, and the methods explains has to address each of these. While the objectives are unique to each task, once fulfilled they provide a platform for the next. They are interlinked and build on each other. To be successful with servitization they will need to be addressed in the order illustrated in Table 8.1; the objectives associated with Engage should only be addressed once those for Explore have been achieved, and so on. To illustrate, the objective of Explore is to establish the permission of the executive leadership to investigate new business models. Once genuine permission is in place, then the programme can move onto Engage. Now, because the servitization programme has the backing of the management team, then the focus can be on demonstrating the potential of a new business model.

Table 8.1 Tasks, objectives and methods of a servitization programme

	Explore servitization and advanced services	Engage in the innovation of an advanced service	Expand to deliver advanced service at scale	Exploit to optimise value creation and capture
Objective	Gain commitment from executive leadership to experiment with advanced services business models	Demonstrate potential of an advanced services business model and gain commitment to incubate	Build capability to scale advanced services business model	Adjust portfolio and optimise delivery of advanced services business model
Method	Search, find out, build a coalition around the possibility of competing through servitization and advanced services	Discover, hypothesise, test and evaluate new service business models and select the most promising	Refine business model, get in place all capabilities to deliver commercially and enter the market	Integrate the business model with the existing portfolio and adjust resourced to achieved efficiencies and economies in service delivery

Care is needed to fulfil the tasks entirely by following the method completely. One danger is that eager executives leading on a servitization programme might be drawn to prematurely skip forwards in the sequence. Our research in the previous chapter shows this to be folly, and can lead to excessive iterations, stalling and premature exits. For example, a promising pilot with just one customer might tempt a team to immediately try to put in place an ambitious business case to scale this across sectors and regions, whereas what should happen is that the team should focus on engaging further pilots with other customer to validate the service proposition and develop a robust operating model (partnerships, people, systems, etc.).

It is also critical not to become distracted by decisions and initiatives that are not key to the task in hand. For example, conversations around the skills and culture of the sales team are important, but a distraction at the programme onset and can be postponed until Expand. The same is true of vision and strategy; early in the programme these need only be concerned with envisioning an compelling service offering to help galvanise the team and build engagement. Ambitions for the wider organisation should come in Exploit.

Activity-cycles and Dynamics

Each task has an objective, and each objective has a method through which it can be fulfilled. To aid the execution of each method we have defined a bespoke activity-cycle (Table 8.2). This is a concise set of generalised activities that need to be cycled through, by the people within the firm who are driving the servitization initiative, until the objective is realised.

Each activity-cycle is defined and expressed in such a way that it can be applied, generically, across industrial firms. For example, in the Explore task the objective focuses on gain commitment from the executive leadership, so the method deals with background research, raising awareness, and motivating a group of stakeholders. We summarise this as an activity-cycle consisting of; coalition, argument and resource. In a short while we will take you through each of these four cycles in some detail.

Our foundational research also provided insights to the most likely dynamics within firms as each of the tasks are executed. Understanding the nature of these dynamics is helpful in preparing the executive team for the servitization journey. We include an icon in Table 8.2 to represent the nature of the dynamics to help you visualise what to expect. To describe the dynamics at play, expect Explore to be particularly turbulent; people

Table 8.2 Activity-cycles and dynamics of a servitization programme

	Explore servitization and advanced services	Engage in the innovation of an advanced service	Expand to deliver advanced service at scale	Exploit to optimise value creation and capture
Activity-cycle	• Coalition • Argument • Resource	• Discover • Hypothesise • Demonstrate	• Strengthen • Invest • Roll out	• Recognise • Adjust • Step back
Dynamics	Questioning & consensus	Driving innovation	Difficult choices & bold decisions	Building & rewarding

will be unsure of the concept and testing their understanding. They will be questioning programme ownership and organisational politics.

Engage will be calmer and more sequential. Markets will be selected and propositions developed, which will then be tested and refined to identify the most promising. During Expand, the challenges of broader organisational change begin to interplay with that of business model innovation. A whole range of factors will need to be dealt with in order to establish a business model viable for scaling. There will be significant tensions and questioning, as the firm wrestles with the new business model and reconciles with the need for organisational change. Finally, Exploit will feel different again as the business model portfolio is adjusted and investments are made to enable market exploitation and economies of scale.

Tracker Topics

The purpose of the tracker topics is to enable progress to be monitored. The topics are symptomatic of the analysis and actions that are typically associated with each task. Table 8.3. They are not though a list of actions that are essential to executed. As we have mentioned previously the context of firms vary. These activities don't need to be competed sequentially and there will be others not included here. Rather, treat this as a checklist that you can use to help you understand where your organisation is on its servitization journey.

Table 8.3 Tracker topics for each task of a servitization programme

	Explore servitization and advanced services	Engage in the innovation of an advanced service	Expand to deliver advanced service at scale	Exploit to optimise value creation and capture
Tracker topics	• Gain foundational education • Form guiding collision • Determine competitive strategy and fit • Identify compelling benchmarks and stories • Establish executive leadership champion • Creative dramatic business case	• Gain service innovation education • Target customer segments • Expose customer profile and value drivers • Propose value propositions & revenue models • Pilot and verify demand • Build business case for incubation	• Gain service scaling education • Review, invest and trial service delivery system, including: - Performance measures and processes - Product and service design - Business processes - Facilities and locations - Suppliers and partnerships - Digital technologies and systems - People, skills, and culture • Ensure and structured for growth	• Gain organisational change education • Review business model portfolio • Commit vision and strategy • Select, educate and train wider salesforce • Integrate business model • Implement, monitor and review • Sustain culture of service business model innovation

Enablers

Every servitization programme will have a unique business context. The conditions in the business environment drive change. Our concern is with the specific circumstances that are particularly helpful in accelerating success with servitization. There are particular enablers that help businesses be good candidates for successful servitization. If these are absent, it may be that remedial actions should be taken to mitigate problems as the programme unfolds.

If the enablers are in place, it means that servitization is likely to proceed quickly and with a good outcome, and if not, then progress will be slow and can stall. This is not to say that servitization cannot take place, but if they are, or can be put in place at the onset, then success is more likely. Table 8.4 captures these enablers, what they mean, and where they can be strengthened

Table 8.4 Enablers of a servitization programme

Enabler	Description	Techniques to help reinforce enabler
Leadership empathy for services	A few senior executives who are sufficiently open-minded and compassionate to the idea that services might offer a competitive business model	Communication to raise awareness, create and galvanise a community Experience room to showcase service and technology innovations and customer experiences Structured 'storytelling' about services opportunities and competitive threats
Services function and partners	Business function already in place offering some services	Engage and work with channel partners Develop and implement performance advisory services
Customers intimacy and intelligence	Familiarity and understanding of the customer and their business environment	Develop and implement performance advisory services Scan and monitor customers own competitive environment Engage and work with channel partners
Proficiency in digital innovations	Familiarity and understanding if technology innovations and their potential opportunity and relevance	Ongoing education and training in digital innovations Experience room to showcase service and technology innovation and customer experiences
Capacity for innovation	Sufficient funding and reliable product platform for service innovation	Raise awareness of dependency on firm financial investment Initiative programmes to ensure product is a reliable platform for service innovation

as part of the servitization programme. Our particular interest is on those key enablers which, if well maintained, help to ensure effective servitization. In other words, we will focus on what to do well to ensure success rather than over burdening you with all the things that can go wrong.

Summarising the Route Planner

In this section, we have taken you through each of the components of the process for a servitization programme to be successful. In Table 8.5 we draw these together to help you to appreciate the whole framework. In the next section we will describe how to go through the process, and we illustrate how to apply this by using evidence from the firms we have studied.

Applying the Route Planner

To take you through this process we will assume that you are new to servitization and advanced services. You might just be inquisitive or committed to a project and anxious to make progress, but nevertheless your interest has been triggered. You may be a very senior executive or a manager reporting into an executive group, either way you want to take your colleagues with you on this journey. We will also assume that to succeed you need to demonstrate to the business that any new business models have been properly conceived and evidenced. As a final word of context setting, you know that no two organisations are identical, and the solutions you come up with will be particular to your firm.

With these points in mind, we will now explain the process revealed by our research. And so as not to make this overly complex, we will focus on the innovation of a single advanced service from inception to becoming embedded in the business model portfolio of an industrial firm. In practice, we see larger firms successfully running this process multiple times in a staggered sequence, so building out a much fuller servitization programme; but explaining that is for another time.

How to Explore Servitization and Advanced Services

Explore is the logical task to begin with if you and your firm have no history of servitization. People around you are also likely to know little about the topic. There is much uncertainty as well as assumptions, and even prejudice. Colleagues may be dismissive; others may see servitization as synonymous with IoT, Industry 4.0, or subscription payments. The challenge is to get started, and the entry point for most is with establishing a coalition of likeminded colleagues within your firm.

The coalition can start small; just you! But then you can build a reason or argument for others to join you, and when you do this successfully and they

Table 8.5 Route planner for a servitization programme

	Explore servitization and advanced services	Engage in the innovation of an advanced service	Expand to deliver advanced service at scale	Exploit to optimise value creation and capture
Objective	Gain commitment from executive leadership to experiment with advanced services business models	Demonstrate potential of an advanced services business model and gain commitment to incubate	Build capability to scale advanced services business model	Adjust portfolio and optimise delivery of advanced services business model
Method	Search, find out, build a coalition around the possibility of competing through servitization and advanced services	Discover, hypothesise, test and evaluate new service business models and select the most promising	Establish readiness for scaling and get in place all necessary commitments, resources and partnerships	Integrate the business model with the existing portfolio and adjust resourced to achieved efficiencies and economies in service delivery
Activity-cycle	• Coalition • Argument • Resource	• Discover • Hypothesise • Demonstrate	• Strengthen • Invest • Roll out	• Recognise • Adjust • Step back
Dynamics	Questioning & consensus	Driving innovation	Difficult choices & bold decisions	Building & rewarding

(continued)

Table 8.5 (continued)

	Explore servitization and advanced services	Engage in the innovation of an advanced service	Expand to deliver advanced service at scale	Exploit to optimise value creation and capture
Tracker topics	• Gain foundational education • Form guiding collision • Determine competitive strategy and fit • Identify compelling benchmarks and stories • Establish executive leadership champion • Creative dramatic business case	• Gain service innovation education • Target customer segments • Expose customer profile and value drivers • Propose value propositions & revenue models • Pilot and verify demand • Build business case for incubation	• Gain service scaling education • Review, invest and trial service delivery system, including: - Performance measures and processes - Product and service design - Business processes - Facilities and locations - Suppliers and partnerships - Digital technologies and systems - People, skills, and culture • Ensure and structured for growth	• Gain organisational change education • Review business model portfolio • Commit vision and strategy • Select, educate and train wider salesforce • Integrate business model • Implement, monitor and review • Sustain culture of service business model innovation

Enablers

Leadership empathy for services

Services function and partners

Customer intimacy and intelligence

Proficiency in digital innovations

Capacity for innovation

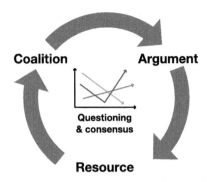

Fig. 8.3 The activity-cycle for the task of explore (© The Advanced Services Group Ltd)

do, then they are adding their own time and resources to yours, and so the coalition grows. You are then able to keep pushing this activity-cycle until the 'coalition' is sufficiently strong, and the 'arguments' sufficiently persuasive, that the business commits sufficient 'resources' to the programme to go onto the next task. Achieve this and then the objective for Explore is complete.

This activity-cycle is illustrated in Fig. 8.3. Some people won't need to go through the task of Explore because they already have the initial coalition, a compelling argument to Engage with servitization, and the resources committed to move forwards with the programme. If you are not in this fortunate position, then you should follow this cycle. Be prepared for a period of uncertainty, questioning and consensus building.

Coalition

Bring together a group of stakeholders, mainly from within the firms, who will support and guide the servitization initiative. Many people will tell you that to get started with servitization requires a very senior executive to lead the way, to initiate and sponsor the programme from the offset. This is desirable but actually not essential. What is needed is a guiding coalition, a core team of willing and motivated individuals. As John Kotter [1] the Harvard Professor has explained this doesn't necessarily need to include the most senior leaders in the company but it must be enough people to create momentum. They don't need to be from a specific business function, and they don't need to have prior knowledge of servitization. But if you are going to make progress, you will need to bring together a group of people who share your interest in exploring the potential of servitization in some depth.

Ross Townshend, the former Business Unit Manager for Ishida, suggested that this is typically a team drawn from project management, product management, finance, engineering or technical, and commercial. They need to be people with enough influence in the company to get things done, to experiment, fail fast and learn quickly, and they need to be resourced with the finances needed to actually go out, talk to customers, set up and test things and make changes internally as a result. Typically, the people in this group will begin to coalesce around discussions about a new service-led business model, reflecting on what new services might be offered, and strengthening their understanding and ambitions. The group needs to be able to wake up colleagues in the wider firm to the opportunities; as Jim Euchner from The Goodyear Tire & Rubber Company once said, *you need to light lots of little fires.*

The size of the coalition will differ from on project/firm to the next. John Kotter suggests that this could be as few as five people to gain traction. Ben Wilson, the Digital Journey Lead at Schneider Electric, told us: *'a coalition was put together by Howard Bowland, the VP of Services at Schneider Electric. It's important to get together a team of adventurers that has the passion and energy to work on something as important as this for the organisation. We brought together a team with one person from every relevant department: sales, marketing, products, supply chain, operations, and digital monitoring. At the start of the project, we devoted about an hour a day to understanding what it means to create a servitized offering, what as-a-service is and isn't (for example, it's not a leasing model). As time went on, some people transitioned into new roles, while for others it became part of their existing job.'*

The coalition will need to be fostered and led. We have seen excellent examples of how to do this in our programme and one of the very best was demonstrated by Chris Borrill, Thales. Chris said: *'Communicate, build awareness, create and galvanise a community and demonstrate the strategic importance.'* Slowly, the coalition can become a much larger services community within the business and help to foster many more innovations. Rinze van Kammen from Yanmar Europe had similar guidance: *'I would advise anyone starting out with servitization to organise the initiative separately from the regular service business, to get traction and focus. Pull in distributors and architects from the onset of the project to build a coalition. You only need a few key advocates.'* We will return to this topic again when discussing the task of Exploit.

As the coalition begins to form there will be a lot of questions, assumptions, challenges, and possibly dismissals. Deal with this by focusing on the objective: gaining commitment from the executive leadership to fully explore the potential of an advanced services business model. Ask no more at this stage, simply permission to explore and evaluate these alternative business models. Avoid becoming distracted with conversations around broader organisational change, culture and investments. Now is not the time for these. Alejandro Chan, the Vice President of Global Services at Tetra Pak put this well: '*There will be many conflicting pressures, viewpoints and alternatives that could be pursued when looking to grow market share. Getting a cross-functional team together, adopting a common language and purpose helped us to build consensus around the topic of servitization. This was critical in making headway with our outcome-based solutions.*'

Engage a range of stakeholders in the coalition to represent the broader activities of the firm. Tom Palmer, former Group Director of Services Strategy of Rolls-Royce, advocated doing just this. He told us: '*You can start mapping out which stakeholders will be needed to provide the customer outcome and how your delivery impacts those around you. The greater the impact, the greater the value of the stakeholder. Think about who's interacting with you, the outputs that you provide and the impact they have on somebody else.*' In some instances, you may be able to engage external stakeholders such as dealers or distributors, especially if these are almost certainly going to be part of the services solution for your firm. This is, of course, a sensitive area, and it may well be that for the moment these should be left until you move to Explore. Even then, a good understanding of these stakeholders and likely allies in the group is very valuable.

You might be fortunate to have a strong coalition already in place, though not necessarily realising this is the case. Goodyear's initial group was of the senior personnel in the innovation team, who were exploring ways to inspire growth. They came to recognise that business model innovation around advanced services could provide a possible route. The group had to engage in a range of activities, from developing and experimenting with customer value propositions through to deciding on relationships with technology suppliers. Jim Euchner, the then Vice President for Global Innovation was also fortunate because at Goodyear they came to the process with a relatively higher level of organisational engagement and a more structured methodology for innovating propositions.

To support the coalition, an education in the basic principles of servitization is vitally important. The guiding coalition need to be well informed and to share the same language and terminology about services so that it can deal with questions and progress in unison. As Tom Palmer explained: '*Rolls-Royce is seen as a leader in servitization, yet still invests in the ongoing education of its people so that they can continue to innovate.*' This education should focus on the language and concepts of servitization and advanced services. The services staircase and roadmap are particularly helpful, as they can illuminate where your business is, where it could go to, and how to get there. Avoid at this stage deeper discussions around the processes of business model innovation or challenges of organisational change. Targeting this education at a small group of people, especially from stakeholders in customer-facing functions, will help to foster a coalition to support for the servitization initiative.

Maintaining momentum with the coalition can be challenging. Ross Townsend spoke to us about his time at Ishida, commenting: '*You've got to be resilient, especially if you keep having to find new ways to communicate the message internally, opening up the journey to the business and nothing really happens because something – the budget, the right software, whatever it might be – isn't there, so you have another setback. You have to be really resilient to keep going in the face of that and it's quite easy to have that confidence eroded.*'

Argument

Develop a strong set of arguments to win support within the leadership of the firm. The strength of the argument should reflect the resources required, but do remember that, here, you are only trying to win the people's time and the permission needed to Engage with the innovation of an advanced service. Nothing more at this point. We find that there are three topics for which it is especially helpful to form arguments.

The first are arguments explaining and relaxing anxieties about servitization. There are a range of common fallacies relating to servitization [2] such as: *We don't own customer assets* (they perceive that the firm will have to own the customers assets on their own books); *We will delay revenue generation* (they suppose that any payments they get for products will extend over the lifetime of the service contract); *We can't take the increased risk* (they worry that failing to meet contracted SLAs will cause penalties); *We are stealing from our partners and they may jump to another competitors' product* (they assume that their partners are not interested in service innovation); and *It's a complex sales cycle* (they worry that they don't have the skills to sell services).

The education we mentioned above will counter many of these fears, for example putting forwards such benefits as first-mover advantage, an opportunity for differentiation and additional revenue generation, especially if you have a large installed base of products that you understand, and that being closer to the customer fosters the innovation of new products and services.

The second are arguments based on a competitive analysis of the firm. This can then be applied to establish how the business currently competes and how this might be changing. Focus on a strategic analysis which pulls in a wide range of stakeholders from within the business. We find the frameworks from Michael Treacy and Fred Wiersema [3] to be particularly helpful. These can be applied with stakeholders to establish the current competitive strategy of the firm and how this might be changing. The stronger the congruence across stakeholders, the stronger the argument you will have for experimentation. Do be aware, though, that the analysis may reveal that a services-led strategy is not appropriate for your business at this time.

The third are arguments based on a competitive threat to the firm. Benchmarks and stories are especially useful for winning the resources needed. Jim Euchner told us how, at Goodyear, organisational commitment to advanced services was enhanced when a principal competitor acquired a network of service providers in South America, which caused anxiety amongst the senior management. The reaction was to significantly increase focus on its own advanced services programme. Similarly, Will Edwards, Director of Channels, Domino Printing said, '*We developed a really good understanding of the megatrends affecting our customer's businesses. Things like labour shortages, greater consumer choice, growth of digitalisation and the move towards access over ownership.*' Finally, Ben Wilson told us how they understood the threat at Schneider Electric. He told us: '*The biggest threat is if somebody else does it first; if somebody provides superior value to our customers before we do, that's a major issue. We need to stay ahead of our competitors.*'

These arguments are especially powerful if they are either developed or endorsed independently. Almudena Marcos Bardera, the EMEA Services Business Development Manager at Omron, told us how the help of independent consultants is very valuable in building an evidence base about the market opportunity. However, they do need to be reputable and to have a good understanding of servitization. Niall Walker, the Sustainability Manager at Diageo, explained how even an academic exercise such as an MBA project can be invaluable in the early days of exploring servitization. Niall said: '*It helped us to really get under the surface of the innovation, to cut through the techno-speak, review the appropriate literature and properly get to grips with the language and concepts of servitization.*'

Finally, our research showed us that you should avoid going too far with your arguments and suggesting and naming a new services offering. Remember you are working to win the resources to do the in-depth analysis. Prematurely suggesting what the results of this might be puts you in danger of people believing that you have the answer for the customers (even though you haven't spoken to them yet). Doing so will create a set of expectations (and so rigidities) within your group may well become problems later. It is better just to give the programme a name and focus on suggesting the art-of-the possible for at this point.

Resources

Get in place the resources that will be needed to Engage with the innovation of an advanced service. The resources needed here are mainly firm commitments for time and authority. This can include for example; permission to properly explore the opportunities of servitization, or permission to engage channel partners and customers in conversation, and even permission for the team and programme to be properly recognised. A commitment might be sought to release staff from some duties so that they can progress, and in some instances extra support may also be needed in the form of seconded staff or advisors. Alejandro Chan, the Vice President of Global Services at Tetra Pak, summed up the type of support you might need: '*Do understand, that before you can talk to any customers, you must create a good case to present to the senior stakeholders in the organisation. Not necessarily a formal report, but certainly [it should be] a strong argument as to why you should be speaking to customers to enable you to build your internal business case.*

These resources are invariably secured by presenting a compelling business case: a clear, and well-constructed proposal that articulates the concept of servitization, provides reflections on the competitive strategy, and gives supporting evidence with compelling stories about other businesses. Again, it is essential to focus on the objective of this task. Remember that this is a business case which is only asking for commitment to engage, and so just the resources and permissions for this. There will be many unknowns, so the case will rely on qualitative assessment, anecdotal evidence, and arguments.

In presenting your case, focus on factors such as the financial opportunity, fit with the strategic vision for the firm, the opportunity in terms of the target market, customer segment and value you might offer to customers. Be upfront about the risks, any early testing around a minimum viable business model, and associated timescales for the programme. Be aware that there will be many times when a business case is needed during a servitization programme. In the task of Explore the business case usually takes the form of presentations and discussions, rather than a formal document. A fuller business case will include the articulation of goals, success metrics, and preparations for operational implications [4]. This though tends to happen more during the Engage task.

Some advisors advocate the development of a vision and strategy from the outset, but our research found this not to be necessary. You are not attempting to re-engineer the firm and, indeed, attempting to do so too early may derail the process. You could, though, put forward a vision of the central ideas; the business model structure we presented in Chapter 2 provides a scaffold to arrange your ideas.

These activities will be helped enormously if there is an empathy for services in the firm. It means that the concepts of servitization and advanced services are more readily accepted, as executives will find it easier to conceive what these might offer. Empathy can be fostered by benchmarking visits to service-based providers, especially dealers and distributors operating in the same supply chain. Similarly, if evidence can be found of demanding customers, then these are especially helpful in suggesting the opportunity.

It is necessary that you achieve a clear commitment from senior leadership. One danger is that because these are 'softer' investments they aren't properly respected – in other words fight hard against "fitting it in with the day job'. Don't let people who are appointed to work exclusively on advanced services get dragged into business-as-usual. Rinze van Kammen initially had such an experience at Yanmar. He told us: *'We didn't make the progress we would have liked because we worked on servitization within our regular service business which requires daily attention and prevents you being able to keep up the necessary consistent pace.'*

Ross Townsend (formerly of Ishida) took invaluable lessons from his first experiences. He said: *'I don't think you'll make progress if one person alone is tasked with servitization for the whole company. I think it should always be a team effort because at the very least you need others to be a sounding board, but I was brought in from outside the company with the specific remit of leading the company's journey into advanced services. My job title was Advanced Services Manager and, as I understood it, this was a core part of the company's strategy and something on which real value was placed. Coming in from outside did bring some challenges; by the time I'd learned the product range there were already people saying, He hasn't done a lot has he? I don't think my role had been communicated well across the company; there was genuine misunderstanding; people thought I was there as a new product manager for our remote management and data analytics software. I soon found myself constantly feeling the need to justify my role, and I increasingly became pulled into managing other, more pressing, and immediate short-term priorities for the business – and to some extent, it was important that I did these things to justify being there, because I had very little to show for all of my efforts on advanced services.'*

This can be offset by a senior executive willing to be a champion or sponsor for the programme. We mentioned earlier Tom Palmer's experience at Rolls-Royce, where he found that having senior people in the business with an empathy for services helped to ensure services thinking and that the business model innovation stayed on track. Every Field Service Conference that we have attended has had, at some point, a discussion or presentation around culture and leadership. There is generally talk about the need for huge commitments and changes. But this is not the type of sponsorship we mean here. All that is needed is a few senior executives who are sufficiently open-minded and compassionate to the idea that services might offer a competitive business model.

Engaging a senior executive can be aided by benchmarking. One of the most powerful ways of achieving this is by benchmarking against businesses which are close to customers. In 2014, we helped Jim Euchner to strengthen engaging with other Goodyear executives by flying with them to Alabama to benchmark visit Thompson Tractors, an excellent Caterpillar dealer based in Birmingham, USA. Bob Bacon and the people at Thompson demonstrated to the Goodyear executives how they worked with customers, listened to their business's challenges, and then worked with them to co-develop integrated products and services that were then readily adopted by these customers. Thompson's enthusiasm was infectious and helped to cement the executive support for Jim inside Goodyear.

How to Engage in the Innovation of an Advanced Service

Engage deals with the task of creating a minimum viable new business model. Sufficient to demonstrate that there is commercial potential for an advanced service. It is important to take your coalition on this journey as many in the group won't have a thorough understanding of business models, what they comprise of, and how they can be developed. It is possible, though, that some may have come across generic tools, such as the business model canvas, and may well have attempted their application in an unfacilitated session and speculating on what the customers may value. Often there will be some confusion about what to do next. Will Edwards at Domino explained this situation to us, sharing with us that thinking through innovative business models had '*helped to engage people*' but lacked the relevance to move them on further'.

The challenge is to establish what to first, and here the entry point is 'discover'. Develop a deep understanding of those customers that are most likely to embrace advanced services. Then, use these insights to co-create with them a selection of new value propositions. Select the most promising as 'hypothesise', then pilot, test and evaluate these to 'demonstrate' the potential value that can be created and captured. Repeat this cycle until you can select, with confidence, the principal features of a business model that you can take forward to business incubation and onto the next task. In this way

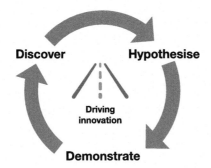

Fig. 8.4 The activity-cycle for the task of engage (© The Advanced Services Group Ltd)

you place a large number of small bets that you gradually reduce, over time, based on the evidence [5]. Achieve this and then the objective for this task is then complete.

This activity-cycle is illustrated in Fig. 8.4. Some people will join the process at this task, having been able to skip the Explore entirely because they already have the team and resources in place. Relatively speaking, this should be straightforward, but expect to cycle around the loop, and if done well you should be able to drive ahead and be quite structured in your thinking.

Discover

Start by exploring what the customer will value. Begin this with a grounded education on advanced services and the relevant processes of business model innovation. This will establish a shared understanding within the coalition of how to go about this task and the most useful and relevant tools. After this, you can begin analysis to understand customer needs and opportunities. Jim Euchner, at Goodyear, reinforced this message, by saying: '*In our case, servitization led us to a business model that best fit by providing solutions to those needs: so, start with customer needs*'. Greg Parker, the Vice President of Innovation and Portfolio Management at Johnson said the same: '*You absolutely have to include customers in the process. Not just in the beginning, but throughout. You need to start by understanding what the customer wants and needs and what their pain points are, and you have to keep listening to them and communicating throughout and include customers in your working team if you can.*'

To do this though you first need to decide which customers to target. Market segmentation will help you to identify customer groups that are most likely to have an appetite for more advanced services. Traditional approaches to segmentation are of little help, as these commonly group customers according to attributes such as industry sector, product type, price point, age, risk aversion or geographic region [6]. For advanced services a more fruitful approach is to differentiate customers based on the strength of relationship. Group customers on this basis and then target a small selection where the relationship is strong. Even then, not every customer is a candidate for advanced services. At Omron, Almudena Marcos Bardera used this approach with her work and told us: '*Some customers are not ready for this journey; for other customers, we do not have the right contact at the right level (technical managers and production managers, for example) to open these business discussions (based on pains and gains) So, segmenting, clarity and focusing on customers where we can start with this consulting approach is fundamental.*'

A small group of customers can then be engaged in 'empathy mapping'. This is a technique for delving into customers' profiles, to richly understand where they would most value help. It also reveals a firm's own internal biases for solutions; and this is a hurdle for executives from firms with a technology or product culture. To help illustrate this, when working with executive groups from industrial firms, we often use the example of a domestic dishwasher company to reflect on the challenges of innovating a new services-based business model in a product-centric firm. We set the scene by telling delegates that they are responsible for 'innovations within a business manufacturing such dishwashers and we ask them about customer needs. Then, we ask them to imagine being a customer and use these insights to inform their thinking, and then ask: *What are the most significant customer needs with a dishwasher?* We usually get the same answers: improved energy efficiencies, reduced detergent usage, made quieter. The delegates think it's all about technology innovation.

Then, we reinforce the question: *Where is the biggest pain for you as a customer with a dishwasher? At home, as a family? What causes arguments?* Universally the answer is: loading and unloading. We then point out that this should be the focus of innovation. Sometimes this is dismissed by the group: they struggle to envisage how a robot arm might be fitted to load and unload dishes. We then reveal how they only see innovation as a technology challenge, how they may struggle with services, and that they need to overcome this if they want to innovate a new business model. Shortly, we will give a practical example taken from Goodyear to show how this bias led to corrupting an executive's hypothesis of a viable service offering.

To understand the customers' needs, you will need to get out into the field As Almudena Marcos Bardera, at Omron, told us: '*You can't just innovate advanced services from the office. Go out and visit customers, understand the environment in which they're operating, find out their pains and gains and make sure you use this information to inform your service offering. This is about empathising with the customer's situation and challenges, understanding the barriers to success and what would help overcome these.* Do empathise with the customer and don't be tempted to sell. A common mistake that practitioners make, is to treat this as an opportunity to prematurely test their ideas about services that might offer, or worse still to discuss what's wrong with current services and products. Do not do this as it will entirely undermine the innovation process. Love the problem not your solution [7]. Focus on discovery, listening to the customer, and challenging your assumptions.

You might be surprised at what you find. Philippe Chassin, the Strategy & Service Solutions Director at Thales, explained that '*We discovered that one half of one customer's team plans to retire in the next five years. This opened the door for us to provide a single contract based on a single point of contact with Thales that provides full training and onboarding of their new resources ... and that facilitates the digital continuity between the customer, Thales and our suppliers.*' Similarly at Omron, Andy Bates, the Service and Solutions Manager, found that: '*Industry faces increasingly complex manufacturing issues such as the growing labour shortage, the rising cost of energy and the environmental priority to reduce energy consumption. In addition, there is the pursuit of ever higher quality, greater efficiency and the decentralisation of production.*'

Executives from Nederman engaged with a large number of customer visits and quickly discovered that they wanted to move to a clean-air-as-a-service offer. To do this, they had to prove that the air was clean coming out of the other side of the filtration process. As they needed to provide measurements as evidence to their customers, they acquired two companies: one that could measure air at the particle level, and one at a level lower (probably nano level). They did this to identify what was clean air, and to prove to customers that was what they were delivering as a service. So, there was a significant impact from talking to customers, developing the service and making significant investment in buying companies rather than partnering or subcontracting.

At this point, you may need to expand your stakeholder group, and possibly recruit them into your coalition. Ben Wilson explained to us how he did this at Schneider: '*In my experience, you can get access to customers without upsetting the relationship with distributors, as long as you don't make the distributors feel threatened. Your brand and reputation as the manufacturer are very valuable to distributors and they want the customer to relate to the brand, but you must remember that ultimately, it's the distributors' customer. You need to all act like a family – if the manufacturer doesn't want to compete with its distributors. As long as the relationship is mutually beneficial, it's useful, and it's easy to recognise when it is becoming non-beneficial to one of the parties.*' Paul

Jennings, the former Managing Director at JCB Finance, also suggested that new product introductions are also a valuable and non-threatening platform on which to engage distributors.

Where objectivity is a concern external advisors can be helpful. Again, Ben Wilson, at Schneider, explained '*We used consultants to interview customers, because they came from an independent, un-biased standpoint, and also because at the time we didn't have the dedicated resources to give this the time and attention it needed. We wanted not just to understand the pain points but to figure out the end-to-end process: what their decision processes were, why they chose certain solutions, what the individual steps were to make buying decisions. We learned that people don't want to think about the technology and in some cases not even to own it. We also learned that capital expenditure takes a long time to get signed off within customer businesses.*'

Hypothesise

Hypothesise a small set of product-service offerings as customer value propositions. The insights from discovery provide the basis for these. Here, it is important to decouple the development of the customer value proposition from conversations about how this might be paid for and how much to charge. What you are seeking to establish is, typically, two to three service offerings that you can take forwards for experimentation.

Begin by recognising that customers are often results and outcomes driven. Examine the evidence from Discovery to look at jobs they are trying to get done (their value drivers) and study how they are doing it. Obstacles or problems preventing customers from achieving their desired outcomes is where you will find the space for innovation [7]. In an outcome-driven paradigm, companies do not brainstorm hundreds of ideas and then attempt to figure out which, if any, have value. Instead they identify a small set of outcomes for a given job that are important but are not being completed satisfactorily, and then, systematically, devise ideas that will satisfy those underserved outcomes [6]. In other words, only after knowing what jobs customers are trying to get done and what outcomes they are trying to achieve are firms able to systematically and predictably identify opportunities to deliver significant new value.

The process should also avoid, for the moment, an overly detailed assessment of the service delivery process and associated technologies. For example, to deliver an advanced service at scale might necessitate a financial partner, but at this stage firms should self-finance the offering and deal with partnering a little later. This task will be enabled, particularly, through customer intimacy. This will mean there is already a good relationship with customers, and so it is likely that they are willing to engage in empathy mapping and experimentation. Indeed, if there is also a demand for innovative services from these customers, then the whole evaluation process will be much accelerated.

Avoid the temptation of apparently quick-fix technology solutions. Will Edwards, Director of Channels, Domino, explained the challenge precisely: '*We had explored the opportunities and got a good indication that advanced services represented a significant opportunity. People were engaged with the concept, but we didn't know how to move this onto the next stage and do more detailed, targeted and real-world work taking towards actually designing and delivering such services. It would have been easy at this point to fall back on designing new digital technologies, but we knew this needed to be a much wider reconsideration of our business model.*

To illustrate this problem a little further, a few years ago we shared the challenges that were motivating Jim Euchner's team, at Goodyear, to explore more advanced services, with the Technical Director of a Japanese-owned manufacturer (best if we don't name them!). The company excelled in producing high-speed weighing and packaging machinery for the food industry, and the director had been educated as an engineer and had a long career within the organisation. We were reflecting on the process led by Jim. His team had followed a process of empathising with their customers, revealing 'pains' associated with maintaining optimum tyre pressures, checking wear, dealing with roadside failures, and conveniently arranging a replacement. As we explained this situation, we could see the director become more and more anxious to share with us his 'no-brainer' solution: – Jim was wrong, what Goodyear needed to deal with this situation was to sell their customers an App, the killer App.

We were intrigued. We knew how hard Jim's innovation team had worked to explore, qualify and validate their understanding of their customers. How they knew in intimate detail the systems that modern cars and trucks have to alert drivers to problems with tyres, and how they had sought to understand that even with these, some customers still failed to properly maintain their tyres. Our guest had a credible executive position, so why had he suggested an App? Had the Goodyear team missed the obvious?

As we delved into the director's reasoning, he explained that his company was actively innovating a new digital system for its customers. He enthusiastically told us about this system, what it meant to his business, and how they had piloted it by monitoring one of their machines located in their customer's operations. He took us through the intelligence the system gave them about their machines and how they were being operated, and the potential it had to record any faults that might arise to indicate the need for maintenance. And how the 'obvious' next step was to 'sell' an online portal or App to customers, so that they could better maintain their machines. It was an opportunity for revenue both through sales of the App and increased sales of spares and repairs to the customer. The 'killer App, a no-brainer'.

We are today in the enviable position of being able to look back on this conversation and what followed. Jim Euchner had succeeded. Goodyear did indeed develop a solution which in part was digital, but they combined this with services that took away the customers' need to be 'bothered' about the pains we mentioned above. In effect, Goodyear focused on 'keeping the truck on the road' and selling the customer 'peace of mind'. As for success, Goodyear's Proactive Solutions was launched in ten markets in Europe in around 2014 and rolled out to North America and Brazil in 2015. Today, over 200 people are employed in this division. By contrast, our Japanese-owned manufacturer sold just a few portals, or killer Apps, before becoming so frustrated with the lack of uptake by customers that these are now given away free with every machine purchased. Just one person was employed.

Demonstrate

Establish the value that can potentially be created and captured by each hypothesis. These are the business experiments. A small set of service offerings can be piloted with willing customers. The pilots should be designed to assess whether the propositions deliver value to the targeted customers. Maurizio Poli, General Manager Strategy Implementation, explained the approach that Omron took: 'We pitched for three pilots in three different geographic regions, as a way of engaging local management in each region, delivering local insights and testing alternative routes to market and partner requirements. The insights that these experiments allow will then enable the original business case to be enriched with evidence and reviewed.

With care, alternative approaches to value capture can begin to be explored. As we described earlier, there are four ways of capturing value: economic, strategic, knowledge and relational. The pilots provide an opportunity to test customer sensitivity to each of these. The value drivers that come from understanding the customers' pains and gains provide a foundation for identifying which approach to follow. For example, if the value driver for customers is 'good-parts-produced', the 'number of good parts produced' becomes the basis to explore a revenue model. Price sensitivity can be explored by asking targeted customers questions such as: *What price would be so low that you question the offerings quality? What price do you begin to think that the offering is a bargain? At what price does it begin to seem expensive, and what price is it too expensive?* [7]

Demonstration might start as piloting but can grow into partial business incubation. This will require further resources to be committed by the firms. These may largely time and authority, but the business exposure will have increased, although marginally. You may need to revisit your business case. James Galloway did this at Baxi. He told us: '*Initially, we created a case around B2C segments, but when our pilots revealed that B2B was a better opportunity, we needed to build a second case to enable the piloting and pre-scaling work.*' Business case can be evaluated on the basis of strategic fit (does the innovation fit with the vision, image and culture of the firm), risk (is there evidence that the idea is likely to work in the real world) and opportunity (is their some evidence about the financial opportunity) [5].

If customers have an outstanding experience through piloting, this can create the foundation of a whole subset of superusers: loyal evangelists who can help to educate the market about the new service, while providing helpful feedback to the company [8]. Greg Parker, Vice President of Innovation and Portfolio Management at Johnson Controls, did exactly this and was able to feedback the success of a pilot to his team. He told us: '*When you've experimented and tested out a service, and you have a successful test case with that particular customer, channel or geography, make sure to celebrate it and let people know. This is important for your team who are working on the service initiative, but even more so because it really starts to open people's minds and make things real in the rest of the organisation. When you can demonstrate the outcomes and perhaps the financial performance and how it might fit into the P&L of the business, you will really start to get somewhere.*

How to Expand and Deliver Advanced Services at Scale

Expand is the task of refining the business model, putting in place all capabilities to deliver the service commercially, and beginning to enter the market. You enter with a principal business model hypothesis on which to now focus; the variants have been filtered out, there is clarity around what is on offer to the customer and how value might be recouped, but there is much uncertainty about how to deliver this in practice. This is a transitional period where successful pilots become the basis of incubated business models and these, in turn, become commercial businesses in targeted markets.

To illustrate, your advanced service might have a name, such as heat-as-service or code-as-a-service, and you have explored likely risks, costs and contract durations, though some of the details around these are still to be firmed. By now, you will also have the executive go-ahead and some resources to further incubate the business model. This will now lead you to a whole raft of questions about partnerships with financiers, contracts, people, skills, etc., all of which will need to be resolved during this period of the servitization programme.

All this is reflected in the activity-cycle illustrated in Fig. 8.5. The objective is to establish within the firm and its partners the capability to offer and deliver an advanced services business model at scale. The hypothesis developed in the preceding task (Engage) will be focused on the value proposition. The first activity is to 'strengthen' this so that you can describe fully the desired business model, this will identify areas where the firm will need to 'invest' to acquire the necessary capabilities, and this will then allow 'roll-out' of the model to customers. In other words, develop business model, investing in a service delivery system, and then beginning to roll this out in a select market segment.

Expect to cycle around these activities, but here there will be difficult choices and the need for bold decisions. You are entering a period which is no longer just about business model innovation. Challenges around organisational change begin to emerge. Many of the resources needed to bring the new model to market will need to be drawn from the firm. More material investments and commitments will be needed, business cases and priorities will be challenged and expect tensions to arise amongst the executive team.

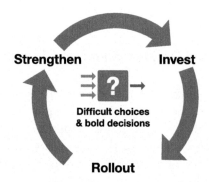

Fig. 8.5 The activity-cycle for the task of expand (© The Advanced Services Group Ltd)

Strengthen

Understand what capabilities will be needed to translate the favoured hypothesis into a fully functional business model. To explain what we mean here, imagine that situation where we had been dealing with the development of a new medical drug, you would recognise the preceding period we have termed 'Engage' as being work carried out within the laboratory and field trials. Assuming the trails were successful, you then want to take it to market. This is then the Expand task. To do this, you need to get in place all the partnerships, supply chains and production facilities. You will need to audit what you have and compare this to what you need. In our world, we think of this as 'strengthening the business model'.

Strengthening begins with education. This should build on earlier and deal with more in-depth analyses of advanced services, business model innovations, value networks and operating models. An introduction to foundational knowledge of broader organisational change will also be helpful to prepare the team for the challenges that will come but avoid drifting prematurely into bigger debates. For example, focus on education that provides some insights into financing and partnering but avoid wider and far reaching discussions around the broader culture within the firm.

The focus then needs to be on understanding the capabilities that need to be in place to deliver the piloted business model at scale. This is the service delivery system we have introduced in Chapter 4. Detailed evaluation will be necessary around:

- Performance measures and processes
- Product and service design
- Business processes
- Facilities and locations
- Suppliers and partnerships
- Digital technologies and systems
- People, skills, and culture.

Approach this evaluation by understanding the value network: the footprint of stakeholders and how they can come together to deliver an advanced service. This is the approach that Tom Palmer adopted at Rolls-Royce. As he told us: '*Thinking through how to deliver advanced services at scale requires you to understand your value network. You need to identify the key stakeholders, their capabilities and how these might fit with your own, as part of your new business model.*' You can start mapping out which stakeholders will be needed to provide the customer outcome and how your delivery impacts those around you. The greater the impact, the greater the value of the stakeholder. Think about who's interacting with you, the outputs that you provide and the impact they have on somebody else.

Invest

Acquire the access to funding, partnerships and resources, need to put in place the necessary capabilities. Where capabilities are lacking and open up the basis for conversations about necessary partnerships, facilities, people, systems, etc., and in particular how these are best acquired. Some capabilities can be provided through sharing those that already exist in the firm; but a whole other set of them may need to be acquired through partnerships and acquisitions. This, then, opens up questions about priorities and investments, and in particular, the autonomy of the business venture while it is incubated and grown.

Do recognise that advanced services business models require capabilities beyond those for production. Business planning processes and financial systems differ significantly and will not support services adequately. James Galloway explained to us how Baxi approached this: '*Making sure our data and systems are ready was crucial to ensuring we are ready to scale at a B2C level. Having a top-down understanding of the new revenue models which surround investment decisions and annual budgeting processes, particularly moving away from upfront transaction-based targets, plays a key role in scaling the business model.*

Also recognise that people involved with the programme might need to change. The best person to launch an offering is not necessarily the same person who established the vision, nor is that person necessarily suited to run the fledgling businesses post-launch [4]. Making innovation work in practice takes people with different skill sets. Skills for discovery are typically drawn from people involved with innovation and design; those for incubation are drawn from people involved with business and entrepreneurship; while those for acceleration depend on people from sales and operations.

New partnerships and acquisitions are almost inevitable for an industrial firm to progress. Will Edwards shared with us an excellent of example of this in practice at Domino: '*In 2019, we recognised a gap in our capabilities and went and purchased a vision system company. Now, we can identify that the right code is on the right product. Having this visibility is a key enabler of the service. Skills in data analytics, predictive analytics and condition monitoring are critical. It's not an area of strength for us and we believe we will have to partner to get this key enabler of a responsive reaction to failure in the field. We can run pilots, and indeed we have in local channels, but we absolutely recognise that if we are going to operate this at scale and scope then the business systems have to support us. Historically, they are built on a traditional model of selling products not services. We are developing a capability at the moment around things like subscription billing. As part of our digital transformation, the ERP upgrade has to be an enabler of our customer interactions.*

Lastly, it should be realised that what is being created is a start-up business venture. The tension is to exploit the firms' resources, while allowing sufficient autonomy for the new business to grow. Our research introduced us to many executives that believe that an entirely new business unit should be created. Dawie Kriel, at Energy Partners Refrigeration, put it to use in this way: '*You must have a separate division driving the development of thereof, one that does not focus on profits now, but long-term investment and optimisation. If your company makes or sells a product or a system, it's very difficult to drive the servitization development business from inside the existing product-focused business. You're almost working against the traditional model of maximum profit now. For example, servitization talks about financing and return on investment, rather than equipment sales and costs – it's a different conversation. Eventually the servitization business becomes a customer to the product business.*'

This autonomy is seen (by many) to be essential for growth. Yet, industrial firms are inevitably challenged to look for economies of scale and this will, mean that there will need to be a reconciliation of the business model portfolio. This though should occur under exploitation and avoid doing so prematurely.

Each investment decision will necessitate a new business case: an articulation of goals, success metrics, and how to prepare for operational implications [1, 4]. These are most formal at this point where significant resources are often needed to scaling and bring the business model to market. Expect to specify such factors as the financial opportunity, the fit with the strategic vision for the firm, the opportunity in terms of target market, customer segment, value offering, and then what is needed to achieve this vision including resources, skills and technologies. The case can express benefits in such areas as economic, strategic and competitive. The economic benefit is principally thought of in terms of revenue growth and improved margins over sales of physical products. Competitive advantage is seen in terms of resilience to economic downturns and overcoming stagnation in mature markets. Strategic benefits focus on differentiation, avoiding commoditisation and creating barriers to competitors [9].

Roll-out

To roll-out the business model means ensuring the capabilities are in place, there is a go to market plan and execution commences. As we mentioned above, the Expand task will be cyclic. The task before, Engage, is relatively linearly driving ahead with innovation; concluding with a piloted innovation, which is possibly well on its way to being incubated as a commercial venture. In contrast, rolling out a new business model will be more organic. Our research showed that rarely is the business model fully developed and then taken into market as the done deal. There are limited periods of further business model incubation, sometimes extended piloting around specific investments (i.e. ensuring that any data collection technologies or financing systems are robust). Here, it is no longer about demonstrating the value of the model (this has been achieved in the Engage task), but rather refining and ensuring the delivery system is fit for scaling. In this way, the business model will be evaluated, investments made, and trialled and improved.

Expect a number of iterations until the business model is fully rolled-out and commercialisation in a targeted market sector. Do be aware though that there are three principal directions such roll-out can make. Either the firm can absorb the new model into existing structures and resources or make minor adjustments and compromises to the firm to accommodate, or indeed radically encourage the new model as an ambitious business venture. Those people who are advocates of servitization will often push for the third of these, though much will depend on the strength of the business case and situation of the firm. Invariably which ever route is taken it will be revisited later during the exploit task.

Assuming that the firm is supportive of the new business model then an executive leader for growth will be needed. This is perhaps one of the most challenging tasks for people who have been involved with the stimulation and incubation of the new business model, as their independence will begin to be challenged. This is the point where the initial coalition might dissolve: in the best cases they will be allowed and encouraged to start again with a new business model; in the worse they will exit the organisation.

To illustrate, having spent four years working with Jim Euchner at Goodyear, we were delighted to see the progress that he had made. He had led a team that enabled a service-based business model to take root in Goodyear, worked with that team to hypothesise and test a range of new customer value propositions, before the settling on one in particular. He helped to incubate and encourage this particular proposition, fighting small battles internally for the resources necessary for it to grow and flourish into a viable business unit.

At the end of this journey, we met again with the Goodyear team. As we spoke, Jim introduced us to the new team leader whom he had helped to appoint. Also, the extended team was now much larger, and included secondees from marketing and commercial, some of which Jim had not met before himself. There was a new reporting structure, with a financial budget no longer part of the original innovation team. Overall, it was clear that this was now a viable and independent business unit, and the early trials and tribulations of business model innovation were becoming a distant memory.

A growth and services mindset are needed. Avoid the temptation to second sales staff from production unless they can demonstrate they have a services mindset. Salespeople differ in the way they act within the firm; they are driven by different priorities, say different things, interact with customers differently, and adopt different behavioural patterns. To sell a service you need to have an intimate knowledge of the customers (their plant, workflow, metrics, etc.) and the way they operate. Their business models and their operations [10].

There also needs to be a more formal set of Key Performance Indicators in place. Targets for the commercialisation of the new business model. Will Edwards told us how this was done at Domino: '*We included metrics about service growth and commitment into the corporate strategy. This demonstrates our determination to do this, and it's a reminder to all of our executives of the commitment we have made.*' This then is reflected in the priorities for the sales team. Ben Wilson explained to us how they had achieved this at Schneider: '*We now have two sales teams. The new team, selling outcome-based services, is well integrated in the existing service sales team and we have KPIs and targets pushing us to introduce this offer to customers.*

How to Exploit Value Created Through Advanced Services

Exploit is the task of adjusting the firms' business model portfolio to optimise the delivery of the advanced services business model to maximise returns to the business. You begin with having in place an advanced services business model that is growing in the market segment. The task now is to integrate the business model with the existing portfolio and adjust resources to achieve efficiencies and economies in service delivery.

Ultimately, this task is about taking actions that ensure a strong and balanced business model portfolio for the firm. This includes protecting and improving existing business models, continuously growing new ones, and decommissioning those that are no longer viable [5]. Any adjustments invariably mean broader organisational change. In this section deal with

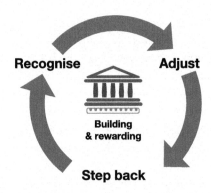

Fig. 8.6 The activity-cycle for the task of exploit (© The Advanced Services Group Ltd)

this though our focus remains on those aspects that stand out to support servitization.

Various models exist to assist the change process [1]. Typically these consist of a series of steps that should be followed when implementing change and includes such topics as forming a powerful coalition of individuals, communicating the vision, and consolidating improvements. All this is reflected in the activity-cycle illustrated in Fig. 8.6. This begins with the need to 'recognise' the potential of the new business model and evaluating it's potential, then making changes to 'adjust' the business model portfolio, and then taking a 'step back' to monitor performance. Reflecting on the process that has taken place and looking out for the next business model opportunity. Again, expect to cycle around these activities, but here the organisation is building and rewarding success.

Recognise

Recognise deals with reviewing the context and opportunities of the firm, so as to form an evidence base on which to underpin adjustments and repositioning of the business model portfolio. change and this needs to be recognised. There are a variety of generic tools to help in understanding the broader business environment within which the business model portfolio should be reviewed.

Education in these tools and the broader mechanisms of organisational change is most helpful. Almudena Marcos Bardera, explained to us how they approached recognising the changes that Omron needed: '*You need to do some analysis, like SWOT, PESTEL and SAF (suitability, acceptability and feasibility). Ask yourself some questions: As this is a successful business what are our traditional and current competitive threats? Change is a constant. Are threats getting worse? If so, do we need to do something more about it? What disruptive threats are we starting to see? Is somebody else practising servitization and stealing a march on us? Can we 'out-discount' low-cost production importers? There is no future in going head-to-head on price; the customer is the only beneficiary. Think about the current trends: What is the market like post-Covid? What impact is working from home having? How are we affected by current and future supply chain disruption? What opportunities does the drive to Net Zero provide? And ask yourself what distinctive advantages do we have or could we leverage? Some businesses have advantages they don't realise or leverage; what could you explore that might be novel and innovative? In complex multi-country and multi-region businesses where local General Managers have the responsibility for sales, you need their involvement in the process of understanding the big picture.*

Now is the time to again review the extent to which the business venture should be integrated into the firm to help better achieve economies of scale. To build an invincible company you may need to create, manage and harmonise two completely antagonistic cultures under one roof—and they both have an important role to play [5]. Potential moves to reconcile a business model portfolio will lead to fear around cannibalisation—that current 'best customers' will transition to a less expensive model and lighter customers won't upgrade [4, 7]. To illustrate, we were told by the senior vice president at Nederman how there was consideration of an advanced services business unit but there was also a strong product-based organisation and strong regional organisation around the world. When looking to create even a light-touch central services unit there was fear that this was threatening the sales and financial performance of those existing product-based structures.

Analysis may lead executives to seek redefine the business model portfolio. This should then be reflected in the formal vision and strategy of the firm. All too often, however, in business the notion of a vision and mission is translated into a somewhat meaningless statement, embedded in a plaque in the reception of a business and of little practical value. Research on successful organisational change is relentless in emphasising the importance of having a well-explained and compelling vision. If anything, our work has shown us that, for servitization, such a vision is an essential underpinning to a change programme. Done well, it can provide an overview of the complete business model portfolio and reveal how these integrate and complement each other. When such a vision features alongside a strategic plan it helps to provide structure and assurance to a change programme.

Adjust

Adjust potentially means making changes. Given the circumstances of the company and the potential presented by the new business model, there are again three primary paths that this can take. The company can either integrate the new model within its current structures and resources, make slight modifications to adapt, or completely reshape its existing business model portfolio to align with the new model. Adjusting a new business model portfolio of an industrial firm can mean challenging the very DNA that has made that firm successful. Established firms have the advantage because they know their existing products and customers, while the new entrants may be advantaged by their enterprise and agility [6].

One of biggest areas where change is most acute is with the front-office staff and salesforce. The salesforce, strongly influenced by technology-induced change processes, plays a key role in a firm moving towards value-creating business models, as it conveys top management's strategic directions to the market [11–13]. To be a successful services business, there had to be a different language in sales, starting with the desired customer outcomes and working backwards to the differentiating features of products and services, rather than leading with them. The sales team need to speak the language of the customer. Building a capability around customer analytics, to support marketing and sales can become critically important.

The experiences of Maurizio Poli at Omron explained this well: '*We aren't trying to just sell services or products; we want to sell Omron's full capability. One sale of a service can be followed by a product sale, and vice versa. Although a product might win the first sale with a customer, it might be service and services that sell the next product. It's about services as well as products, and not rather than.*' Ben Wilson had similar experiences at Schneider Electric. He told us: '*Eventually new roles were created: consumption sales manager (assisting the sales team to move towards bespoke solutions and consumption billing), digital transformation manager (digitally optimising legacy business processes), customer success manager (non-sales engagement, helping the customer be successful using the offer)*'. Andy Bates at Omron, stressed to us the magnitude of the task: '*One of the largest barriers you will face is transitioning the salesforce and partners to start to have conversations about value rather than product. Asking a sales business to move to selling the intangible, based on a service offer and promised 'outcomes' is probably a product-led business's largest challenge.*'

Selection, education and training of the salesforce, if done well, can really unlock the opportunity presented by the new advanced services business model. Will Edwards at Domino explained: '*Our salespeople understand that the conversation has moved and it's about creating value around the product. We have to continue to train and develop them to sell services. Speaking as a former salesperson, I know that solutions and services selling is very different to product selling, that you have to understand customer problems and the value you can add in addressing those problems. The other element is ensuring you align rewards. We have aligned our reward structures, using commission pillars to guide our sales teams and make sure our rewards are geared towards selling services. We don't seek to have uniform commission schemes across the world, but we provide guidance around how to evolve schemes to incentivise selling services. Our salespeople get the fact this is a way to move up the value chain.*

Step Back

Step back is about reviewing, reflecting and deciding on what to do next. As we mentioned earlier, we have focused on describing the innovation of a single advanced services business model as a pathway to servitization, though in practice we expect that firms, overtime, will have perhaps multiple innovations running in a staggered sequence. Executive teams leading on the initiation, management and learning from their experiences, to sustaining a culture of services business model innovation. Our research showed us that there are three important components that need to be in place for this to be achieved.

First is the ongoing education in what it means to excel as a services-led firm. Tom Palmer provided a compelling explanation: '*We all know that Rolls-Royce is a leader in advanced services, and yet we also know that people move on, and experience and knowledge can be lost. Any company needs to keep innovating, so service innovation education is critical to being able to design a sustainable business model for future flight.*' He goes onto explain why this is the case: '*Recently Rolls-Royce celebrated 60 years of offering a service model. In 60 years, things have changed massively, and customers are a lot more focused on getting value. They have, understandably, become more demanding. We are more demanding in our everyday lives and that translates to industry. You see it in everyday life, so to think industry would be any different is naïve. You don't see a set of requirements for these data-enabled advanced services. It's an unwritten expectation because that's how we live today.*

Second, a firm should put aside financial resources and commitments towards ongoing advanced services business model innovation. Chris Borrill explained to us that Thales, which is fostering multiple innovations in advanced services, have created a services research and development budget to help expand and sustain development. Similarly, Kate Rattigan, Product

Manager at Domino, explained to us the value of the commitments to innovation, saying that '*The three-year strategy calls out critical and specific targets for outcome-based contracts ... that means we've got this high-level strategic goal that's called out, that everyone's aware of, and we've got some ringfenced funding. So, it's a huge step forward from where we were and is driving all our activity.*'

Third is to sustain a services community within the firm. Again, we saw at Thales how actions by Chris, Phillipe and his team brought together and galvanised people from services functions into a cohesive community and developed their competencies. This has been critically important to sustaining services innovation at Thales. Chris explains this as follows: '*Share knowledge and best practice from parts of the organisation more advanced in services. Do it tactfully and constructively. In services you are always looking for a network and allies. We have a complex structure with senior managers responsible for this initiative in different departments, sometimes we need to hunt as a pack if we're going to move further and faster and knock down the obstacles, persuade people that services need to be taken more seriously. It's better that a few of us are saying the same thing at senior level, so finding broader channels to repeat the same messaging to the point where services became accepted at the senior management level as a key contributor to business success and customer satisfaction.*'

Chris went onto explain that at the outset the service community '*was diffuse and difficult to define because different business lines and units treated services so differently, some much more distinguishable from products, some much less defined.*' He goes onto explain: '*To bring all that together needed some imagination. The approach had to be adapted to the circumstances. There was a top-down belief that services could deliver more to the business. You have to continually reinvent the messaging, you have to celebrate the successes, reinforce the link between service success, customer satisfaction and business success. Seize on every dissatisfied customer as evidence of a lack of services culture. Spend time understanding the approach and logic of subgroups within the organisation is a key part of the job. If you don't understand them, you can't convince them to do something. You can't disenfranchise any of the communities who do the component parts of the service within the organisation, they all have a part to play. You have to be sensitive to and aware of the people you are putting at risk and address that directly.*'

Finally, all the education, resources and community building need to be done in such a way that it 'embraces, recognises and complements' the firm. It is not adversarial. As Tom Palmer, at Rolls-Royce, told us: '*You have to work with the organisation you've got, and the culture of that organisation. You can't change it completely. I think you need to be more pragmatic than idealistic, accept that good is ok and perfect is rarely, if ever, achievable. It won't all fall into your lap after the first speech you give. You will always have detractors and cynics. To move an organisation you don't need to convince everyone, just enough of the right people. The challenge is to work out who they are, where they are and what it takes to move them.*

Chapter Summary

In this chapter we have presented and illustrated a generic process we term the "route planner" to guide industrial firms, particularly those with a product-oriented heritage, through the development and execution of a servitization programme (Table 8.5). Our intention is that this will enable firms to initiate, develop, and exploit advanced services business models, thereby accelerating the exploitation of servitization. The process is intended to be relevant to all industrial firms interested in servitization, irrespective of whether their heritage is routed in the production of products or in the provision of more conventional services.

The route planner is a comprehensive framework, offering instructions for establishing a servitization programme within a firm. It is structured around four principal tasks: Explore, Engage, Expand, and Exploit, with each task building upon the completion of the previous one. Objectives and methods are defined for each task, and these are intended to be completed sequentially. An activity cycle has been created to operationalise the method and enable the realisation of each objective (Fig. 8.2). The dynamics within the firm vary throughout the tasks, with turbulence characterising the early tasks. To monitor progress, tracker topics are provided, and specific enablers are presented to facilitate effective servitization. Our goal is that by adopting the route planner, firms can navigate the servitization journey with clarity and purpose, ensuring a successful outcome from their servitization journey into advanced services.

References

1 Kotter, J.P., *Leading change.* 2012: Harvard Business Press.
2 Lah, T. and J. Wood, *Technology-as-a-service playbook: How to grow a profitable subscription business.* 2016: Point B, Inc.
3 Treacy, M. and F. Wiersema, *The discipline of market leaders: Choose your customers, narrow your focus, dominate your market.* 2007: Hachette UK.

4 Baxter, R.K., *The forever transaction: How to build a subscription model so compelling, your customers will never want to leave.* 2020: McGraw-Hill Education.

5 Osterwalder, A., et al., *The invincible company: how to constantly reinvent your organization with inspiration from the world's best business models.* Vol. 4. 2020: John Wiley & Sons.

6 Linz, C., G. Müller-Stewens, and A. Zimmermann, *Radical business model transformation: Gaining the competitive edge in a disruptive world.* 2017: Kogan Page Publishers.

7 Liozu, S.M., *The industrial subscription economy: A practical guide to designing, pricing and scaling your industrial subscription.* 2021: Value Innoruption Advisors Publishing

8 Baxter, R.K., *The membership economy find your superusers, master the forever transaction, and build recurring revenue.* 1st edition ed. 2015: McGraw-Hill. 272.

9 Posselt, T., T. Posselt, and Berg, *Organizational competence for servitization.* 2018: Springer.

10 Kowalkowski, C. and W. Ulaga, *Service strategy in action: A practical guide for growing your B2B service and solution business.* 2017: Service Strategy Press.

11 Harrmann, L.K., A. Eggert, and E. Böhm, *Digital technology usage as a driver of servitization paths in manufacturing industries.* European Journal of Marketing, 2023. **57**(3): p. 834–857.

12 Krämer, M., et al., *The role of salespeople in industrial servitization: how to manage diminishing profit returns from salespeople's increasing industrial service shares.* International Journal of Research in Marketing, 2022. **39**(4): p. 1235–1252.

13 Terho, H., et al., *Selling value in business markets: Individual and organizational factors for turning the idea into action.* Industrial Marketing Management, 2017. **66**: p. 42–55.

9

Close

Recap

When we first put forward our ideas of servitization to executives, back in the early 2000s, we would be asked to explain the concept and describe what it might look like for their business. What services they might offer and what rewards they can expect? We would attempt to ease their understanding by referred to the process as adding services to products. We would then gain traction during conversations, describe the somewhat conventional services they might offer, then slowly introduce more advanced services, such as Rolls-Royce's power-by-the-hour model. Initially they would be enthusiastic, then their sense of reality would kick in and their interest would wane. We would be told that these were too ambitious and irrelevant, and to give them more 'pragmatic' suggestions. A debate would follow, and the result was all too familiar: the executives either felt that servitization was irrelevant, or that they were already doing it.

Our earlier book, *Made to Serve*, helped to bring about a change. It reported on work that had been a key component of the most significant international research programme conducted on servitization. It provided foundations. It painted a picture. It suggested a vision of industry beyond make-sell-dump. Today, the conversations with executives are much more positive. They want to know how to go about embracing servitization so that their businesses can compete through more advanced services. Yet, *Made to Serve* also helped to impact the research community. It provided the catalyst for the first international conference dedicated to servitization. Today, the

T. Baines et al., *Servitization Strategy*, Palgrave Executive Essentials, https://doi.org/10.1007/978-3-031-45426-4_9

Spring Servitization Conference regularly draws in over one hundred contributors from around the globe. It also provided a set of ideas on which we created the Advanced Services Group, the world's largest group of researchers dedicated to servitization, working with businesses large and small. All this goes to show the importance we place on now bringing forwards this text; and we had very specific motivations in doing so.

Our understanding of servitization and advanced services has refined. It has been over ten years since Make-to-Serve, much of our foundational thinking still stands, but through the Advanced Services Group we have now worked with well over 300 firms on the topic of servitization. This exposure has helped us to refine how we think about and express servitization. We wanted to bring this new learning to you, the reader. So, in Chapter 2 we described servitization, advanced services and outcomes. In particular, we explained what we mean by an advanced service, describing it as a business model that is principally outcome-based. We also described what customers typically receive and how they will typically pay.

We particularly wanted to explain the value created by advanced services, as we know that the link between the compensation to provider and the value generated for customers is often problematic. So, in Chapter 3, we delved into the subject, and explained this in the economic terms of the financial compensation structure (the revenue model), covering such topics as 'subscription', 'pay-per-use' or 'pay-per-outcome'. We also explained that revenue models and ownership are, in practice, often blended. We finished this chapter by explaining a wide range of other ways through which value can be captured.

We also wanted to explain the system through which advanced services can be delivered. We know that many readers will be looking at servitization from a background in product manufacture and productions, and that they will be looking at servitization in much the same way as Lean systems have been looked at in the past. Therefore, in Chapter 4, we explored the characteristics of the broader system that needs to be in place to deliver an advanced services business model.

We then wanted to explain the relevance and potential impact of servitization through advanced services. We know that to move a business into a new space is difficult, complex and lengthy, and that executives will only really invest in this route if they are persuaded of the opportunity. In Chapter 5 we, therefore, put forward the financial arguments and evidence, but then also examine resilience, net zero, productivity, international trade, and technology adoption. We looked at each of these from the perspective of moving away from a dependency on product-centric business models. We know that these are grand challenges, and they are reoccurring topics in the conversations we have with executives, so we wanted to spell out clearly the potential offered by these business models.

We wanted to then explain how servitization happens, especially in firms with a production legacy. We know that executives are motivated to change when they see others doing it, but if you look around you might not see many businesses in this space. We wanted to give you confidence that this is happening and how. Therefore, in Chapter 6, we shared research examining businesses that are adopting servitization and we distilled from this deep insights about the process that firms go through when innovating to compete through advanced services. The research disentangled and made sense of this knotty process and, in doing so, created a scientific platform to properly explain and manage servitization in action.

Finally, we wanted to explain how you can bring about servitization in your own firm. We know that servitization can be overwhelming; there is an avalanche of questions to answer and many decisions to be made. We wanted to tell you how to go about making servitization happen successfully. In Chapter 8, we did this by providing a generic and rational framework, summarising the enablers of success, and then showing how this framework can be applied in practice. We focused on the specifics of servitization through advanced services, pointing you to generic resources where we felt they might be helpful, but emphasising the resources most relevant to this particular journey.

In summary, we wanted you to leave this book knowing three things: what is meant by servitization and advanced services, why are these important, and how to go about them. We set out to emphasise these through our three-part structure. We hope we have delivered our goals.

The Future

Across the globe there is increasing attention being given to servitization in both research and practice, and growing awareness that it can deliver improved commercial and environmental performance. Yet the thinking is still largely fragmented. Much of industry is still in the foothills, looking to grow revenues through sales of spare parts, maintenance contracts, and digital platforms that report on asset performance. The trend though is clear: more and more businesses are looking to move up the services staircase in one way or another.

As an indicator, just as we were concluding the writing of this book, two others were published by technology companies: SAP published *Business as Unusual with SAP* [1], which systematically and thoroughly examined the megatrends shaping industry, and IFS published *Moment of Service* [2]. Both books deal with servitization, and the presence of both indicate the direction their publishers expect industry to follow. Simultaneously, research will continue to enrich our understanding of servitization and advanced services, and over the last two decades publications have grown exponentially. There is no sign that this trend will slow, and this means greater awareness, greater communication and a greater number of people leaving universities and colleges with a knowledge of servitization.

Advanced services sit at the top of the services staircase for industrial firms. They have their challenges, they can be tricky to articulate and can appear complex, so, why focus on these? Well, let us ask you this; most people in industrial firms are entirely comfortable with Advanced Manufacturing Technologies, they take them to be exciting and innovative, so why not advanced services? Or should the future for services simply be about cheaper and faster ways to deliver spare parts?

For ourselves at ASG these advanced services cut to the heart of servitization. They passionately embrace the concept of outcomes; *we make money when our customers make money*. Attention given to advanced services lags behind that of servitization but is growing. This is only to be expected as they are a more recent concept, yet the trajectory is again clear, and this is apparent especially in the B2C context. As we have explained in this book there are barriers, particularly around culture, finance and digital. Over the next decade, we expect to see many of these addressed, and so the barriers to adoption will be broken down.

So, where do we expect to see most intense adoption? As we have referred to earlier, there are grand challenges for societies and economies, ranging from dealing with an aging population to the realisation of sustainability, and these all open up market opportunities. But which businesses are most likely to take advantage of these?

Large industrial firms are, in theory, well placed as they have the resources and technical know-how; they know their product, they know how it should be used, they have an installed base, and they know how to repair their product when it breaks. They also have the knowledge, authority and opportunity to change the design of their product so that they are better suited to the service, so that they don't need maintaining so often, break less frequently, and are easier and quicker to repair if they do. But these large firms also have inertia.

In our introduction, we spoke of an executive called Mike; wedded to making things in his work life. We see so many Mikes, we really do. Perhaps these people are simply a legacy of a baby boomer generation which was wedded to the notion of ownership, and their influence is about to recede. We are not so sure. What we do know is that, within large industrial firms, the influence of the incumbent portfolio is such that the adoption of relatively adventurous business models is difficult. A change is much more likely to gain traction if enablers are in place, such as an empathy for services and closeness to the customer as we referred to in the last chapter. Or if firms are facing dramatic shifts in their business environment, such as the introduction of the new net zero regulations, which mean that their old business models are facing extinction. We are not suggesting that these industrial firms are uninterested or can't change—they are, and they can; but their culture is such that change is incremental.

Smaller firms are often much keener adopters. In 2018, we published a compilation of 30 case studies about our work with smaller businesses, and how we had worked with them to capture untapped value from their customers through the adoption of servitization. The average size of businesses engaged in this programme was 26 employees; but they ranged in size from two to 125 employees at the extremes, and none of the businesses at that time had an annual turnover which exceeded £44.5 m (EUR 50 million). These cases were drawn as illustrations taken from a larger programme of business interventions with eighty companies. Across this spread of businesses, we witnessed that their work on servitization resulted in a Gross Value Add of £7,500/employee, an improvement in productivity of 16%, a two- to three- fold improvement in the exploitation of digital technologies, and a 10% increase in the value of exports.

We have now worked with over 300 smaller businesses, helping them to understand and exploit servitization. They are so refreshing to work with, they are anxious to understand advanced services, they readily engage with customers and are happy to pilot ideas and learn from their mistakes. Introducing them to advanced services helps to crystalise their ambitions and structure their strategies: it acts like a North Star, introducing the art of the possible and a direction for their thinking which they enthusiastically and passionately embrace. Quite simply, they lack the incumbent business model portfolio around products, they lack the inertia (they lack the Mikes), but they also lack the resources. Small businesses are invariably constrained by their access to finance, and as yet there are insufficient innovations in the financial sector to unlock these businesses models for smaller companies. As a consequence, there are some, but not as many, examples of advanced services offered by these businesses as they, their customers, and we ourselves would like.

We are, though, beginning to see change. Some financial innovators are stepping forward to work with these smaller businesses, using the insights from digital technologies to de-risk their investments. And, simultaneously, we are seeing digital innovators willing to partner with these smaller businesses and these finance companies. Partnerships are being incubated: small businesses with agility, empathy and customer intimacy; financial innovators looking for growth and exploring new business models for themselves; digital innovators looking to realise returns on their investments and willing to partner. This is one area where we expect to see adoption intensify. There is, though, a second.

We suspect that those firms that really exploit advanced services will not be the manufacturers. Instead, it will be Large-tech firms and their service partners. Manufacturing firms see servitization as their innovation—that the only way up the staircase is to add more and more services to their products, and that the only competitors to look out for are their traditional competitors. They believe that, as long as they outpace these competitors, they will be fine. That is not the case. Large tech is looking at this services space; they already provide the business systems for these firms and their customers. For customers, in particular, they provide the frameworks for procuring and managing the supply chains which feed their operations. When coupled with outsourcing and third-party logistics providers, they can create a supply chain architecture within which manufacturing firms have to operate, boxing them into the second and third tier and putting them under intense pressure to improve cost, quality and delivery.

To illustrate what we mean here, imagine the scenario where your firm produces machine tools used in automotive production. A large-tech firm provides the platform through which the customer manages the machining capability, acquisition, operation, decommissioning. Your value network has been disintermediated. Oh, and these newcomers they will be contracting on the basis of outcomes; so you need to put in place all the investments associated with servitization but you have lost many of the benefits. But it's not large tech alone that is eyeing up this space. Firms that we more usually associate with services and utilities are aligning with the opportunity. They often have the customer intimacy, resources, and culture, so they are only inhibited by their lack of technical know-how; but, when working with large-tech firms they can also gain access to this resource. So, our message to industrial firms with a production heritage is simple: embrace advanced service business models while you still have some influence.

So, what next? The subtext of this book indicates how we see servitization and advanced services evolving. We have explained that we see servitization as the bridgehead to management by outcomes. Our advice is: run your business on the basis of outcomes. Think about the outcomes for your customers, the way you manage your business and those that supply you. and create an alignment of outcomes up and down the value chain. Although this is undoubtably a somewhat amorphous topic to grapple, we believe it is the natural trajectory for companies, and one that we ourselves will continue to embrace and follow—while, as ever, keeping one foot firmly rooted in the practicalities of business.

References

1 Saueressig, T. and P. Maier, *Business as unusual with SAP: How leaders navigate industry megatrends*. 2022: SAP Press.
2 Roos, D., *Moment of service*. 2023: Park Communications Ltd.

Resources

To support this book, we have created a website with complementary learning resources that can be accessed here: www.servitizationstrategy.com.

In addition, if your research interests align with servitization, you can join us at the Spring Servitization Conference that is held annually. For more information, see: https://www.advancedservicesgroup.co.uk/research/spring-servitization-conference/.

Finally, if you are a business and want to be involved with our thought leadership programmes, then please visit: https://www.advancedservicesgroup.co.uk/partnering/as-partnership/.

T. Baines et al., *Servitization Strategy*, Palgrave Executive Essentials, https://doi.org/10.1007/978-3-031-45426-4

Index

© The Editor(s) (if applicable) and The Author(s), under exclusive license to Springer Nature Switzerland AG 2024
T. Baines et al., *Servitization Strategy*, Palgrave Executive Essentials,
https://doi.org/10.1007/978-3-031-45426-4

Printed by Printforce, United Kingdom